162-0

IMAGINE A SEASON IN WHICH THE YANKEES NEVER LOSE

MARTY APPEL

TRIUMPH
BOOKS

To Babe, Lou, Joe, Mickey, Thurm, Bobby, Don, and Derek.
Thanks for being there as each generation of
Yankee fans has come along.

Copyright © 2010 by Marty Appel

No part of this publication may be reproduced, stored in a retrieval system, or transmitted in any form by any means, electronic, mechanical, photocopying, or otherwise, without the prior written permission of the publisher, Triumph Books, 542 South Dearborn Street, Suite 750, Chicago, Illinois 60605.

Triumph Books and colophon are registered trademarks of Random House, Inc.

Library of Congress Cataloging-in-Publication Data

Appel, Martin.
  162–0 : imagine a season in which the Yankees never lose / Marty
Appel.
     p. cm.
  ISBN 978-1-60078-325-8
  1. New York Yankees (Baseball team)—History. I. Title. II. Title:
One hundred sixty two to zero. III. Title: Imagine a season in which the
Yankees never lose.
  GV875.N4A66 2010
  796.357'64097471—dc22
                              2009043088

This book is available in quantity at special discounts for your group or organization. For further information, contact:

Triumph Books
542 South Dearborn Street
Suite 750
Chicago, Illinois 60605
(312) 939-3330
Fax (312) 663-3557
www.triumphbooks.com

Printed in U.S.A.

ISBN: 978-1-60078-325-8

Editorial and page production by Red Line Editorial

Photos courtesy of AP Images and Getty Images unless indicated otherwise

CONTENTS

FOREWORD

It's a well-established fact in Major League Baseball that although you go out and give your all every day, with rare exceptions all teams are going to win 60 and lose 60, and it's the remaining 42 games that separate the good teams from the bad. When you win or lose a close game, you say to yourself, "That was one of the 42 that a good team would have won."

What you do about it also determines good from bad. If you accept it, you're not going to be very successful. If you work to make sure the mistakes that cost you the game don't happen again, you're on to a good thing.

When I moved from the Chicago White Sox to the New York Yankees in 1977, I knew I was moving to a team that didn't like losing any of those 42, and that was part of what made them the historically successful franchise that they were.

I enjoyed my years with the White Sox, but we were realistic—the team hadn't won a pennant since 1959, and before that, 1919, when they were the scandal-ridden Black Sox.

With the Yankees, winning was always expected. It was then, and it remains so today. And with that comes a mindset that makes you feel like somehow 162–0 is not unrealistic as you enter a new season. You figure every loss is going to be an upset.

Despite their success and all the records they hold, the Yankees do not own the record for most victories in a season, nor the most to start a season.

The best regular-season record was 116 victories by the 1906 Chicago Cubs, later matched by the 2001 Seattle Mariners, managed by my old Yankees teammate Lou Piniella. Because of a shorter schedule, the Cubs only lost 36, while the Mariners lost 46. The best record to start a season was 13–0, first by the 1982 Atlanta Braves, and then by the 1987 Milwaukee Brewers. The Braves were managed by Joe Torre that season, and they wound up winning only 89 and getting swept in the National League Championship Series. So after the big start, they were only 76–73, not exactly primed and ready to win a world championship. Finishing strong is better than starting strong.

As for the Brewers, they wound up third in the American League's Eastern Division, and were only 78–71 after the 13–0 start. Again, a fast start did not guarantee a big finish.

The idea of a book about going 162–0 could only be a fantasy, and this is exactly that. To piece it together based on real games required picking games from different seasons. That technique not only made this fun—tying together different eras of Yankees baseball as though the guys were all teammates—but it gives the reader a chance to get to know many long-forgotten Yankee stars of the past. In an age of short-term memory, it's good to remember just how good some of those old-timers were—names like Earle Combs, Tony Lazzeri, Joe Gordon, Waite Hoyt, and Bill Dickey—Hall of Famers all, but from a long-ago time and now largely forgotten.

Of course the big stars rise to have their big moments again—Babe Ruth, Lou Gehrig, Joe DiMaggio, Yogi Berra, Mickey Mantle, Bobby Murcer, Thurman Munson, Reggie Jackson, Dave Winfield, Don Mattingly, Paul O'Neill, Bernie Williams, Derek Jeter, and A-Rod. And the supporting cast gets to take another bow as well—hey, I'm in there too a few times!

So this is the ultimate dream book for a Yankee fan. A whole season without losing. Could it ever really happen?

Almost certainly not. But, if it ever does . . . this will be the franchise to watch.

—Bucky Dent

INTRODUCTION

Anyone who follows Major League Baseball knows it's impossible for a team to go undefeated for an entire 162-game season—at least until you read this book.

Using real games, but from different seasons, we've prepared a mythical year in which the Yankees win every single game to go 162–0. (And thanks to Bucky Dent, there is even a 163rd win).

We have reached back across all decades so that most of the great names in Yankees history get to make a figurative "curtain call" (although "curtain calls" really became popular in 1976—see July 25, 1976), as is Yankees style, encouraged by their fans.

Yankees fans are often called "The Greatest Fans in the World" because of their knowledge of the game and also because of their response to great emotional moments. We try to pack those in as well.

If you've lived through these glorious times, or even if you're too young to have experienced these games first-hand, you will enjoy the memories and moments that we have put together to form this perfect season.

Yankee Stadium Hosts a Winner on Its Final Opening Day

There were 83 previous home openers in the history of the edifice known as Yankee Stadium, but with the brand new stadium set to open across the street in 2009, the 84th home opener would be its last.

More than 55,000 fans packed the ballpark to watch the Yankees host the Toronto Blue Jays, who were starting former Cy Young Award winner Roy Halladay.

Taiwanese pitcher Chien-Ming Wang got the start and tossed seven solid innings as the Yankees rallied against Halladay to post a 3–2 victory.

At a Glance

WP: Wang (1–0)

S: Rivera (1)

HR: Cabrera (1)

Key stats: Wang 7 IP, 6 H; Rodriguez 2-for-3, RBI

Halladay brought a 10–4 lifetime record against the Yankees into the contest, but after getting two stress-free outs to start the game, a Bobby Abreu single and an Alex Rodriguez double produced a 1–0 lead in the first inning.

Halladay and the Jays had a 2–1 lead when Melky Cabrera led off the sixth inning with a game-tying home run.

"It was a patented Yankee Stadium home run," said Blue Jays manager John Gibbons.

The Yankees took the lead for good on a Hideki Matsui RBI groundout in the seventh.

Joba Chamberlain and Mariano Rivera delivered two scoreless innings of relief to lock up the Yankees' 11th straight home-opening win. —⁓—

Jeter's Debut Includes Homer, First Yanks Win for New Manager Torre

A new era in Yankees history was ushered in at "The Jake" in Cleveland. Derek Jeter was making his initial Opening Day start at shortstop as a 21 year old for the Yankees, while veteran baseball man Joe Torre made his Yankee managerial debut.

It was a complete success as Jeter homered and made an outstanding over-the-shoulder catch to help the Yankees topple the Indians 7–1, giving Torre his first win as Yankees manager.

Jeter batted ninth and was 1-for-4 while Bernie Williams clubbed a three-run homer to break the game open.

"I didn't know what to expect from Derek," Torre said. "The only thing I require and hopefully come to expect is that he play solid defense."

In the fifth inning, Jeter took a 2–0 pitch from Indians pitcher Dennis Martinez and launched it into the left-field seats for his first major league home run and a 2–0 lead.

In the seventh, the Yankees still led by two when Roberto Alomar reached second with a two-out double. Omar Vizquel then lifted a pop-up into short center field. Center fielder Bernie Williams was too deep, but Jeter used his range to make a terrific over-the-shoulder grab and end the threat.

Yankees	AB	R	H	RBI
Boggs 3b	5	0	0	0
Duncan 2b	4	2	1	0
O'Neill rf	4	1	3	2
Sierra dh	5	1	2	1
Martinez 1b	4	0	1	0
B. Williams cf	4	1	1	3
G. Williams lf	4	0	0	0
Girardi c	3	1	1	0
Jeter ss	4	1	1	1
Totals	37	7	10	7

Indians	AB	R	H	RBI
Lofton cf	4	1	1	0
Franco 1b	2	0	1	0
Baerga 2b	4	0	0	1
Belle lf	2	0	1	0
Murray dh	3	0	0	0
Thome 3b	2	0	0	0
Ramirez rf	4	0	0	0
Alomar c	3	0	1	0
Burnitz ph	1	0	0	0
Vizquel ss	4	0	0	0
Totals	29	1	4	1

												R	H	E
NY	0	0	1	0	1	0	0	3	2	-	7	10	0
CLE	0	0	0	0	0	0	1	0	-	1	4	0

Yankees	IP	H	R	ER	BB	SO
Cone W(1–0)	7	2	0	0	6	4
Wickman	0.1	2	1	1	1	0
Howe	0.2	0	0	0	0	0
Wetteland	1	0	0	0	0	1
Totals	9	4	1	1	7	5

Indians	IP	H	R	ER	BB	SO
Martinez L(0–1)	7	5	2	2	2	5
Embree	1	2	3	3	1	2
Plunk	0.1	1	1	1	0	1
Assenmacher	0.2	2	1	1	1	0
Totals	9	10	7	7	4	8

DP—New York 2. 2B—New York O'Neill 2, Sierra; Cleveland Alomar. HR—New York Jeter (1), B. Williams (1). LOB—New York 7; Cleveland 8. SB—New York Girardi; Cleveland Murray, Lofton 2. Attendance: 42,289.

Johnson's Debut with Yankees a Success

This Sunday night home game marked the Yankee debut of pitcher Randy Johnson.

The Yankees were still feeling the effects of their crushing loss to Boston in the 2004 American League Championship Series, and Johnson was acquired during the winter to help ease the pain.

Before an announced crowd of 54,818, the 6-foot-10 lefty went six innings, giving up a run on five hits while striking out six and walking two in the 9–2 win.

Former Yankee David Wells started for Boston but his ex-teammates treated him rudely, scoring four runs on 10 hits in 4 1/3 innings.

Hideki Matsui paced the offense with three hits and a two-run homer, while taking a home run away from Boston's Kevin Millar in the second inning with a leaping grab over the left-field wall.

"I went into the game the way I always do," Matsui said through an interpreter. "You naturally feel a little excited going into this game. That may have had a part in the way I played."

Johnson threw 95 pitches in his six innings of work and downplayed the significance of this win, which was the first meeting of the teams since the infamous 2004 playoff series. "I didn't build this up," Johnson said. "I just had a job to do." —

Red Sox	AB	R	H	RBI
Damon cf	4	0	0	0
Renteria ss	4	0	0	0
M. Ramirez lf	4	0	0	0
Ortiz dh	4	1	1	0
Millar 1b	2	0	0	0
Varitek c	4	0	3	0
Payton rf	3	0	1	1
Nixon ph	0	0	0	1
Mueller 3b	3	0	0	0
Bellhorn 2b	4	0	1	0
Totals	32	2	6	2

Yankees	AB	R	H	RBI
Jeter ss	5	2	2	0
A. Rodriguez 3b	6	1	2	1
Sheffield rf	4	2	1	1
Sierra dh	5	0	1	1
Matsui lf	5	3	3	3
Posada c	4	0	2	0
Giambi 1b	2	0	1	0
Martinez 1b	0	1	0	0
Williams cf	2	0	0	1
Crosby pr,cf	0	0	0	0
Womack 2b	5	0	3	0
Totals	38	9	15	7

```
BOS  0 1 0 0 0 0 0 1 - 2 6 2
NY   0 1 3 0 0 2 0 3 X - 9 15 1
```

Red Sox	IP	H	R	ER	BB	SO
Wells L(0–1)	4.1	10	4	4	1	4
Myers	0.2	0	0	0	0	0
Neal	0.1	1	2	1	1	0
Embree	0.2	1	0	0	1	0
Timlin	1	1	0	0	0	1
Mantei	0.2	1	3	2	3	1
Halama	0.1	1	0	0	0	0
Totals	8	15	9	7	6	6

Yankees	IP	H	R	ER	BB	SO
Randy Johnson W(1–0)	6	5	1	1	2	6
Sturtze	2	0	0	0	0	3
Gordon	1	1	1	1	1	1
Totals	9	6	2	2	3	10

E—Boston Damon, Halama; New York Giambi. DP—Boston 1; New York 1. 2B—Boston Ortiz, Varitek, Bellhorn; New York Jeter, Sheffield, Posada, Sierra. HR—New York Matsui (1). SF—Boston Nixon; New York Williams. HBP—New York Giambi 2. LOB—Boston 7; New York 14. SB—New York Jeter, Womack. Attendance: 54,818.

Wells Shows No Signs of Wear as He Nears 40

The Yankees pounded out 18 hits and smoked five home runs en route to a 12–2 thrashing of the Tampa Bay Devil Rays.

David Wells gave up a run in eight innings to win his first start of the year. The burly lefty made waves during spring training with the release of a book he wrote that upset some of his teammates.

"Despite all that happened during spring training, to go out there and pitch, get it under your belt and move on, it makes everything fade away," Wells said.

Wells, a month shy of his 40th birthday, got off to a slow start, but found his rhythm as the game wore on.

"He was a little rusty at the start but I think his stuff got better after the first inning," Yankees manager Joe Torre said.

Bernie Williams had four hits, including a home run, and three RBIs. Yankees right fielder Raul Mondesi also had four hits and scored twice.

The Yankees broke the game open with four runs in the sixth inning and five more in the ninth, thanks to homers from Jorge Posada, Alfonso Soriano, and Jason Giambi. Robin Ventura added a solo shot in the fourth.

The Yankees were without shortstop Derek Jeter, who was sidelined with a dislocated left shoulder. Erick Almonte replaced Jeter in the lineup and went 1-for-4.

Yankees	AB	R	H	RBI
Soriano 2b	6	2	3	2
Johnson 1b	6	2	2	1
Giambi dh	5	2	1	2
Williams cf	6	1	4	3
Matsui lf	5	0	1	0
Posada c	3	1	1	2
Ventura 3b	5	1	1	1
Mondesi rf	5	2	4	0
Almonte ss	4	1	1	0
Totals	45	12	18	11

Devil Rays	AB	R	H	RBI
Crawford lf	5	1	1	0
Baldelli cf	4	0	2	0
Huff 3b	4	0	1	1
Easley 2b	4	0	1	0
Lee 1b	4	0	1	0
Rolls rf	4	1	1	0
Grieve dh	3	0	0	0
Hall c	4	0	1	0
Ordonez ss	4	0	1	1
Totals	36	2	9	2

NY 2 0 0 1 0 4 0 0 5 - 12 18 1
TB 1 0 0 0 0 0 0 0 1 - 2 9 2

Yankees	IP	H	R	ER	BB	SO
Wells W(1–0)	8	7	1	1	0	4
Hitchcock	1	2	1	1	0	1
Totals	9	9	2	2	0	5

Devil Rays	IP	H	R	ER	BB	SO
Parris L(0–1)	5	9	3	3	1	3
McClung	2	3	4	4	3	2
Venafro	1	0	0	0	0	0
Colome	1	6	5	5	0	1
Totals	9	18	12	12	4	6

E—New York Almonte; Tampa Bay Crawford, Huff. 2B—New York Soriano, Johnson 2, Mondesi; Tampa Bay Lee. HR—New York Ventura (2), Williams (1), Posada (2), Soriano (2), Giambi (3). SF—New York Posada. HBP—Tampa Bay Grieve. LOB—New York 11; Tampa Bay 8. Attendance: 15,169.

Key Starts Big Apple Tenure on Right Foot

After missing out on free-agent pitcher Greg Maddux during the offseason, the Yankees signed pitcher Jimmy Key, who had won 116 games in nine seasons with the Toronto Blue Jays.

The lefty made his Yankee debut against the Indians in Cleveland and didn't disappoint. In front of 73,290 fans (the second-largest Opening Day crowd in American League history), Key gave up one run on three hits over eight innings to lead the Yankees over the Tribe 9–1.

Home runs by the Yankees' Danny Tartabull, Matt Nokes and Pat Kelly made things a little easier for their new teammate.

Pitching in 36-degree weather, Key was economical, throwing 71 pitches in eight innings and retiring the final 11 hitters he faced.

Yankees third baseman Wade Boggs, who had seen the crafty Key from the other side, said: "You just bang your head against the wall when he pitches. He frustrates you. He doesn't just throw, he pitches. He's one of the best."

Key was in trouble only once. In the third inning, the Indians had tied the game at one and were looking for more with a runner on first, but Key induced the speedy Kenny Lofton to hit into an inning-ending double play. —

Yankees	AB	R	H	RBI
B. Williams cf	5	0	1	0
Boggs 3b	4	0	1	2
Mattingly 1b	5	1	2	0
Tartabull rf	5	1	3	1
O'Neill lf	5	1	2	0
Nokes c	5	1	1	3
Maas dh	4	0	0	0
Owen ss	5	3	3	0
Kelly 2b	4	2	3	3
Totals	42	9	16	9

Indians	AB	R	H	RBI
Lofton cf	4	0	0	0
Fermin ss	3	0	0	0
Howard ph	1	0	0	0
Baerga 2b	3	0	0	0
Belle lf	3	0	0	0
Sorrento 1b	3	0	0	0
Jefferson dh	3	0	1	0
Martinez 3b	3	1	1	0
Hill rf	3	0	1	0
Alomar c	2	0	0	1
Totals	28	1	3	1

NY	0	1	0	0	1	5	0	2	0	-	9	16	0
CLE	0	0	1	0	0	0	0	0	0	-	1	3	0

Yankees	IP	H	R	ER	BB	SO
Key W(1–0)	8	3	1	1	0	3
Habyan	1	0	0	0	0	0
Totals	9	3	1	1	0	3

Indians	IP	H	R	ER	BB	SO
Nagy L(0–1)	5.2	11	7	7	1	3
Wickander	0.1	1	0	0	0	0
Cook	1.1	4	2	2	1	1
Plunk	0.2	0	0	0	0	0
Lilliquist	1	0	0	0	0	1
Totals	9	16	9	9	2	5

DP—New York 1, Cleveland 1. 2B—New York Kelly, Tartabull, Owen; Cleveland Martinez, Jefferson. HR—New York Tartabull (1), Nokes (1), Kelly (1). SF—Cleveland Alomar. LOB—New York 8; Cleveland 1. Attendance: 73,290.

Shea Provides Home Away from Home

During the 1972 season, it was decided that the Yankees would play their home games at Shea Stadium for the 1974 and 1975 campaigns while the original Yankee Stadium underwent a drastic and much-needed renovation.

So when the Yankees took the field at Shea before a crowd of 20,744, it was the first home game the Yankees had played outside of Yankee Stadium since it opened in 1923.

Mel Stottlemyre was the first Yankee pitcher to grace the mound at Shea. He didn't skip a beat as he went the distance on a seven-hitter in a 6–1 win over Cleveland.

Bill Sudakis was the first home-team designated hitter to ever appear in a game at Shea, while Yankees center fielder Bobby Murcer played his first game at a place that was destined to be his Yankee downfall.

With his left-handed swing, Murcer was able to take advantage of the short right-field porch at Yankee Stadium. But at Shea, the distances were not that generous, and it eventually affected his power numbers. (The Yankees ended up trading Murcer to the San Francisco Giants following the 1974 season for Bobby Bonds.)

Hall of Famer Gaylord Perry was the starter and loser for the Indians, but not without some controversy.

Home plate umpire Marty Springstead issued a warning to Perry in the bottom of the sixth inning for allegedly throwing a spitball.

The right-hander had always been suspected of doctoring the ball, but he was never really called on it until this game.

The Yankees took a 2–0 lead in the fourth inning when Graig Nettles hit a two-run homer off Perry. At that point, the fans began chanting "We're number one!" in reference to the Mets, the "landlord" of the building.

Indians	AB	R	H	RBI
Lowenstein lf	4	0	1	0
Gamble dh	4	0	1	0
Hendrick cf	4	0	0	0
Ellis c	3	0	1	0
Spikes rf	4	1	2	0
Chambliss 1b	4	0	1	1
Bell 3b	4	0	0	0
Duffy ss	3	0	0	0
Hermoso 2b	3	0	1	0
Totals	33	1	7	1

Yankees	AB	R	H	RBI
White lf	4	1	1	0
Hegan 1b	3	0	1	0
Munson c	5	1	2	0
Murcer cf	4	2	2	1
Blomberg rf	3	1	0	0
Maddox ph,rf	2	0	1	1
Nettles 3b	2	1	1	2
Sudakis dh	3	0	1	0
Michael 2b	2	0	0	2
Mason ss	3	0	0	0
Totals	31	6	9	6

CLE	0	0	0	0	0	0	0	0	1	-	1	7 1
NY	0	0	0	2	0	1	3	0	X	-	6	9 1

Indians	IP	H	R	ER	BB	SO
G. Perry L(0–1)	6.1	6	5	5	4	4
Hilgendorf	0.2	2	1	1	2	2
Upshaw	1	1	0	0	1	1
Totals	8	9	6	6	7	7

Yankees	IP	H	R	ER	BB	SO
Stottlemyre W(1–0)	9	7	1	1	1	4

E—Cleveland Chambliss; New York Munson. DP—New York 1. 2B—Cleveland Hermoso; New York Hegan. 3B—Cleveland Spikes. HR—New York Nettles (1). SH—New York White, Hegan. SF—New York Michael. LOB—Cleveland 6; New York 11. SB—New York Munson, Murcer 2, Hegan. Attendance: 20,744.

The Yankees made it 3–0 in the sixth inning on a sacrifice fly by Gene Michael.

Stottlemyre was cruising, retiring seven in a row at one point, as he kept the Indians off the board until the ninth inning, when they scored their lone run on a ground out.

The Yankees added three more runs in the seventh inning. Murcer and Elliott Maddox had run-scoring singles, and Michael added a bases-loaded walk.

Before the game, workers at Shea had to scramble to replace the "Mets" sign atop the scoreboard with one that read "Yankees."

When the score of the Mets' 5–4 loss in Philadelphia was posted on the Shea scoreboard, Yankee fans cheered lustily.

Mike Hegan, who would go on to become a longtime Indians broadcaster, started at first base for the Yankees and went 1-for-3 with a double.

During their stay at Shea, the Yankees used the New York Jets' locker room as their home clubhouse.

Senator Ted Kennedy's son, Teddy, a 12 year old who had his leg amputated because of cancer, threw out the first ball.

Horace Clarke, of the less-than-stellar "Horace Clarke Era" of the Yankees, and wife-swapping Yankee Fritz Peterson were booed during pregame introductions. —⚬—

Hunter, Reg-gie Show Hall of Fame Stuff

It was vintage Catfish Hunter as the Hall of Famer tossed seven shutout innings to lead the Yankees to a 3–0 win over the Milwaukee Brewers.

Hunter gave up three hits, struck out five, and did not walk a batter.

In the fifth inning, Brewers second baseman Don Money singled, but Hunter retired the final nine batters he faced before turning it over to Sparky Lyle. Lyle pitched the final two innings for the save.

"It's nice to go in the clubhouse knowing you have some runs," Hunter said after he departed with the lead.

In the second inning, Yankees designated hitter Jimmy Wynn hit a home run that cleared the 430-foot mark in left-center field and was measured at an estimated 450 feet.

Reggie Jackson made his Yankees debut and was 2-for-4 with two runs scored. An announced crowd of more than 43,000 chanted, "Reg-gie, Reg-gie, Reg-gie" when the slugger came to bat in the eighth inning.

Jackson admitted that he had never heard anything like that in his 10 years in the big leagues. The previous year, he had been traded from Oakland to Baltimore, where he played out his contract before filing for free agency.

—m—

At a Glance

WP: Hunter (1–0)

S: Lyle (1)

HR: Wynn (1)

Key stats: Hunter 7 IP, 3 H, 0 R; Wynn 2-for-3, RBI

Reggie Jackson shows the form that made him one of the most feared hitters in baseball. In his debut game on April 7, 1977, Jackson went 2-for-4 and scored twice.

P Sparky Lyle

In March of 1972, the Yankees acquired left-handed closer Sparky Lyle from the Red Sox in exchange for 1B Danny Cater and a player to be named later (infielder Mario Guerrero). It turned into one of the best trades in Yankees history.

Lyle became one of the best closers during the decade of the 1970s. In 1972, the southpaw led the AL with 35 saves, which was a league record at the time. He also became the first left-hander to record 100 saves.

When Lyle was brought into a game via a sponsored car, Yankee organist, the late Toby Wright, would play "Pomp and Circumstance" (a famous military march).

In 1977, Lyle became the first American League reliever to win the Cy Young Award.

Matsui Begins Career with a Grand Slam and a Curtain Call

There was great anticipation for the Yankee Stadium debut of left-handed-hitting outfielder Hideki Matsui from Japan.

The Yankees signed the Japanese star to take advantage of the short right-field porch at Yankee Stadium and to promote the Yankee brand throughout Japan.

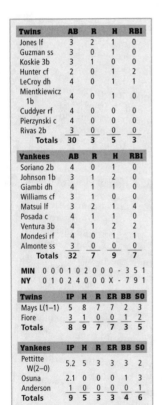

Twins	AB	R	H	RBI
Jones lf	3	2	1	0
Guzman ss	3	0	1	0
Koskie 3b	3	1	0	0
Hunter cf	2	0	1	2
LeCroy dh	4	0	1	1
Mientkiewicz 1b	4	0	1	0
Cuddyer rf	4	0	0	0
Pierzynski c	4	0	0	0
Rivas 2b	3	0	0	0
Totals	30	3	5	3

Yankees	AB	R	H	RBI
Soriano 2b	4	0	1	0
Johnson 1b	3	1	2	0
Giambi dh	4	1	1	0
Williams cf	3	1	0	0
Matsui lf	3	2	1	4
Posada c	4	1	1	0
Ventura 3b	4	1	2	2
Mondesi rf	4	0	1	0
Almonte ss	3	0	0	0
Totals	32	7	9	7

											R	H	E
MIN	0	0	0	1	0	2	0	0	0	-	3	5	1
NY	0	1	0	2	4	0	0	0	X	-	7	9	1

Twins	IP	H	R	ER	BB	SO
Mays L(1–1)	5	8	7	7	2	3
Fiore	3	1	0	0	1	2
Totals	8	9	7	7	3	5

Yankees	IP	H	R	ER	BB	SO
Pettitte W(2–0)	5.2	5	3	3	3	2
Osuna	2.1	0	0	0	1	3
Anderson	1	0	0	0	0	1
Totals	9	5	3	3	4	6

E—Minnesota Pierzynski; New York Almonte. DP—New York 2. 2B—Minnesota Jones; New York Posada. HR—New York Ventura (3), Matsui (1). SF—Minnesota Hunter. LOB—Minnesota 5; New York 4. SB—New York Johnson. Attendance: 33,109.

On this date, both intentions were fulfilled to the max.

Matsui clubbed a grand slam to right-center field to power the Yankees to a 7–3 win over the Minnesota Twins.

The game was tied at two in the bottom of the fifth inning. The crowd anticipated something special after the Twins intentionally walked Bernie Williams to load the bases.

Yankees third baseman Robin Ventura, who had hit his share of grand slams, told teammate Roger Clemens on the bench that "this is the perfect time for him [Matsui] to come up there."

The Japanese icon made Ventura and the fans look good when he drove a 3–2 changeup from Twins pitcher Joe Mays into the right-field bleachers for his first Yankee home run.

"He stayed on it," Mays said.

As Matsui rounded the bases, the scoreboard flashed "Home Run" in English and Japanese.

The appreciative hometown crowd, which was looking to stay warm in a 35-degree chill, urged the Japanese star out of the dugout for his first American curtain call.

Speaking through an interpreter, Matsui said, "When I hit the ball, I kind of figured it was going to be a homer."

Matsui contributed in the field as well. In the fourth inning, Twins center fielder Torii Hunter lined a ball to left. Matsui was able to save a run by keeping the ball from rolling to the wall after it took a funny bounce.

Matsui's father, Masao, was in the stands and nearly came to tears when the fans started chanting "Mat-sue-ee, Mat-sue-ee."

Matsui became the first Yankee to hit a grand slam in his first game at Yankee Stadium. "When I hit it, it didn't feel like I actually hit it on my own," the first-year Bomber said.

Matsui couldn't help but get caught up in the mystique of Yankee Stadium.

"It felt like there were other energies, other powers, that helped me," Matsui said.

In a rare moment from a player, Matsui admitted he was thinking home run in that spot.

"I go up there thinking just do something for the team," Matsui said, "but if you ask me, I think somewhat I was thinking about it."

Yankee starter and winner Andy Pettitte had seen his share of remarkable events at Yankee Stadium. Add this one to the list.

"It's mind-boggling the things that happen here at the Stadium," Pettitte said. —⁓—

Murcer Comes Through in the Clutch with Slam

Dave Winfield was upstaged in his Yankees debut by an old favorite.

Bobby Murcer's pinch-hit grand slam off Texas pitcher Steve Comer led the Yankees to a 10–3 win over the Rangers.

Winfield, who signed a 10-year, $23 million contract that made him among the highest paid players in the game during the offseason, hit third in the order and was 2-for-3 in his first game, but it was the fan favorite who stole the show.

Rangers	AB	R	H	RBI
Wills 2b	5	1	1	0
Rivers cf	4	1	0	0
Oliver dh	5	0	1	1
Bell 3b	5	0	2	0
Sample lf	2	1	0	1
Grubb rf	3	0	1	0
Putnam 1b	4	0	2	0
Sundberg c	3	0	1	1
Mendoza ss	2	0	0	0
Ellis ph	1	0	0	0
Wagner ss	0	0	0	0
Totals	**34**	**3**	**8**	**3**

Yankees	AB	R	H	RBI
Randolph 2b	4	0	2	0
Mumphrey cf	5	0	1	0
Winfield lf	3	1	2	0
Watson 1b	4	2	2	0
Piniella rf	4	2	2	1
Cerone c	4	0	1	2
Nettles 3b	4	2	0	0
Werth dh	2	1	0	0
Murcer ph,dh	1	1	1	4
Dent ss	4	1	3	3
Totals	**35**	**10**	**14**	**10**

TEX	0	1	1	0	1	0	0	0	0	-	3 8 0
NY	0	3	2	0	0	0	5	0	X	-	10 14 1

Rangers	IP	H	R	ER	BB	SO
Matlack L(0–1)	5.2	8	5	5	4	2
Comer	1	5	5	5	1	0
Hough	1.1	1	0	0	2	1
Totals	**8**	**14**	**10**	**10**	**7**	**3**

Yankees	IP	H	R	ER	BB	SO
John W(1–0)	8	7	3	2	4	2
Underwood	1	1	0	0	0	0
Totals	**9**	**8**	**3**	**2**	**4**	**2**

E—New York Mumphrey. DP—Texas 1. 2B—Texas Grubb; New York Piniella, Cerone. 3B—New York Randolph. HR—New York Dent (1), Murcer (1). SH—New York Cerone. SF—Texas Sample. HBP—Texas Sample. LOB—Texas 10; New York 9. SB—New York Mumphrey. Attendance: 55,123.

The Yankees had a 5–3 lead with the bases loaded and one out in the bottom of the seventh inning. Manager Gene Michael, making his managerial debut, elected to use the left-handed hitting Murcer against the righty Comer.

"He [Murcer] comes off the bench well, he's a disciplined hitter, and he's a contact hitter," Michael said in explaining why he chose Murcer over Oscar Gamble or Jim Spencer. "There were two low pitches that he could've swung at and hit into a double play but he held off."

When Murcer stepped out of the dugout to hit, the crowd of 55,123 was on its feet, offering a standing ovation.

"It got me going," Murcer said.

Murcer worked the count full and then drove a fastball from Comer over the right-field fence to boost the Yankees' lead to 9–3.

Murcer nearly did not make the team out of spring training. The popular Yankee struggled in camp and his status was in severe jeopardy. As fate would have it, Reggie Jackson landed on the disabled list with a torn tendon in his calf, so Murcer stuck, and it paid off handsomely in this game.

Bucky Dent's three-run homer off former Met Jon Matlack gave the Yankees a 3–1 lead in the second inning. The irony of the blow was that Don Zimmer, who had been managing the Red Sox the day of Dent's famous three-run homer at Fenway

Park, was occupying the visitors' dugout as the manager of the Rangers.

Tommy John went eight innings, allowing two earned runs (three in all) on seven hits. Lefty Tom Underwood pitched a scoreless ninth inning.

Winfield, who began the rally in the seventh that set up Murcer's heroics with a line-drive single, had wowed the hometown fans with a hard slide into Texas shortstop Mario Mendoza to break up a potential double play.

After the game, he was asked if he was relieved to have his first game as a Yankee behind him.

The 6-foot-6 Winfield, who played left field, said, "Nothing is behind me, it's all in front of me."

In a prophetic moment on what was yet to come, Winfield added, "There will be good and bad. More good than bad." Finally, he said, "There will be plenty of big games."

The game was played under overcast skies and damp conditions, but that didn't bother the new Yankee manager. "I enjoyed it," Michael said. "You can't anticipate anything like that, but getting that kind of lead certainly made it easier." —◊—

Did You Know?

Only 22 players in Major League history have hit a walk-off grand slam with their team trailing by three runs, and two were Yankees.

In 1925, Babe Ruth hit a 10th-inning, walk-off grand slam to beat the White Sox. In 2002, Jason Giambi equaled the feat against the Twins in the 14th inning.

Timeout Call Negates Home Run, Gives Yanks New Life vs. Brewers

Yankees	AB	R	H	RBI
Rivers cf	5	1	1	1
White lf	5	1	3	1
Munson dh	5	2	2	2
Chambliss 1b	5	1	1	2
Piniella rf	4	1	3	1
Nettles 3b	3	1	0	0
Dempsey c	5	0	1	1
Randolph 2b	3	1	0	1
Stanley ss	1	0	1	0
Gamble ph	1	1	1	0
Mason ss	0	0	0	0
Velez ph	1	0	0	0
Alomar ss	1	0	0	0
Totals	**39**	**9**	**13**	**9**

Brewers	AB	R	H	RBI
Moore lf	2	0	0	0
G. Thomas cf	1	0	1	0
Darwin ph	1	0	0	0
Money 3b	6	1	2	0
Scott 1b	4	2	2	3
Porter c	5	1	2	0
Aaron dh	4	0	2	1
Lezcano cf,lf	4	0	2	2
Sharp rf	5	1	0	0
Yount ss	5	1	3	0
Garcia 2b	4	1	1	1
Totals	**41**	**7**	**15**	**7**

NY	0 0 0	0 0 0	4 0 5	-	9 13 3
MIL	0 0 0	1 2 3	0 0 1	-	7 15 0

Yankees	IP	H	R	ER	BB	SO
Figueroa	5.1	11	6	4	3	2
Martinez	0.1	0	0	0	0	1
Tidrow	2	3	0	0	2	2
Lyle W(1–0)	0.1	1	1	0	1	0
Pagan	0.2	0	0	0	0	0
Brett SV(1)	0.1	0	0	0	0	0
Totals	**9**	**15**	**7**	**4**	**6**	**5**

Brewers	IP	H	R	ER	BB	SO
Travers	5.2	4	0	0	3	4
Rodriguez	0.2	3	4	4	1	0
Augustine	1.2	2	1	1	0	1
Murphy L(0–1)	0.1	3	4	4	1	1
Champion	0.2	1	0	0	0	0
Totals	**9**	**13**	**9**	**9**	**5**	**6**

E—New York Nettles 2, Randolph. DP—New York 1. 2B—New York Gamble, Chambliss; Milwaukee Garcia. 3B—New York Piniella; Milwaukee Scott. HR—New York Munson (1). SH—Milwaukee Moore. SF—New York Randolph. LOB—New York 9; Milwaukee 15. SB—New York White, Rivers. Attendance: 10,871.

In one of the most bizarre games in their history, the Yankees outlasted the Brewers 9–7, but not before an umpire's timeout call saved the day.

The Yankees led 9–6 entering the bottom of the ninth inning. With the bases loaded and no outs, Brewers third baseman Don Money hit an apparent game-winning grand slam off Yankee reliever Dave Pagan. The blast, however, did not count because first base umpire Jim McKean had signaled time before the pitch was thrown.

Money drove a 1–0 pitch from Pagan into the left-field seats, but Yankees manager Billy Martin signaled from the dugout to first baseman Chris Chambliss to call for time. McKean granted the request.

"Chambliss turned around and said, 'Jim time-out,'" McKean said. "I called time out with my right hand up in the air. Then he threw the pitch."

After the pitch was hit into the stands, Martin bolted from the dugout to speak to McKean.

Within a few minutes, the umpires instructed the teams to go back onto the field to resume play with Money batting, but no game-winning slam in the books.

The hometown fans were understandably irate, and they took out their frustrations by booing loudly and throwing things on the field.

There are differing accounts of what actually happened.

Bobby Darwin was the runner at first base for Milwaukee when Money hit his called-back home run.

"I heard Chambliss call time out but I didn't hear the umpire say anything," Darwin said.

"I heard Chambliss ask for time out, but by then the pitch was on its way," Milwaukee first base coach Harvey Kuenn said.

Some observers felt Martin intimidated McKean into making the call because it took a few minutes before the result was decided upon.

"He's the best intimidator in the league," the Brewers' Kurt Bevacqua said. "There are a few managers like that. I think Martin caught him by surprise."

McKean hastily denied that Martin had influenced him.

"That has nothing to do with it," he said. "I already had made the call."

Money got back into batter's box and flied out to right without a run scoring. The crowd got even more incensed at this point, prompting then-Brewers president Bud Selig to inform a security guard, "You better give these guys [the umpires] a police escort. They're going to get hurt."

The next batter, George Scott, hit a sacrifice fly to score a run.

Lefty Ken Brett replaced Pagan and got Darrell Porter to ground out for a most unusual save.

The Yankees had staged a five-run rally in the top of the ninth inning to grab the lead. Chambliss' two-run double tied the game at six. He then scored the lead run on Lou Piniella's triple.

Despite Selig's fears, the umpiring crew did not have to leave the ballpark with a police escort.

Milwaukee manager Alex Grammas was tossed in the ninth inning and said he would file a protest, which was never upheld. —⁓—

12-Run Seventh Inning Does Plenty of Damage

The Yankees scored 12 times in the seventh inning to blow open a close game as they cruised to a 15–2 demolition of the Royals in Kansas City.

The remarkable rally was two runs short of the Yankees record for the most runs in one inning, and it was the largest single-inning output since 1949.

First baseman Don Mattingly was one of three Yankees hitters with three hits, and "Donnie Baseball" also drove in five. Dennis Rasmussen was the beneficiary of all this offense as he pitched 8 1/3 innings.

The Yankees led 2–0 before the dam broke in the seventh inning.

Mattingly, who was mired in an 0-for-12 slump as part of a 1-for-19 skid, cleared the bases with a double to make it 5–0. Later in the seventh inning, Mattingly would hit a two-run double as Royals center fielder Willie Wilson lost the ball in the Missouri sun. Mattingly ended with five RBIs in the inning.

Gary Ward, Wayne Tolleson, and Rickey Henderson all had two hits during the seventh-inning barrage.

The 12-run seventh ended with the most runs scored by the Yankees in a single inning since they scored 12 in the third inning of a 20–5 blowout of Washington on September 11, 1949. —

Yankees	AB	R	H	RBI
Henderson cf	5	2	2	1
Washington cf	1	0	0	0
Mattingly 1b	6	3	3	5
Winfield rf	3	2	2	1
Pasqua rf	0	0	0	0
Ward lf	5	1	3	2
Kittle dh	5	2	3	2
Sakata 2b	5	0	0	0
Pagliarulo 3b	5	1	2	1
Cerone c	3	2	0	0
Tolleson ss	4	2	2	2
Zuvella ph,ss	1	0	0	0
Totals	43	15	17	14

Royals	AB	R	H	RBI
Wilson cf	4	0	0	0
Seitzer 1b	4	0	1	0
Tartabull rf	3	1	0	0
White 2b	3	0	1	0
Beniquez 3b	4	0	1	1
B. Jackson lf	3	1	2	1
Balboni dh	4	0	0	0
Owen c	2	0	0	0
Biancalana ss	1	0	0	0
Hearn ph	1	0	0	0
Salazar ss	1	0	0	0
Totals	30	2	5	2

```
NY   1 0 0 1 0 0 12 0 1  -  15 17 0
KC   0 0 0 0 0 0  0 1 1  -   2  5 0
```

Yankees	IP	H	R	ER	BB	SO
Rasmussen W(1–0)	8.1	5	2	2	3	4
Clements	0.2	0	0	0	1	0
Totals	9	5	2	2	4	4

Royals	IP	H	R	ER	BB	SO
D. Jackson L(0–2)	6.1	7	6	6	4	1
Farr	0.1	4	6	6	2	1
Gumpert	2.1	6	3	3	1	2
Totals	9	17	15	15	7	4

DP—New York 2. 2B—New York Kittle, Mattingly 3, Ward 2; Kansas City B. Jackson, Beniquez. HR—Kansas City B. Jackson (1). LOB—New York 8; Kansas City 5. Attendance: 31,303.

Mantle, Berra, and Skowron a Formidable Murderers' Row

Past Yankee lineups have been known as "Murderers' Row" for their vaunted power and offensive ability.

The Yankees' "Murderers' Row" this day consisted of Mickey Mantle, Yogi Berra, and Bill "Moose" Skowron, who combined to go 7-for-15 with nine RBIs and seven runs scored as the Bombers blasted the Washington Senators 19–1.

Even Whitey Ford was 3-for-5 with four RBIs and two runs scored while tossing a complete game two-hitter.

The Yankees took a 2–0 lead in the third inning on a two-run triple from third baseman Andy Carey. They never stopped scoring as they produced runs in their last six times at bat.

The game was played in a steady, cold drizzle but the Yankees' bats stayed hot.

Mantle spoiled the major league debut of side-arming righty Ted Abernathy with a three-run homer into the right-center-field bleachers to cap off a five-run fourth inning that made it 7–0.

Ford out-hit Washington by himself and would have had a shutout were it not for the weather. In the sixth inning, Ford balked in the only Washington run of the game because he slipped on the wet rubber while facing Roy Sievers. Sievers got one of the two Washington hits in the game off Ford. —∿—

Senators	AB	R	H	RBI
Yost 3b	4	0	0	0
Bushy cf	3	0	0	0
Vernon 1b	3	1	0	0
Runnels 2b	4	0	1	0
Sievers lf	3	0	1	0
Umphlett rf	3	0	0	0
Fitz Gerald c	2	0	0	0
Oldis c	0	0	0	0
Kline ss	3	0	0	0
McDermott p	1	0	0	0
Paula ph	1	0	0	0
Roig ph	1	0	0	0
Totals	28	1	2	0

Yankees	AB	R	H	RBI
McDougald 2b	3	2	1	0
J. Coleman 2b	2	0	0	0
Carey 3b	6	1	2	2
Mantle cf	5	3	3	4
Berra c	4	2	1	2
Skowron 1b	6	2	3	3
Bauer rf	3	3	1	0
Cerv lf	5	2	2	4
Rizzuto ss	0	2	0	0
Hunter ph,ss	1	0	0	0
Ford p	5	2	3	4
Totals	40	19	16	19

```
WAS  0 0 0 0 0 1 0 0 0 - 1 2 2
NY   0 0 2 5 2 4 3 3 X - 19 16 1
```

Senators	IP	H	R	ER	BB	SO
McDermott L(0–1)	3.1	4	6	6	3	0
Abernathy	0.2	1	1	1	0	1
Currie	2	5	6	5	2	1
Gonzales	2	6	6	6	3	1
Totals	8	16	19	18	8	3

Yankees	IP	H	R	ER	BB	SO
Ford W(1–0)	9	2	1	1	5	8

E—Washington Kline, McDermott; New York Berra. 3B—New York Carey, Cerv. HR—New York Mantle (1), Berra (1), Skowron (1). SH—New York Rizzuto. HBP—New York Mantle, Rizzuto, Cerv. LOB—Washington 5; New York 9. SB—New York Rizzuto. Attendance: 11,251.

Yanks Able to Stomach the Babe's Absence

It was an early test for the Yankees against the defending World Champion Washington Senators (yes, they won one World Series). The Bronx Bombers did not disappoint the home fans as they scored a 5–1 victory without the services of Babe Ruth.

Ruth, the defending American League home run champion with 46, was hospitalized with what was termed indigestion.

Ruth's replacement was a 29-year-old journeyman named Ben Paschal, who batted leadoff and played right field in place of the Yankee legend.

Paschal pleased the home folks who were missing Ruth when he launched a two-run homer into the left-field bleachers in the sixth inning off the Senators' George Mogridge. The blast gave the Yankees a 4–1 lead.

Right-hander Urban Shocker went the distance, giving up a run on seven hits. The pitcher, who was acquired from the St. Louis Browns during the winter, contributed at the plate with a bases-loaded walk to drive in the first run in the second inning and a triple in the fifth inning.

More than 50,000 fans packed the Stadium on a dreary day to enjoy the game, which lasted less than two hours. ~⚏~

Senators	AB	R	H	RBI
McNeely cf	4	0	0	0
B. Harris 2b	4	0	1	0
Rice rf	4	0	0	0
Goslin lf	4	1	1	0
Judge 1b	3	0	1	0
Bluege 3b	2	0	2	1
Peckinpaugh ss	3	0	0	0
Ruel c	3	0	0	0
Mogridge p	2	0	2	0
Leibold ph	1	0	0	0
Totals	30	1	7	1

Yankees	AB	R	H	RBI
Paschal rf	4	1	2	3
Dugan 3b	3	0	0	0
Combs cf	4	0	0	0
Meusel lf	4	1	2	1
Pipp 1b	4	0	0	0
Ward 2b	4	1	2	0
Scott ss	4	1	2	0
O'Neill c	3	0	0	0
Shocker p	2	1	1	1
Totals	32	5	9	5

```
WAS  0 0 0 1 0 0 0 0 0 - 1 7 1
NY   0 1 0 0 1 2 1 0 X - 5 9 0
```

Senators	IP	H	R	ER	BB	SO
Mogridge L(0–1)	7	9	5	5	2	2
Russell	1	0	0	0	0	0
Totals	8	9	5	5	2	2

Yankees	IP	H	R	ER	BB	SO
Shocker W(1–0)	9	7	1	1	2	3

E—Washington Mogridge. DP—New York 3. 3B—New York Shocker. HR—New York Paschal (1), Meusel (1). SH—New York Dugan, Shocker. LOB—Washington 4; New York 7. SB—Washington Goslin. Attendance: 55,000.

Stadium's Structural Issues Send Yankees Packing to Shea

A day before the Yankees were scheduled to open a three-game series at home against the Anaheim Angels, the 75-year-old structure known as Yankee Stadium, rebuilt two decades earlier, began showing some serious warts. What was described as "a heavy chunk of steel and concrete" came loose and crashed into empty seats below the upper deck.

A day later, a loose piece of concrete slab on the upper deck was discovered, so the game against Anaheim was called due to unsafe conditions at the stadium.

It was going to take some time to get the stadium inspected and declared "risk free" in order to play ball again, so the Yankees worked out an agreement with the New York Mets to play one of their games against the Angels at Shea Stadium.

For the first time in the 20th century, one ballpark would play home to two games with four different teams. After the Yankees vs. Angels game, the Mets played their regularly scheduled night game against the Chicago Cubs.

The Yankees gathered at Yankee Stadium for an 11-mile bus trip (in full uniform) that lasted only 16 minutes, thanks to a police escort.

> ## At a Glance
>
> **WP:** Wells (2–1)
>
> **S:** Nelson (1)
>
> **HR:** Strawberry (4)
>
> **Key stats:** O'Neill 3-for-4, 2 RBIs; Martinez 2-for-4, 2 RBIs

David Wells got the start, but there was some irony for a couple of Yankees in playing the game at Shea.

Pitcher David Cone and designated hitter Darryl Strawberry both had prominent careers for the New York Mets, so Shea Stadium felt like home to the two Yankees.

Cone didn't appear in the game, but Strawberry felt like he never left Queens when he blasted a run homer off the Angels' Omar Olivares in the fifth inning to give the Yankees a 6–0 lead. —⌇—

Mantle's Debut Includes Meeting with Williams

A pair of Yankees legends—one on the field and one off the field—made their debuts in a 5–0 win over the Red Sox, but no one in the crowd of more than 44,000 or the fans following the game knew it at the time.

Nineteen-year-old Mickey Mantle put on the Yankee pinstripes for the first time amidst an extraordinary amount of fanfare.

Mantle was being tabbed as the next great Yankee, the man who would one day fill the shoes of the great Joe DiMaggio, who was planning to retire at the end of the 1951 season.

According to the *New York Times*, while on the field before the game, Mantle was in awe of big stars like DiMaggio and Ted Williams. The young slugger blushed when a photographer asked if he would pose with the "Yankee Clipper" and the "Splendid Splinter."

Williams was the one who broke the ice when he said to Mantle, "You must be Mick" and then, with an appreciated smile, shook the young slugger's hand to officially "welcome" him into an exclusive club.

At a Glance

WP: Raschi (1–0)

HR: Jensen (1)

Key stats: Mantle debuts with run-scoring single; Jensen 2-run HR; Raschi 6-hitter

Any anxiety didn't carry over to the game. Mantle started in right field and drove in a run with a single in the sixth inning off Boston lefty Bill Wight. Ironically, Mantle would later name Wight one of the toughest pitchers he ever faced.

Jackie Jensen opened the scoring with a two-run homer off Wight in the third inning and started the sixth inning with a double. Mantle, DiMaggio, and Yogi Berra—three future Hall of Famers—drove in runs to chase Wight during the three-run rally.

Vic Raschi (a.k.a. "the Springfield Rifle" because he was from Springfield, Massachusetts) got the win and was aided right away by an old friend in center field. Dom DiMaggio led off the game with a single. The next batter, Billy Goodman, blooped one into short center field, but Joe DiMaggio made a shoe-string catch and threw to Johnny Mize at first base to double-up his brother.

There were more spectacular defensive plays in the infield. Shortstop Phil

Mickey Mantle, a fresh-faced rookie at age 19 in this image from spring training, made his debut on April 17, 1951. Mantle drove in a run with a single in his first game in the majors.

Rizzuto and second baseman Jerry Coleman combined on two sparkling double plays to snuff out Red Sox rallies and help Raschi go the distance on a six-hitter.

Before the game, Yankees manager Casey Stengel, whose team was in the midst of a streak of five straight World Series titles, was lamenting the fact he had some very young players like Jensen and Mantle in his lineup.

"I just wish I didn't have to play so many green peas today," Stengel said. "I like to use veterans and not a couple of untried kids like Jackie Jensen and Mickey Mantle."

After the game, Stengel probably changed his tune. In the years to come, Stengel was hard on Mantle because of the expectations that were placed on his young superstar.

A crowd of 44,860 had the privilege of seeing eight future Hall of Famers in the lineups that day. Three Boston players and five Yankees who were destined for enshrinement in Cooperstown made the box score that day. (Casey Stengel and coach Bill Dickey were not in the lineups but were on the field.)

The Red Sox contingent featured Williams, along with second baseman Bobby Doerr and shortstop Lou Boudreau. Boudreau, the former player/manager, was in his first year with the Red Sox after a stellar 13-year career in Cleveland.

Five Hall of Famers occupied the Nos. 2–6 spots in the Yankees batting order. Shortstop Phil Rizzuto began the all-time procession of hitters. Right fielder Mantle hit third; Joe DiMaggio was cleanup in center field, followed by catcher Yogi Berra and first baseman Johnny "Big Cat" Mize.

Stengel's biggest problem that day was raising the 1950 World Championship flag to the top of the flagstaff in left-center field. During the ceremony before the

OF Mickey Mantle

Considered the greatest switch-hitter of all time, Mickey Mantle thrilled baseball fans with his ability to hit monstrous home runs from either side of the plate.

Mantle was a three-time MVP Award winner and a 16-time All Star. He still holds the record for the most World Series home runs with 18.

When Mantle first joined the Yankees in 1951, he played right field because Joe DiMaggio was still manning center.

Mantle not only had tremendous power, but he had blazing speed that was cut short by the numerous leg injuries he suffered over his 18-year career.

In 1956, Mantle won the Triple Crown by leading the American League in batting average (.353), home runs (52), and runs batted in (130).

The slugging switch-hitter blasted 536 home runs in his career and played in 12 World Series, winning seven times.

game, Stengel got tangled in the ropes and the banner refused to elevate.

A few fans yelled out to Red Sox manager Steve O'Neill, who, out of respect, was standing alongside.

"Give 'im a hand, Steve."

"Nuts to you, Case," he defiantly responded. "I'm not helping you win any pennant."

The game also marked the debut of "The Voice of Yankee Stadium."

Bob Sheppard, the world's most famous public address announcer, was behind the mic at Yankee Stadium for the first time on April 17, 1951 and put in just under 60 years in the Bronx prior to his retirement at age 99 in 2009. ᐳᐳᐸ

Did You Know?

The Yankees have hosted Game 7 of the World Series four times. In 1947, the Yankees beat the Dodgers for their only Game 7 win. They lost to the St. Louis Cardinals in 1926, the Brooklyn Dodgers in 1955 and the Milwaukee Braves in 1957.

Ruth Homer Part of Original Yankee Stadium's Debut

What a grand opening it was. More than 74,000 fans were on hand for the first game at the brand new Yankee Stadium to see the Yankees christen the new ballpark in style as they beat their archrivals, the Boston Red Sox, 4–1.

Surprisingly, only 18,000 reserved seats were sold beforehand, so there were 52,000 seats still available on the morning of the game.

Yankees business manager Ed Barrow opened 36 ticket windows at noon in anticipation of the great demand for the seats.

There were small sections of empty seats in the right- and left-field bleachers, but every seat in the actual grandstand was filled. Many fans were seen standing four and five deep behind each of the three tiers.

The stadium was filled with dignitaries and celebrities. John Philip Sousa, who was the "honorary director" of the "Seventh Regiment Band," played the "Star Spangled Banner," New York Governor Al Smith made a perfect "first pitch" toss to Yankees catcher Wally Schang, and the game was ready to start.

Yankees starter Bob Shawkey faced Boston's Chick Fewster, and at 3:31 in the afternoon he threw ball one for the first official pitch at the grand structure.

The first hit in the stadium came off the bat of Red Sox first baseman George Burns in the second inning, but he was cut down trying to steal.

The first Yankees hit was produced by second baseman Aaron Ward, who singled to lead off the third inning. Later in the inning, Joe Dugan drove in the first ever run at the Stadium with a single, and then Babe Ruth stepped to the plate with two on and two out.

The day before at a workout, Ruth said, "Looks pretty far out to that right-field fence."

The distance to right field in the first game was 370 feet.

"I'd give a year of my life if I could hit the first home run there," the Bambino said.

Center field was 490 feet, while left field was 395, but 281 down the left-field line.

The gaps were expansive as well. Left-center field was 460 feet, while in right-center, it was 429. Down the right-field line, the distance was 295 feet.

On a 2–2 pitch from Red Sox pitcher Howard Ehmke, Ruth slammed a line drive three-run homer into the right-field bleachers to give the Yankees a 4–0 lead.

The Bambino flied out in the first inning and walked his other two times up.

Ruth committed the first Yankees error at the Stadium when he dropped a fly ball in the fifth inning, but the Red Sox did not score.

The 32-year-old Shawkey pitched one of his

Red Sox	AB	R	H	RBI
Fewster ss	3	0	0	0
Collins rf	4	0	0	0
Skinner cf	4	0	0	0
Harris lf	4	0	0	0
Burns 1b	3	1	1	0
McMillan 2b	2	0	1	1
Shanks 3b	3	0	0	0
DeVormer c	3	0	0	0
Ehmke p	2	0	1	0
Menosky ph	1	0	0	0
Totals	29	1	3	1

Yankees	AB	R	H	RBI
Witt cf	3	1	1	0
Dugan 3b	4	1	1	1
Ruth rf	2	1	1	3
Pipp 1b	3	0	0	0
Meusel lf	4	0	1	0
Schang c	4	0	0	0
Ward 2b	3	0	1	0
Scott ss	2	0	1	0
Shawkey p	3	1	1	0
Totals	28	4	7	4

											R	H	E
BOS	0	0	0	0	0	0	1	0	0	-	1	3	1
NY	0	0	4	0	0	0	0	0	X	-	4	7	1

Red Sox	IP	H	R	ER	BB	SO
Ehmke L(0–1)	7	7	4	4	3	4
Fullerton	1	0	0	0	1	1
Totals	8	7	4	4	4	5

Yankees	IP	H	R	ER	BB	SO
Shawkey W(1–0)	9	3	1	1	2	5

E—Boston Burns; New York Ruth. DP—New York 1. 2B—New York Meusel, Scott. 3B—Boston McMillan. HR—New York Ruth (1). SH—New York Scott. HBP—Boston Fewster. LOB—Boston 4; New York 5. Attendance: 74,200.

best games in the stadium opener. He gave up one run on three hits while walking two and striking out five in going the distance. The Yankees' first winning pitcher also contributed a home run.

The Sox got a run off the veteran hurler in the seventh inning. Burns walked and then scored on a Norm McMillan triple.

The Yankees had a potential run cut down at the plate in the fifth inning. Schang tried to score from first on an Everett Scott double, but was thrown out on a perfect relay from Boston left fielder Shano Collins to Burns to catcher Al DeVormer.

The Yankees nearly had to forfeit the game in the ninth inning because a number of fans had come onto the field and surrounded Ruth in right field. The field was cleared, and play resumed.

The first game at Yankee Stadium also resulted in the first arrests of ticket scalpers. A ticket priced at $1.10 was being sold for $1.25 or $1.50, depending on the buyer.

The first game always produces some notable "firsts." Besides Ruth's first home run and Burns' first hit, Collins recorded the first outfield putout when he snared Ruth's ball in the first inning.

Yankees shortstop Everett Scott, who played in his 987th consecutive game, recorded the first assist, and first baseman Wally Pipp had the first putout, retiring Chick Fewster for the first out of the game.

Every Yankee in the lineup, including Shawkey (who homered), got a hit except for Pipp and Schang.

Three umpires were used for this historic game. American League president Ban Johnson had previously announced that Billy Evans would be umpire-in-chief and work behind the plate, but Tommy Connolly, the veteran arbiter of the crew, who had worked the very first game of the New York Highlanders in 1903, took his spot behind the dish just before the game began.

The game ended at 5:36 in the afternoon and the fans filed out of the cavernous ballpark pleased that they had seen a special moment in Yankees history. —⁓—

McDonald's Star Shines Brightest with One-Hitter vs. Red Sox

"Every dog has his day" is an old sports expression used to describe a surprising performance.

Yankee pitcher Jim McDonald was no dog, but he had his day as he one-hit the Red Sox in a 5–0 Bombers victory at Fenway Park.

It was the sinker-baller's best game in three seasons in pinstripes.

Only a bloop single in the second inning by Boston first baseman Harry Agganis prevented the 26-year-old right-hander from gaining entry to the record books.

Hank Bauer and Mickey Mantle supported the effort with home runs.

Phil Rizzuto opened the third inning with a double off of loser Mel Parnell and scored on an infield single by Bauer, who had three RBIs in the game.

McDonald helped his own cause with a single and a run scored in the ninth.

Despite walking five, the Oregon native was never really in trouble, as only one Red Sox base runner reached second.

McDonald only made 10 starts that season because he was limited by a groin injury. He posted a 16–12 record overall for the Yankees.

After the season, the right-hander was part of the famous 16-player trade with Baltimore that netted the Yankees pitchers Bob Turley and Don Larsen. —⁓—

Yankees	AB	R	H	RBI
McDougald 3b	5	0	1	1
Bauer rf	5	1	3	3
Mantle cf	5	1	2	1
Berra c	4	0	0	0
Robinson 1b	3	0	1	0
Collins pr,1b	0	0	0	0
Woodling lf	4	0	1	0
Coleman 2b	4	0	0	0
Rizzuto ss	3	2	2	0
McDonald p	3	1	1	0
Totals	**36**	**5**	**11**	**5**

Red Sox	AB	R	H	RBI
Goodman 2b	3	0	0	0
Maxwell lf	4	0	0	0
Jensen cf	2	0	0	0
Kell 3b	3	0	0	0
Agganis 1b	4	0	1	0
White c	3	0	0	0
Piersall rf	3	0	0	0
Lepcio ss	3	0	0	0
Parnell p	1	0	0	0
Baker ph	1	0	0	0
Totals	**27**	**0**	**1**	**0**

											R	H	E
NY	0	0	1	0	0	1	1	1	1	-	5	11	1
BOS	0	0	0	0	0	0	0	0	0	-	0	1	0

Yankees	IP	H	R	ER	BB	SO
McDonald W(1–0)	9	1	0	0	5	4

Red Sox	IP	H	R	ER	BB	SO
Parnell L(0–2)	8	9	4	4	2	5
Herrin	1	2	1	1	0	1
Totals	**9**	**11**	**5**	**5**	**2**	**6**

E—New York Robinson. DP—New York 2. 2B—New York Rizzuto 2, McDougald, Robinson. HR—New York Bauer (3), Mantle (1). SH—New York McDonald. LOB—New York 7; Boston 5. SB—Boston Parnell. Attendance: 27,762.

April 20, 1926
Yankees 18, Senators 5

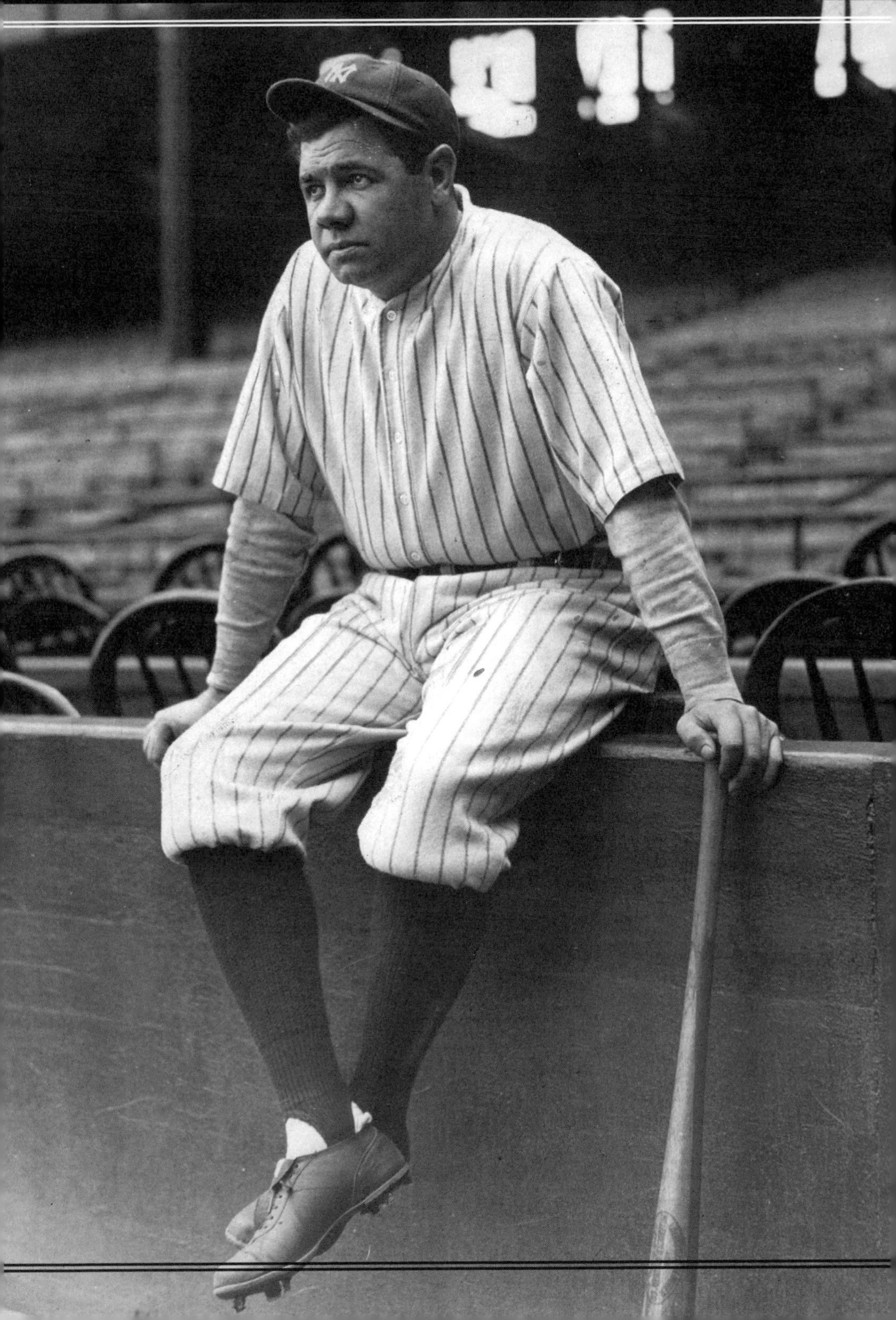

'Big Train' Gets Derailed after Outburst by Ruth

Babe Ruth was 5-for-6 to pace a 22-hit attack as the Yankees destroyed the Washington Senators and future Hall of Famer Walter Johnson 18–5.

Ruth was a big reason that Johnson lasted only three innings.

The Bambino hit a monstrous two-run homer off Johnson in the top of the first inning to get the Yankees off and running.

The shot was described in the April 21, 1926, edition of the *New York Times:* "People who were taking their afternoon constitutional saw the stranger in the sky and thought it was an army dirigible."

Johnson, a.k.a. "The Big Train," gave up five runs on six hits in the third inning and was finished after three.

Babe was not done, however. In the fifth inning, he doubled in two more runs and by the time it was over, Ruth had five hits, five runs scored, and six RBIs.

The Sultan of Swat had tied his career high for hits in a single game while setting a personal best in runs scored.

> ## At a Glance
>
> **WP:** Shocker (1–0)
>
> **HR:** Ruth (1)
>
> **Key stats:** Shocker 8 IP, 7 H; Ruth 5-for-6, 6 RBIs, 5 runs; Gehrig 2-for-4, 2 RBIs, 4 runs

Yankees center fielder Earle Combs (4-for-7) hit safely in his first four times at the plate, while first baseman Lou Gehrig got into the mix with two hits and four runs scored.

Johnson's ERA soared to a "whopping" 2.50. In his previous start, he had pitched a 15-inning shutout against the Philadelphia Athletics. —∽—

A matchup of future Hall of Famers went the way of the Babe on April 20, 1926. Babe Ruth hit a two-run homer off Walter Johnson in the first inning of the Yankees' 18–5 win over the Washington Senators. When "The Big Train" was dispatched after three innings, Ruth continued his assault and finished the game 5-for-6 with six RBIs and five runs scored.

'Louisiana Lightning' Strikes Down White Sox with 3-Hitter

Lefthander Ron Guidry was brilliant as he tossed a three-hit shutout and the Yankees held off the White Sox in Chicago 1–0.

It was vintage "Louisiana Lightning." The Cajun southpaw retired 15 straight hitters at one stretch and 24 of the last 25 he faced.

Willie Randolph's RBI single in the fifth inning scored Dave Revering with the only run the Yankees would need.

"Gator" worked out of a first-inning jam when he struck out Tom Paciorek with two on and two out.

White Sox designated hitter Greg Luzinski ended Guidry's streak of 15 consecutive batters retired when he doubled to lead off the seventh inning, but the left-hander got Paciorek to fly out to center, and he ended the threat by striking out Carlton Fisk and Jerry Hairston with his patented slider.

"The slider is here early," Guidry said after the game. "Usually, it's not here that early, [and] that's been the biggest factor."

The White Sox never saw another base runner after Luzinski's double.

In the ninth inning, Guidry set down Tony Bernazard on a fly to center. After Steve Kemp struck out, Luzinski hit a lazy fly to right to give Guidry his first shutout in nearly two years. —⁓—

Yankees	AB	R	H	RBI
Randolph 2b	4	0	1	1
Mumphrey cf	4	0	2	0
Griffey rf	4	0	0	0
Gamble lf	1	0	0	0
Collins lf	3	0	1	0
Winfield dh	3	0	1	0
Nettles 3b	3	0	2	0
Revering 1b	3	1	1	0
Piniella ph	1	0	0	0
Watson 1b	0	0	0	0
Cerone c	3	0	1	0
Dent ss	3	0	0	0
Murcer ph	1	0	0	0
Milbourne ss	0	0	0	0
Totals	33	1	9	1

White Sox	AB	R	H	RBI
LeFlore cf	4	0	0	0
Bernazard 2b	4	0	1	0
Kemp lf	4	0	0	0
Luzinski dh	4	0	2	0
Paciorek 1b	3	0	0	0
Fisk c	2	0	0	0
Baines rf	2	0	0	0
Hairston ph,rf	1	0	0	0
Morrison 3b	3	0	0	0
Almon ss	3	0	0	0
Totals	30	0	3	0

NY	0	0	0	1	0	0	0	0	- 1	9	0
CHI	0	0	0	0	0	0	0	0	- 0	3	0

Yankees	IP	H	R	ER	BB	SO
Guidry W(2–0)	9	3	0	0	1	9

White Sox	IP	H	R	ER	BB	SO
Dotson L(1–1)	5	5	1	1	1	2
Hickey	1	1	0	0	2	0
Hoyt	2	1	0	0	0	1
Koosman	0	1	0	0	0	0
Barojas	1	1	0	0	0	0
Totals	9	9	1	1	3	3

DP—Chicago 3. 2B—Chicago Luzinski. LOB—New York 8; Chicago 4. SB—New York Mumphrey, Collins. Attendance: 13,700.

Skowron's Blast in 14th Ends a Complete-Game Shutout for Ford

It was one of the best games pitched in the 16-year career of Hall of Famer Whitey Ford. It also came in the first season in which the crafty southpaw would lose 10 games.

"The Chairman of the Board" went the distance and struck out a career-high 15 batters as the Yankees shut out the Washington Senators 1–0 in 14 innings.

Ford gave up seven hits and seven walks but nary a Senators hitter reached third base and only four runners made second.

Bill "Moose" Skowron's solo home run in the top of the 14th inning made Ford a winner in a tremendous overall pitching performance.

Washington pitcher Bill Fischer matched Ford for 10 shutout innings. Senators lefty Chuck Stobbs tossed three more scoreless innings but gave up Skowron's homer with two out in the 14th inning.

Washington manager Cookie Lavagetto took a shot to win the game and lifted Fischer for a pinch-hitter in the 10th inning, but Ed Fitzgerald grounded out and center fielder Albie Pearson popped out with the winning run on second.

Taking into account that Ford came to the plate six times and was on base via three walks, it was amazing he could pitch the whole 14 innings.

Washington second baseman Reno Bertoia led off the bottom of the first inning with a double but was left stranded. The Senators had two runners on base against Ford in the third, 10th, and 14th innings, but could not score a run.

Yankees shortstop Tony Kubek had three of the team's eight hits overall, while Mickey Mantle and Yogi Berra were a combined 0-for-10. Washington rookie outfielder Bob Allison went 0-for-6.

Yankees	AB	R	H	RBI
Bauer rf	6	0	1	0
Kubek ss	6	0	3	0
Mantle cf	5	0	0	0
Berra c	5	0	0	0
Siebern lf	5	0	1	0
Howard ph,lf	1	0	0	0
Skowron 1b	6	1	1	1
Carey 3b	5	0	0	0
Richardson 2b	6	0	1	0
Ford p	3	0	1	0
Totals	**48**	**1**	**8**	**1**

Senators	AB	R	H	RBI
Bertoia 2b	5	0	1	0
Pearson cf	4	0	0	0
Allison lf	6	0	0	0
Lemon rf	5	0	1	0
Zauchin 1b	6	0	1	0
Malkmus pr	0	0	0	0
Killebrew 3b	5	0	2	0
Aspromonte ss	4	0	0	0
Porter c	5	0	2	0
Fischer p	3	0	0	0
Fitz Gerald ph	1	0	0	0
Stobbs p	1	0	0	0
Samford ph	1	0	0	0
Totals	**46**	**0**	**7**	**0**

NY 0 0 0 0 0 0 0 0 0 0 0 0 0 1 - 1 8 0
WAS 0 0 0 0 0 0 0 0 0 0 0 0 0 0 - 0 7 1

Yankees	IP	H	R	ER	BB	SO
Ford W(2–0)	14	7	0	0	7	15

Senators	IP	H	R	ER	BB	SO
Fischer	10	6	0	0	4	3
Stobbs L(0–2)	3.2	2	1	1	2	0
Hyde	0.1	0	0	0	0	0
Totals	14	8	1	1	6	3

E—Washington Aspromonte. DP—New York 2; Washington 2. 2B—New York Ford, Richardson; Washington Bertoia. HR New York Skowron (3). SH—New York Bauer; Washington Porter. LOB—New York 12; Washington 12. SB—New York Siebern. Attendance: 7,337.

The Yankees had chances to score in the fourth and sixth innings, but a line drive into a double play killed the latter threat. In the eighth, Berra walked with two out to load the bases, but Fischer got Norm Siebern to ground out to second to end the threat.

The Yankees had another golden opportunity to take the lead in the 10th. Ford led off with a double and was bunted to third by Hank Bauer. With the infield in, Kubek grounded out to second. Mantle ended the inning with a ground out to second as well.

With one out and the bases empty in the 14th, Skowron parked his third home run of the year into the left-field bleachers at Griffith Stadium. The crowd of a little more than 7,000 went home unhappy after Ford retired pinch-hitter Ron Samford on a grounder to second with the tying and winning runs on base.

Ford was threatened in the third inning when the Senators put two on with two out, but the Yankees southpaw got Allison to ground into an inning-ending force play.

After Skowron's homer in the top half of the 14th, Washington's Norm Zauchin led off with a single. Bobby Malkmus ran for Zauchin and was forced at second on a sacrifice bunt attempt from slugger Harmon Killebrew.

With two out, Washington's J. W. Porter singled to put the tying run in scoring position. Samford batted for pitcher Dick Hyde and grounded out to second base to end a thrilling win for the Yankees. —⁓—

Switch-Hitters Williams, Posada Go Long from Both Sides of the Plate

At a Glance

WP: Hernandez (4–0)

S: Rivera (6)

HR: Williams 2 (6); Posada 2 (5)

Key stats: Williams 3-for-4, 5 RBIs; Posada 3-for-5, 3 RBIs

One of the rare occurrences in baseball is when a switch-hitter smacks a home run batting from both sides of the plate in the same game. It's an even more un-likely occurrence when two players do it in the same game.

Bernie Williams and Jorge Posada became the first pair of switch-hitters to homer from both sides of the plate in the same game as the Yankees outslugged the Blue Jays in Toronto 10–7.

In the top of the first inning, Williams hit a two-run homer from the left side off Blue Jays right-hander Frank Castillo. Posada clubbed his first homer of the game, also left-handed, off Castillo in the second inning.

In the fourth inning, the Yankees' dynamic duo completed the feat as each homered right-handed off Toronto southpaw Clayton Andrews.

After Williams hit his right-handed shot, he passed Posada on the way to the dugout and suggested that the Yankees catcher match his production. Posada obliged, taking the first pitch from Andrews over the right-center-field wall at SkyDome.

Orlando "El Duque" Hernandez was victim-ized for four Blue Jays homers and despite giv-ing up seven runs in a little over six innings pitched, he still picked up the win. —ᴡᴡ—

Bernabe' (Bernie) Figueroa Williams was one of the more underrated Yankees. He an-chored a team that won four World Series championships.

Williams began his big-league career in 1991 and played his entire 16-year career in pinstripes.

The popular Yankees outfielder was a five-time All-Star, won four Gold Gloves, and was named the 1996 American League Cham-pionship Series MVP. In the five-game series vs. Baltimore, Williams batted .474 with 2 home runs and 6 RBIs.

In the 1998 season, Williams won the Amer-ican League batting title with a .339 average. He also became the first player to win a bat-ting crown and Gold Glove and be on a World Series champion team in the same season.

OF Bernie Williams

Mogridge Throws First Yankees No-Hitter

To accomplish a "first" in the history of the New York Yankees is pretty special.

Four years and two weeks after the New York Highlanders officially changed their name to the New York Yankees, left-hander George Mogridge became the first pitcher to throw a no-hit game for the Bronx Bombers in a 2–1 win.

The gem came at Fenway Park against the defending World Champion Red Sox, but it wasn't easy.

The 28 year old from Rochester, New York, stymied the Sox all game long by changing speeds and keeping the hitters off-balance.

The Yankees took a 1–0 lead in the sixth inning. Angel Aragon, the first Hispanic to play for the Yankees, led off with a double and scored on a single by Lee Magee.

Boston tied it in the seventh inning with an unearned run thanks to a pair of walks, an error by second baseman Fritz Maisel, and a sacrifice fly.

The Yankees took the lead for good in the top of the ninth inning.

Shortstop Roger Peckinpaugh singled, stole second, and took third on a throwing error from Red Sox catcher Hick Cady.

> ## At a Glance
>
> **WP:** Mogridge
>
> **Key stats:** Mogridge becomes first Yankee to throw a no-hitter, RBI; Magee, 2–4, RBI

"Peck" scored when Red Sox shortstop Mike McNally threw a ball in the dirt trying for a double play at first on a pop-up by Yankees catcher Les Nunamaker.

Red Sox pitcher Dutch Leonard was the tough-luck loser. The Boston lefty gave up both runs on eight hits with three walks and six strikeouts. —⁓—

Paulie Gets a Standing-O after Fifth Hit of Game

Jimmy Key tossed seven scoreless innings and Paul O'Neill tied a career high with five hits as the Yankees walloped the California Angels at Yankee Stadium 11–1.

The fiery Yankees right fielder singled in the first inning to drive in a run and give the Yanks an early 2–0 lead.

Key was brilliant as he limited the Angels to three hits. The only two times that California had two men on were in the third and fifth innings, but Key induced rally-killing double plays to stymie both of those threats.

The offense made it easy for the wily veteran to go seven innings. Key walked two and struck out four in lowering his ERA to 3.38.

After lining a single to center for his fifth hit in the eighth inning, O'Neill was lifted by manager Buck Showalter for pinch-runner Gerald Williams. The announced crowd of 14,782 gave "Paulie" (whose popularity was growing in leaps and bounds) a standing ovation.

O'Neill added a stolen base, one of five he would swipe on the season. —⚏—

Angels	AB	R	H	RBI
Easley 3b	3	0	1	0
Curtis cf	4	0	1	0
Salmon rf	4	0	0	0
Davis dh	4	1	2	0
Jackson lf	3	0	0	0
Edmonds lf	1	0	0	0
Perez 1b	4	0	0	0
Turner c	3	0	1	0
Fabregas ph	1	0	1	1
Hudler 2b	4	0	1	0
Owen ss	3	0	0	0
Totals	34	1	7	1

Yankees	AB	R	H	RBI
Polonia lf	5	1	2	0
Boggs 3b	4	2	2	2
Mattingly 1b	4	2	1	1
Stanley 1b	0	0	0	0
Tartabull dh	3	1	0	0
O'Neill rf	5	1	5	2
G. Williams pr,cf	0	0	0	0
Nokes c	4	1	1	5
Leyritz c	1	0	0	0
B. Williams cf	4	1	1	1
Boston ph,rf	0	0	0	0
Velarde ss	4	1	1	0
Kelly 2b	3	1	1	0
Totals	37	11	14	11

```
CAL  0 0 0 0 0 0 0 0 1 - 1 7 3
NY   2 0 5 0 0 3 1 0 X - 11 14 1
```

Angels	IP	H	R	ER	BB	SO
Leiter L(2–1)	5	8	7	7	2	3
Sampen	1	4	4	4	3	1
Lewis	2	2	0	0	1	0
Totals	8	14	11	11	6	4

Yankees	IP	H	R	ER	BB	SO
Key W(3–1)	7	3	0	0	2	4
Wickman	2	4	1	1	0	3
Totals	9	7	1	1	2	7

E—California Salmon, Jackson, Hudler; New York Kelly. DP—California 1; New York 2. 2B—New York Polonia, Velarde. HR—New York Nokes (2), B. Williams (4). HBP—New York Velarde. LOB—California 8; New York 9. SB—New York O'Neill. Attendance: 14,782.

A-Rod's First Magical Game: 3 Homers, 10 RBIs

The stars couldn't have been more perfectly aligned for a coming out party for Alex Rodriguez.

"A-Rod" had a tough first year with the Yankees in 2004 and the fans were losing their patience, but Angels pitcher Bartolo Colon provided the tonic for a memorable game in a 12–4 Yankees victory.

Going into the game, A-Rod had always had good numbers against the burly right-hander. Rodriguez was 14-for-38 with three home runs in his career against Colon when he approached the plate for the first time in the first inning.

Before the game, Rodriguez and Yankees captain Derek Jeter were discussing the wind, which was blowing out to right.

"No human alive could hit a ball out to left tonight," Jeter said.

"I think I called 'Jeet' every name in the book," A-Rod said.

After stroking this three-run homer in the first inning, Alex Rodriguez popped two more longballs, including a grand slam, to lead the Yankees to a 12–4 win over the Angels on April 26, 2005. Rodriguez finished the game with three homers and 10 RBIs. Only Lou Gehrig has hit four homers in a game for the Yankees.

Rodriguez unloaded a three-run bomb to left-center field in the first to give the Yankees a 3–0 lead, but it was just the beginning of what was to be a special night.

In the third inning, Rodriguez homered again, this time into the left-field corner, to account for all five Yankee runs and a 5–2 lead. After he got back to the dugout, the crowd demanded a curtain call, and he acknowledged it.

Angels second baseman Chone Figgins made two errors to set up a big fourth inning. Then there was A-Rod, stepping to the plate with the bases loaded.

Anaheim skipper Mike Scioscia decided to stick with Colon—who had thrown 94 pitches—for one more chance, but it backfired big time. "I thought Bart had enough in his tank," Scioscia said.

Rodriguez drove a pitch to dead center field for a grand slam. The blast, Rodriguez's third of the game off Colon, gave the Yankees an astounding 10–2 lead. What was even more astounding was that A-Rod had nine RBIs and was threatening the Yankees' all-time single-game record.

The Yankees' record for most RBIs in a single game is 11 (see: May 24, 1936). Tony Lazzeri had set the mark. Here was Rodriguez with nine, and the game was only in the fourth inning. The legendary Lou Gehrig is the only Yankee to have hit four home runs in a game (see: June 3, 1932).

All things being equal, A-Rod would be getting, at least, two more at-bats. After giving up 10 runs (five earned) in less than four innings, Colon was finally lifted.

In the sixth inning, Rodriguez delivered his fourth hit and 10th RBI with a single to center. For one night, standing ovations were the norm. "After the last base hit up the middle, it just felt like you're on top of a cloud," Rodriguez said. "You don't want the moment to end."

Angels	AB	R	H	RBI
Erstad 1b	3	2	1	0
Merloni 1b	1	0	0	0
Figgins 2b	4	0	3	1
Guerrero rf	4	0	2	2
Paul ph	1	0	0	0
Anderson lf	3	0	0	1
Rivera rf	1	0	0	0
Finley cf	3	0	0	0
Quinlan lf	1	0	0	0
Cabrera ss	4	0	0	0
McPherson 3b	3	1	1	0
J. Molina c	3	0	0	0
DaVanon dh-cf	4	1	1	0
Totals	**35**	**4**	**8**	**4**

Yankees	AB	R	H	RBI
Jeter ss	4	2	1	0
Williams cf	5	2	1	1
Crosby pr-rf	0	0	0	0
Sheffield rf	4	1	1	0
Matsui lf	2	3	0	0
A. Rodriguez 3b	5	3	4	10
Sanchez 3b	0	0	0	0
Giambi dh	3	0	1	0
Posada c	5	0	0	1
Phillips 1b	5	1	1	0
Womack 2b	4	0	3	0
Totals	**37**	**12**	**12**	**12**

ANA	0	0	2	0	1	0	0	0	1	-	4	8	3
NY	3	0	2	5	0	2	0	0	X	-	12	12	0

Angels	IP	H	R	ER	BB	SO
Colon L(3–2)	3.2	5	10	5	5	3
Gregg	3.1	6	2	2	2	2
Woods	1	1	0	0	0	0
Totals	**8**	**12**	**12**	**7**	**7**	**5**

Yankees	IP	H	R	ER	BB	SO
Pavano W(2–2)	7	7	3	3	2	2
Bean	2	1	1	1	2	2
Totals	**9**	**8**	**4**	**4**	**4**	**4**

E—Anaheim, Figgins 2, McPherson. DP—Anaheim 1. 2B—Anaheim, McPherson, Figgins; New York, Womack, Phillips. HR—New York, A. Rodriguez 3 (7). LOB—Anaheim 8; New York 8. SB—Anaheim, DaVanon, McPherson. Attendance—36,328.

Neither did the crowd of 36,328 at Yankee Stadium. In the eighth inning, with the crowd on its feet, Rodriguez approached the plate one more time to face Angels left-hander Jake Woods, who was pitching in only his seventh major league game.

The crowd was greedy. They certainly wanted one more moment, and A-Rod nearly delivered.

Rodriguez led off the inning and lined a Woods pitch into deep center field, but the ball would come up short in his attempt at a record-tying fourth home run and 11th RBI.

Rodriguez stole the show in such a way that reportedly some of the media members who were 11 miles away covering the New York Mets and Atlanta Braves in Queens abandoned a pitching matchup of Pedro Martinez and John Smoltz to witness what was occurring in the Bronx.

Yankees right fielder Gary Sheffield, who scored on one of A-Rod's three homers, said, "He was definitely the A-Rod everybody's been waiting to see."

Yankees manager Joe Torre, who had seen his share of great moments throughout his long career, had an insightful response to what he has just witnessed.

"I don't think there's anybody in baseball that doesn't know," Torre said. "They all understand that Alex has no ceiling. He can rewrite a few things with his ability to hit a ball out anywhere in the ballpark."

Jeter admired what his teammate did.

"You don't see too many days like that," Jeter said. "That's once in a life-time."

The final numbers: 4 hits, 3 home runs, and 10 RBIs. Some players don't see those power numbers in a month. Alex Rodriguez added those stats to his career ledger in less than three hours. —⚌—

3B Alex Rodriguez

Alex Rodriguez joined the Yankees in 2004 and is on the way to becoming the club's greatest third baseman.

Rodriguez has won three American League MVP Awards, two of those with the Yankees.

In 2007, Rodriguez became the youngest player in baseball history to reach the coveted 500 home run plateau (see: August 4, 2007).

On the final day of the 2009 season, "A-Rod" hit two home runs in one inning and drove in an American League record-setting seven runs. Rodriguez also reached 30 home runs and 100 RBIs for a 12th consecutive season, and 13th overall, which is a major league mark.

Key Impressive during Second Career 1-Hitter

Left-handed pitcher Jimmy Key was in the process of justifying his free-agent signing when he tossed a 5–0, one-hit shutout of the Angels at Anaheim Stadium.

The Yankees had always had trouble winning in Anaheim, so this one was extra sweet.

Angels shortstop Gary DiSarcina had the lone hit off Key, a leadoff single to center in the sixth inning.

Key was mowing 'em down, but he left a fastball out over the plate on a 3–1 pitch to DiSarcina, and the gem was spoiled.

"I never think I have no-hit stuff," said Key, who had signed a four-year, $17 million deal. "I'm not that kind of pitcher. I didn't go out in the sixth inning thinking about it. I was just trying to get people out."

Mike Gallego got a rare start at third base and cashed in on his opportunity with two home runs off Angels loser Chuck Finley.

Key struck out eight and walked one in a 117-pitch gem. Only six Angels hit the ball out of the infield and only two reached second base.

"It's fun to watch him pitch. He had great command and great presence," Yankees manager Buck Showalter said.

Key lowered his ERA to 0.93 in winning his third straight for the Bombers.

The Angels had won nine of 11 home games coming in and they had Yankees killer Finley on the hill, but the Bombers touched him for four home runs, including shots from Danny Tartabull and Bernie Williams.

It was the second career one-hitter for Key, who turned the trick as a member of the Toronto Blue Jays on May 22, 1986, when he pitched a one-hitter against the Chicago White Sox. —⁓—

Yankees	AB	R	H	RBI
B. Williams cf	3	1	1	1
Owen ss	5	0	1	0
Mattingly 1b	3	0	1	0
Tartabull rf	4	1	1	1
Stanley c	4	0	0	0
Leyritz dh	4	1	1	0
Velarde lf	4	0	2	0
Gallego 3b	4	2	2	2
Kelly 2b	3	0	0	0
Totals	34	5	9	4

Angels	AB	R	H	RBI
Polonia lf	4	0	0	0
Curtis cf	4	0	0	0
Salmon rf	3	0	0	0
Gaetti dh	3	0	0	0
Snow 1b	3	0	0	0
R. Gonzalez 3b	3	0	0	0
Easley 2b	3	0	0	0
DiSarcina ss	3	0	1	0
Orton c	3	0	0	0
Totals	29	0	1	0

											R	H	E
NY	1	1	0	0	1	0	0	1	1	-	5	9	1
CAL	0	0	0	0	0	0	0	0	0	-	0	1	0

Yankees	IP	H	R	ER	BB	SO
Key W(3–0)	9	1	0	0	1	8

Angels	IP	H	R	ER	BB	SO
Finley L(2–1)	9	9	5	5	4	7

E—New York Key. DP—California 1. HR—New York B. Williams (2), Gallego 2 (1,2), Tartabull (4). LOB—New York 6; California 3. Attendance: 24,261.

Melee at Sportsman's Park Brings Out the Fireworks

Yankees	AB	R	H	RBI
Rizzuto ss	5	0	2	0
Martin 2b	6	1	1	0
Bauer rf	4	2	1	2
Mantle cf	5	2	2	3
Woodling lf	3	0	0	0
Berra c	4	0	1	1
McDougald 3b	5	1	1	0
Collins 1b	2	0	0	0
Raschi p	1	1	0	0
Reynolds p	1	0	0	0
Totals	36	7	8	6

Browns	AB	R	H	RBI
Groth cf	3	1	0	0
Edwards ph,lf	2	0	1	2
Young 2b	3	1	3	1
Kokos lf	2	1	0	0
Dyck ph,cf	1	0	0	0
Wertz rf	4	0	1	3
Kryhoski 1b	4	0	0	0
Sievers ph,1b	1	0	0	0
Elliott 3b	3	1	1	0
Courtney c	5	0	1	0
Hunter ss	4	1	0	0
White p	1	0	0	0
Upright ph	0	1	0	0
Brecheen p	1	0	0	0
Moss ph	1	0	0	0
Totals	35	6	7	6

NY	2 0 3 0 1 0 0 0 0 1 - 7										8 0
STL	0 0 0 0 3 3 0 0 0 0 - 6										7 3

Yankees	IP	H	R	ER	BB	SO
Raschi	5.1	4	6	6	6	3
Scarborough	0	2	0	0	0	0
Schmitz	3	0	0	0	3	0
Reynolds W(3–1)	1.2	1	0	0	0	2
Totals	10	7	6	6	9	5

Browns	IP	H	R	ER	BB	SO
Cain	2.2	3	5	5	4	0
White	3.1	3	1	1	1	0
Brecheen (L(0–3)	4	2	1	0	3	4
Totals	10	8	7	6	8	4

E—St. Louis Elliott, Courtney, White. DP—New York 1; St. Louis 1. 2B—New York Martin, Mantle, McDougald; St. Louis Young 2, Wertz, Elliott. HR—New York Bauer (1), Mantle (3). SH—New York Rizzuto, Raschi, Schmitz. HBP—St. Louis Hunter. LOB—New York 10; St. Louis 9. Attendance: 13,463.

A wild free-for-all erupted in the 10th inning during the Yankees' 7–6 victory over the Browns at Sportsman's Park.

With the game deadlocked at six in the top of the 10th, the Yankees had runners at first and second with one out.

Allie Reynolds hit a come-backer to the mound. St. Louis pitcher Harry Breechen threw to Billy Hunter at second base for a force play, but the Yankees' Gil McDougald, who had been at second, tried to score. Hunter's throw to Browns catcher Clint Courtney at the plate was perfect, but McDougald crashed into the catcher to jar the ball loose, so the go-ahead run scored.

In the bottom half of the inning, Courtney hit a ball off the right-field wall. Yankees right fielder Hank Bauer nailed Courtney trying to stretch the hit into a double, but the Browns' backstop, obviously smarting from getting the ball knocked out of his glove by McDougald, slid hard into Yankees shortstop Phil Rizzuto.

"The Scooter" held onto the ball but was spiked in the leg in two places.

As Rizzuto walked off the field, the remainder of the Yankees infield surrounded Courtney and within seconds, punches were flying and a melee ensued.

Both benches emptied and after a few minutes, the umpires restored order on the field. But the incident was far from over.

Some overzealous fans in the stands began throwing bottles on the field at the Yankees. Pitcher Whitey Ford nearly got hit while left fielder Gene

Woodling left the field three separate times as he refused to be a target.

The bottle tossing brought back memories of Yankees center fielder Whitey Witt, who was hit by a soda bottle in the ninth inning of a game at Sportsman's Park 30 years earlier (see: September 16, 1922).

The umpires were threatening to forfeit the game to the Yankees unless the fans behaved themselves.

It took a gesture of goodwill from Browns manager Marty Marion to get things calmed down.

When the final out was made, more bottles came flying out of the stands. Marion and some of the other Browns players had to walk with the Yankees back into their clubhouse.

It took two police cars to escort the team bus back to the hotel. Fans became rowdy outside the ballpark while the Yankees departed.

During the game, Mickey Mantle blasted a mammoth home run off Browns pitcher Bob Cain that went out of the ballpark over left-center field for a 5–0 lead in the third inning.

Yankees starter Vic Raschi could not hold the lead as he walked six and gave up six earned runs in 5 1/3 innings pitched. The Browns tied it in the sixth inning, setting up the fireworks between the two clubs in extra innings. —∞—

Did You Know?

A total of 11 Yankees have combined to hit for the cycle 15 times in franchise history. Melky Cabrera became the latest to join that list when the accomplished the feat during the 2009 season. Three Yankees have done it more than once, including Bob Meusel (three times), Lou Gehrig and Joe DiMaggio (twice each).

A Run in Every Inning Makes Big Unit a Winner

The Yankees scored in all eight innings to help a support a less-than-stellar Randy Johnson in a 17–6 thrashing of Toronto.

Johnny Damon paced a 15-hit attack with two home runs, while Jason Giambi had four RBIs.

"Not a bad time to get things going," Damon said.

"The Big Unit" lasted only five innings, but it was enough for the win. The 6-foot-10 left-hander gave up six runs on six hits.

"When we score runs, it's great," Johnson said. "But my job is to pitch and that's what I care about."

The Yankees took a 4–2 lead in the first inning off Jays starter and loser Josh Towers thanks to a three-run home run by Giambi.

Damon's first home run made it 5–2 in the second inning. From there, the Yankees scored two runs in the third inning, two in the fourth, three in the fifth, one in the sixth, three in the seventh, and one more in the eighth on a Miguel Cairo RBI single.

Damon tied a career high with five runs scored. Gary Sheffield was 3-for-3, but had to leave the game in the fifth inning after a collision with Jays first baseman Shea Hillenbrand.

After Toronto second baseman Aaron Hill fielded Sheffield's grounder in short right field, the throw forced Hillenbrand into the path of the Yankees' right fielder. Sheffield's right knee hit the back of Hillenbrand's head, and both players were on the ground as medical personnel came rushing out to the field. Both proved to have minor injuries. —m—

At a Glance

WP: Johnson (4–2)

HR: Giambi (8), Damon 2 (2, 3), Posada (3)

Key stats: Giambi 2-for-3, 4 RBIs; Damon 3-for-5, 3 RBIs; Sheffield 3-for-3, 2 RBIs

15th-Inning Grand Slam Allows Martinez to Make New Fans

First baseman Tino Martinez was stepping into some big shoes. It wouldn't be easy trying to "replace" Don Mattingly, who was immensely popular with the Yankee fans.

Martinez got off to a slow start, but on what turned into a rainy night in Baltimore, he may have finally won over the Yankee loyalists when his grand slam in the top of the 15th inning gave the Yankees a huge 11–6 win over the Orioles.

Andy Pettitte made a rare relief appearance as New York stopped Baltimore 11–6 in 15 innings. The Yankees went on to win the World Series that year.

Why was this game so significant? In the minds of many, this was the "bookmark" regular season game that propelled the Yankees to a memorable season that ended with the team's 23rd World Championship.

The teams combined to use 13 pitchers, but in the end it was Andy Pettitte, making his only relief appearance of the season, who tossed three scoreless innings to get the win.

In the 15th inning, the Yankees had runners on second and third with one out when Ruben Sierra was walked intentionally to load the bases for Martinez.

The teams were racing an American League curfew that stated no inning could begin after 1 a.m. local time.

At a little before 1 a.m., Martinez unloaded on a Jimmy Myers pitch and belted it into the left-center-field seats for his biggest hit to date as a Yankee.

The game took numerous twists and turns before it was finally settled.

The Yankees saw leads of 5–1 and 6–3 go down the drain and watched the Orioles tie it in the bottom of the ninth.

With John Wetteland trying to preserve a 6–5 lead, Orioles catcher Gregg Zaun reached on an error by Yankees second baseman Mariano Duncan. A sacrifice bunt and a wild pitch put Zaun at third. He scored the tying run on a sacrifice fly from Robbie Alomar.

In the 10th inning, the Orioles had a golden opportunity to end the game against rookie pitcher Jim Mecir, who was making his Yankee debut. The Birds had the bases loaded with one out, but Mecir got Jeffrey Hammonds to pop to first and ended the inning by striking out Brady Anderson.

Mecir was like a magician as he dodged trouble in the 11th and 12th by leaving two runners on in each of those innings.

The night before, the Yankees outlasted the Orioles 13–10 in the longest nine-inning game (4 hours, 21 minutes) ever played thanks to a three-run

Yankees	AB	R	H	RBI
Boggs 3b	8	1	3	0
Jeter ss	5	2	1	0
O'Neill rf	7	0	0	0
Sierra dh	5	1	0	0
Martinez 1b	7	2	2	5
B. Williams cf	8	2	5	1
Duncan 2b	5	2	2	0
Fox 2b	1	0	0	0
G. Williams lf	8	1	6	3
Girardi c	6	0	1	1
Totals	60	11	20	10

Orioles	AB	R	H	RBI
Anderson cf	6	1	1	1
Alomar 2b	7	1	2	1
Palmeiro 1b	5	1	1	0
Bonilla rf	7	0	2	0
C. Ripken ss	4	0	2	2
Alexander pr-ss	3	0	1	0
Surhoff 3b	5	1	0	0
Devereaux dh	3	0	0	0
Tarasco dh-ph	3	0	1	0
Hoiles c	1	0	0	0
Zaun c	5	2	2	2
Hammonds lf	5	0	1	0
Totals	54	6	13	6

NY 0 3 0 1 1 1 0 0 0 0 0 0 0 0 5 - 11 20 4
BAL 1 0 0 0 2 2 0 0 1 0 0 0 0 0 0 - 6 13 4

Yankees	IP	H	R	ER	BB	SO
Rogers	5	3	5	5	3	5
Wickman	1.1	2	0	0	0	0
Howe	0.2	0	0	0	0	0
Nelson	1	2	0	0	0	0
Wetteland	1	0	1	0	2	1
Mecir	3	3	0	0	4	2
Pettitte W(4–1)	3	3	0	0	0	2
Totals	15	13	6	5	9	10

Orioles	IP	H	R	ER	BB	SO
Wells	7	10	6	6	1	4
McDowell	0.2	2	0	0	1	1
Orosco	2.1	0	0	0	0	3
R. Myers	2	2	0	0	3	2
Mercker L(2–2)	2	3	2	2	1	1
J. Myers	1	3	3	3	1	0
Totals	15	20	11	11	7	11

E—New York, Duncan 3, Fox; Baltimore, Alomar, Zaun 2, Mercker. DP— New York 2; Baltimore 2. 2B— New York, B. Williams 3; Baltimore, Alomar. HR— New York, G. Williams (3), B. Williams (5), Martinez (4); Baltimore, Anderson (12), Zaun (1). SH— New York, Girardi, Jeter, Fox; Baltimore, Hammonds, Tarasco. SF— New York, Martinez; Baltimore, Alomar. HBP— New York Jeter. LOB— New York 16; Baltimore 15. SB— New York, Duncan, Girardi; Baltimore, Anderson. Attendance—47,472.

homer from Martinez that snapped a 9–9 tie. This one took 5 hours and 34 minutes to complete and ended at 1:09 a.m. Even though they must've been exhausted from two grueling games in two days, the Yankees had to feel good about what they accomplished.

"I think after these two games, nobody can question the chemistry, class or ruggedness of this team," Yankees manager Joe Torre said. "These two games were special."

A couple of Yankees had special games themselves. Bernie Williams was 5-for-8 with two runs scored and an RBI, but it was another Williams who stole the offensive show.

Gerald Williams (no relation to Bernie) became the second Yankee in franchise history to record six hits in a game when he went 6-for-8 with three RBIs. The last Yankee to have six hits in a game was Myril Hoag (see: June 6, 1934, and June 7, 2008, when Johnny Damon was 6-for-6 vs. Kansas City).

The Yankees took a 3–1 lead in the second inning, keyed by a two-run homer from Gerald Williams.

The two teams combined for 17 runs and 33 hits. There were 31 runners left on base, and there were eight errors, including three by Duncan.

There was an interesting side note to the game.

Orioles manager Davey Johnson used Manny Alexander to pinch run for Cal Ripken Jr. in the bottom of the eighth inning of a one-run game.

Whenever Ripken was removed from a game during his consecutive games streak (except for when he was ejected), it came with the Orioles far ahead or far behind. Ripken seemed miffed as he sat on the bench and did not speak to reporters after the game.

"I didn't think anything about it. I wanted to steal a base and I knew he [Alexander] could steal it," Johnson said. —⟋⟍—

Andy Pettitte

Standing 6-foot-5, out of Baton Rouge, Louisiana, Andy Pettitte burst on the Yankees scene in 1995 and, except for a three-year stint in Houston, he's been a staple of the Yankees ever since.

Pettitte has won 192 games in a Yankees uniform through the end of the 2009 season and is a two-time 20-game winner.

In the 1996 World Series, Pettitte outpitched John Smoltz to win Game 5 1–0 and put the Yankees on the brink of their first World Championship in 18 years.

The tall southpaw is a two-time All-Star and was named the MVP of the 2001 American League Championship Series win over Seattle.

Gehrig's Streak Comes to an End after 2,130 Straight Games

For the first time since May 31, 1925, the Yankees' lineup would not have Lou Gehrig's name in it.

"The Iron Horse" voluntarily took himself out of the lineup and ended his record-setting consecutive games streak at 2,130. (It was a mark that stood for 56 years until it was broken by Baltimore's Cal Ripken Jr. in 1995.)

The Yankees appropriately honored their captain by pounding out 17 hits en route to a 22–2 mauling of the Tigers in Detroit.

The Yankees batted around in three different innings. Gehrig's replacement, Babe Dahlgren, made his first start at first base since joining the club in 1937. He made the most of his opportunity with a home run, a double, and two RBIs.

However, the story was Gehrig's absence from the lineup. The Columbia University graduate spoke to manager Joe McCarthy, in private, about not playing.

"Lou just told me he felt it would be best for the club if he took himself out of the lineup," McCarthy said.

At a pre-arranged news conference, Gehrig admitted he was hurting the team.

"I haven't been a bit of good to the team since the season started," the long-time first baseman said.

> ## At a Glance
>
> **WP:** Ruffing
>
> **HR:** Dahlgren (1), Selkirk (2), Henrich (1), Keller (1)
>
> **Key stats:** Gehrig's consecutive games played streak ends at 2,130; Keller 2–5, 6 RBIs

Gehrig came to grips with his situation as a result of what turned out to be his final game on April 30. He was 0-for-4 and failed to deliver in the clutch.

"I went up there four times with men on base," Gehrig said. "A hit would've won the ballgame for the Yankees but I missed, leaving five stranded."

The proud ballplayer knew he was done and he didn't need to hang around to erase any doubts. —ᴡ—

DiMaggio's Delayed Debut One to Remember

The major league debut of Joe DiMaggio was delayed by a problem with his left foot that occurred during spring training.

At a Glance

WP: Murphy (1–1)

Key stats: Murphy 5 shutout IP in relief; Chapman 4-for-4; 5 RBIs; Gehrig 4-for-5, 2 RBIs; DiMaggio 3-for-6, RBI

But his long-awaited first appearance in pinstripes was indeed memorable, as DiMaggio went 3-for 6 with an RBI in the Yankees' 14–5 rout of St. Louis.

"Joltin' Joe" started in left field and batted third in the order ahead of the cleanup batter, Lou Gehrig.

The graceful outfielder immediately won over the crowd with a single in the second inning as the Yankees scored three times to go up 7–3 on the lowly Browns.

In the sixth inning, "The Yankee Clipper" drove in his first run with a triple as the Yanks took a 13–5 lead. He completed his impressive first game with a single in the eighth inning off Browns pitcher Russ Van Atta.

The Yankees were in the midst of a stretch that would see them win 21 of 28 games to take a 2½-game lead over Boston in the race for the American League pennant.

Gehrig did not have to take a backseat to the "rook" because he had four hits, scored five, and drove in two to power the 17-hit attack.

Lefty Gomez started for the Yankees but was ineffective as he yielded four runs on nine hits in four innings of work. Reliever Johnny Murphy gave up a run on four hits over the final five to pick up the victory. —

P Lefty Gomez

Vernon Louis (Lefty) Gomez played 13 seasons for the Yankees and was a four-time 20-game winner.

Gomez was the winning pitcher for the American League in the first All-Star Game played in 1933 and he also drove in the very first run in All-Star competition.

In 1934 and 1937, Gomez won the pitching version of the Triple Crown when he led the league in wins, strikeouts, and earned run average.

The left-hander from Rodeo, California won 189 games for the Yankees.

In February 1972, the Veterans Committee unanimously inducted Gomez into the Hall of Fame. Gomez became the second Hispanic player to be inducted into the Hall.

Davis Strikes Out Final Eight for Dominant Save

For one day, a journeyman reliever named Ron Davis had his moment in the sun (despite the fact it was a night game).

The Yankees doubled up the Angels 4–2 at Anaheim Stadium. Rookie pitcher Gene Nelson went six innings to pick up a win in his major league debut, but Davis struck out the final eight Angel batters to earn a spectacular save.

The 6-foot-4 side-arming right-hander relieved Nelson to start the seventh inning. The first batter to face Davis was Don Baylor, who popped to second base. After that, no California Angel batter put the ball in play.

The stretch began with strikeouts of catcher Ed Ott and second baseman Bobby Grich to end the seventh. In the eighth, Davis caught Butch Hobson and Rod Carew looking. Rick Burleson swung and missed at strike three to become the fifth victim.

Dan Ford looked at a third strike to start the ninth inning, while Fred Lynn and John Harris struck out swinging to end an amazing stretch of power pitching.

Davis tied the American League record for most consecutive strikeouts with Nolan Ryan, who accomplished the feat twice in his illustrious career.

In his previous appearance in Oakland, Davis had struck out all five A's batters he faced. The back-to-back dominant outings gave Davis 13 strikeouts out of the last 14 batters he faced.

The Yankees took a 2–0 lead in the second inning. Graig Nettles and Barry Foote singled before Bucky Dent drove in two with a double into the left-field corner. The Angels rallied to tie the game before Lou Piniella, who was batting .160, and Foote hit solo home runs in the sixth inning to make it a two-run advantage.

After the game, Davis downplayed his success of late.

"I'm not a strikeout pitcher," the Houston native said. "I just get lucky every once in a while." —⚞—

Yankees	AB	R	H	RBI
Randolph 2b	5	0	2	0
Mumphrey cf	5	0	2	0
Winfield lf	3	0	0	0
Jackson dh	4	0	0	0
Watson 1b	3	0	1	0
Spencer 1b	0	0	0	0
Piniella rf	4	1	1	1
Nettles 3b	3	1	1	0
Foote c	4	2	2	1
Dent ss	4	0	2	2
Totals	35	4	11	4

Angels	AB	R	H	RBI
Carew 1b	3	0	0	0
Burleson ss	4	0	0	0
Ford rf	4	0	1	0
Lynn cf	3	0	0	0
Harris lf	4	1	1	0
Baylor dh	3	1	1	1
Ott c	3	0	0	1
Grich 2b	3	0	1	0
Hobson 3b	3	0	0	0
Totals	30	2	4	2

```
NY   0 2 0 0 0 2 0 0 0 - 4 11 0
CAL  0 1 0 0 1 0 0 0 0 - 2  4 1
```

Yankees	IP	H	R	ER	BB	SO
Nelson W(1–0)	6	4	2	2	2	4
Davis SV(2)	3	0	0	0	0	8
Totals	9	4	2	2	2	12

Angels	IP	H	R	ER	BB	SO
Zahn L(3–3)	5.2	9	4	4	4	2
Sanchez	2.2	2	0	0	1	1
Hassler	0.2	0	0	0	0	0
Totals	9	11	4	4	5	3

E—California Lynn. DP—New York 1; California 4. 2B—New York Dent, Watson, Mumphrey; California Ford, Harris. HR—New York Piniella (1), Foote (4); California Baylor (3). LOB—New York 9; California 3. Attendance: 30,897.

Posada's Walk-Off Blast Finishes Baltimore

In a game that was destined to be won by the team with the last at-bat, Jorge Posada slammed a three-run walk-off home run in the bottom of the ninth inning to give the Yankees a wild 12–10 victory over the Baltimore Orioles.

The Birds battled back from a 3–0 deficit to grab a 10–8 lead heading into the last of the ninth inning. Paul O'Neill led off the fateful frame with a solo home run off Orioles pitcher Mike Timlin to cut Baltimore's lead to 10–9.

After Bernie Williams singled, Orioles closer B. J. Ryan relieved Timlin and walked Tino Martinez to put two runners on with no one out.

Posada was the next batter, and the Orioles were thinking bunt. The Yankees had a better idea. Posada wanted to be sure that he knew the game plan, so he walked up the third-base line for a pow-wow with third base coach Willie Randolph. Posada asked Randolph if he was bunting.

"As of now you're not," Randolph said. "Look for a good pitch and drive it up the middle."

The Orioles put on the wheel play (a defensive maneuver used to negate a sacrifice bunt attempt) and Ryan delivered a fastball that Posada ripped into the left-field stands for a stunning come-from-behind win.

The Yankees had blown two leads and fell behind 7–5 thanks to two-run homers from the Orioles' B. J. Surhoff and Harold Baines in the top of the fourth inning.

In the seventh, Williams hit a three-run homer to tie the game at eight before Baltimore retook the lead in the eighth inning on an RBI double by Delino DeShields and a sacrifice fly from Surhoff.

Posada had four hits and four RBIs, while Williams was one of three other Yankees in the lineup with three hits apiece. The teams combined for 22 runs and 30 hits —ᴡᴡ—

Orioles	AB	R	H	RBI
Anderson cf	4	1	1	0
DeShields 2b	5	4	4	1
Surhoff lf	4	1	2	4
Belle rf	4	1	1	0
Baines dh	4	1	1	2
Amaral pr,dh	0	0	0	0
Ripken 3b	4	1	1	1
Conine 1b	5	0	2	0
C. Johnson c	4	0	0	0
Bordick ss	4	1	2	0
Totals	38	10	14	8

Yankees	AB	R	H	RBI
Ledee lf	5	0	3	0
Jeter ss	5	2	0	0
O'Neill rf	5	3	3	1
Williams cf	5	3	3	4
Martinez 1b	4	0	0	1
Bellinger pr	0	1	0	0
Posada c	5	2	4	4
Spencer dh	4	1	1	0
Brosius 3b	3	0	1	1
Delgado 2b	2	0	1	1
Totals	38	12	16	12

```
BAL   0 1 2 0 4 1 0 2 0 - 10 14 0
NY    3 0 0 2 0 0 3 0 4 - 12 16 1
```

Orioles	IP	H	R	ER	BB	SO
Erickson	6	8	5	5	0	0
Groom	0.2	4	3	3	0	1
Trombley	1.1	1	0	0	1	1
Timlin	0	2	2	2	0	0
Ryan L(1–2)	0	1	2	2	1	0
Totals	8	16	12	12	2	2

Yankees	IP	H	R	ER	BB	SO
Hernandez	4	9	7	6	1	3
Grimsley	3	3	1	1	1	1
Stanton	0.2	2	2	2	0	0
Nelson W(5–0)	1.1	0	0	0	2	2
Totals	9	14	10	9	4	6

E—New York Delgado. DP—Baltimore 1; New York 1. 2B—Baltimore Conine, DeShields 2, Surhoff; New York Williams, Spencer. HR—Baltimore Ripken (5), Surhoff (4), Baines (3); New York Williams (8), O'Neill (2), Posada (7). SH—Baltimore Anderson. SF—Baltimore Surhoff; New York Delgado. HBP—New York Brosius. LOB—Baltimore 7; New York 6. SB—Baltimore DeShields. Attendance: 42,244.

Mays Makes Quick Work of Athletics with 2-Hitter

Yankees pitcher Carl Mays was masterful in twirling a two-hit shutout in a 2–0 victory at Philadelphia's Shibe Park during a game that lasted 1 hour and 11 minutes.

The 30-year-old side-arm pitcher stymied the A's hitters with a variety of off-speed pitches while facing only 29 Philadelphia batters.

Philadelphia pitcher Slim Harriss was matching zeros with Mays until the eighth inning.

Yankees first baseman Wally Pipp opened the inning with a triple to deep center field. Aaron Ward bounced a single off the leg of shortstop Chick Galloway and the Yankees had a 1–0 lead. After a sacrifice bunt and an error left Ward at third base, Mays drove in the run with a ground out.

Mays dodged a bullet in the bottom half of the inning. A's center fielder Ed Miller, who had both hits off the right-hander, led off with a double. Miller took third on a ground out, but he was left stranded as Mays got Jimmy Dykes and Galloway to pop out to second.

In the seventh inning, Yankees left fielder Chick Fewster was ejected by umpire Frank Wilson for arguing balls and strikes.

The win, combined with the St. Louis Browns' loss in Cleveland, left the Yanks in sole possession of first place in the American League.

Yankees	AB	R	H	RBI
Witt rf	4	0	0	0
Fewster lf	3	0	0	0
Skinner lf	1	0	1	0
Baker 3b	4	0	0	0
Miller cf	4	0	0	0
Pipp 1b	3	1	2	0
Ward 2b	3	1	2	1
Scott ss	2	0	0	0
DeVormer c	3	0	0	0
Mays p	2	0	0	1
Totals	**29**	**2**	**5**	**2**

Athletics	AB	R	H	RBI
Young 2b	4	0	0	0
Johnston 1b	4	0	0	0
Walker lf	3	0	0	0
Perkins c	3	0	2	0
Miller cf	3	0	0	0
Welch rf	3	0	0	0
Dykes 3b	3	0	0	0
Galloway ss	3	0	0	0
Harriss p	2	0	0	0
Hauser ph	1	0	0	0
Totals	**29**	**0**	**2**	**0**

NY	0	0	0	0	0	0	2	0	-	2	5 1
PHI	0	0	0	0	0	0	0	0	-	0	2 1

Yankees	IP	H	R	ER	BB	SO
Mays W(3–2)	9	2	0	0	0	2

Athletics	IP	H	R	ER	BB	SO
Harriss L(2–3)	9	5	2	1	0	5

E—New York Ward; Philadelphia Dykes. DP—Philadelphia 1. 2B—Philadelphia Miller. 3B—New York Pipp 2. SH—New York Scott, Mays. LOB—New York 2; Philadelphia 2. Attendance: 15,000.

Irabu Shows His Value with Workmanlike Win

Hideki Irabu was pitching for his spot in the rotation, and he responded to the pressure by tossing seven innings in the Yankees' 10–1 thrashing of Seattle.

Irabu gave up a run on four hits. The Japanese right-hander struck out five and did not walk a batter in earning the win.

A Russ Davis home run in the seventh inning broke up the shutout bid, but the Yankees got what they wanted from the enigmatic hurler who worked quickly and was efficient in what he was throwing.

Derek Jeter tied a career high with five RBIs, including a three-run homer off Mariners pitcher Mac Suzuki to break up a scoreless tie in the fifth inning.

"He's special," Yankees interim manager Don Zimmer said of Jeter. "He's a super player."

Irabu was able to work out of trouble in the sixth inning. Seattle had two on with no one out, but Irabu got David Bell on a stress-free fly out to right. He then struck out Ken Griffey Jr. on a nifty 1–2 splitter and ended the threat by getting the dangerous Edgar Martinez on a ground out.

During one dominant stretch, Irabu retired 11 straight Mariner hitters. In the fourth inning, Martinez doubled and took third on a wild pitch, but Irabu struck out David Segui on a 3–2 fastball.

Despite his erratic tenure with the Yankees, Irabu was twice named the American League pitcher of the month. ~⌒~

Mariners	AB	R	H	RBI
Hunter lf,cf	4	0	1	0
Bell 2b	4	0	0	0
Griffey cf	3	0	0	0
Cedeno ss	1	0	0	0
Martinez dh	4	0	1	0
Segui 1b	4	0	0	0
Huskey rf	3	0	0	0
Davis 3b	3	1	1	1
Wilson c	3	0	0	0
Bournigal ss	2	0	1	0
Ibanez ph,lf	1	0	1	0
Totals	**32**	**1**	**5**	**1**

Yankees	AB	R	H	RBI
Curtis lf	2	1	0	0
Jeter ss	5	1	3	5
O'Neill rf	4	0	0	0
Williams cf	4	2	1	0
Martinez 1b	4	1	2	1
Bellinger ph,1b	1	0	0	0
Davis dh	4	0	0	0
Brosius 3b	3	2	2	1
Posada c	2	2	1	0
Sojo 2b	4	1	1	1
Totals	**33**	**10**	**10**	**8**

SEA	0	0	0	0	0	0	1	0	0	-	1	5 2
NY	0	0	0	0	3	5	2	0	X	-	10	10 1

Mariners	IP	H	R	ER	BB	SO
Suzuki L(0–1)	5.1	5	7	4	5	3
Weaver	0.1	1	1	0	0	0
Spencer	1.1	4	2	2	2	1
Halama	1	0	0	0	0	2
Totals	**8**	**10**	**10**	**6**	**7**	**6**

Yankees	IP	H	R	ER	BB	SO
Irabu W(1–0)	7	4	1	1	0	5
Naulty	2	1	0	0	0	1
Totals	**9**	**5**	**1**	**1**	**0**	**6**

E—Seattle Griffey, Weaver; New York Sojo. DP—New York 1. 2B—Seattle Martinez; New York Martinez, Brosius. HR—Seattle Davis (8); New York Jeter (6). HBP—New York Curtis. LOB—Seattle 4; New York 7. SB—Seattle Hunter; New York Jeter. Attendance: 38,476.

Pinch-Hit Homer by Nokes Does the Job

The Yankees blew a 6–0 first-inning lead, but Matt Nokes hit a pinch-hit two-run homer in the top of the 11th to give the Bombers a grueling 10–8 win over the Tigers.

The Yankees put six runs on the board in the first inning as they knocked out Detroit starting pitcher Tom Bolton.

Jim Abbott was the beneficiary of all this offense but he could not hold the lead as he went four-plus innings, giving up seven runs to allow the Tigers to knot the game at seven.

Detroit took an 8–7 lead in the fifth inning on a solo home run by Skeeter Barnes off Scott Kamieniecki.

Danny Tartabull's solo home run in the ninth inning off Tigers closer Mike Henneman tied the game and sent it into extra innings.

In the 11th inning, Paul O'Neill singled to set up Nokes' heroics. The Yankees catcher burned his old team with a two-run shot off pitcher Dave Johnson and the Yanks had a two-run cushion.

Closer Steve Farr worked his second inning of scoreless relief to nail down the win.

It was a strange night all around. Before the game, reliever Steve Howe tripped running down the clubhouse stairs near the dugout and sprained his ankle. —⁓—

Yankees	AB	R	H	RBI
B. Williams cf	6	1	3	0
Boggs 3b	5	1	2	0
Kelly pr,2b	1	0	0	0
Mattingly 1b	6	2	3	1
Tartabull rf	6	2	3	3
Leyritz dh	1	1	1	1
Maas ph,dh	4	0	0	0
Velarde lf	1	1	0	0
O'Neill ph,lf	4	1	1	0
Stanley c	5	0	0	0
Nokes ph,c	1	1	1	2
Owen ss	3	0	1	1
Gallego 2b,3b	5	0	0	2
Totals	48	10	15	10

Tigers	AB	R	H	RBI
Phillips 2b	4	3	2	0
Trammell 3b	6	2	4	3
Fryman ss	4	0	0	0
Fielder dh	5	0	1	2
Deer rf	5	1	1	1
Tettleton 1b	4	0	1	0
Thurman pr,lf	0	0	0	0
Gibson ph	0	0	0	0
Kreuter c	4	0	0	0
Cuyler cf	5	0	2	1
Whitaker ph	1	0	0	0
Barnes lf,1b	3	2	1	1
Totals	41	8	12	8

```
NY   6 0 0 1 0 0 0 0 1 0 2 - 10 15 0
DET  1 3 1 2 1 0 0 0 0 0 0 -  8 12 1
```

Yankees	IP	H	R	ER	BB	SO
Abbott	3	6	7	7	6	2
Kamieniecki	3	3	1	1	1	3
Habyan	2.1	2	0	0	1	1
Heaton	0.2	0	0	0	2	1
Farr W(1–1)	2	1	0	0	1	2
Totals	11	12	8	8	11	9

Tigers	IP	H	R	ER	BB	SO
Bolton	0	5	5	5	0	0
Grater	1	1	1	1	1	1
Gohr	3	3	1	1	0	4
Leiter	3.2	2	0	0	2	3
Henneman	2.1	2	1	1	1	1
Johnson L(1–1)	1	2	2	2	1	1
Totals	11	15	10	10	5	10

E—Detroit Phillips. DP—New York 1. 2B—New York Leyritz, Mattingly. HR—New York Tartabull (5), Nokes (2); Detroit Trammell (2), Barnes (1). SF—Detroit Fielder. HBP—New York Leyritz, Gallego. LOB—New York 12; Detroit 12. SB—Detroit Cuyler. Attendance: 27,350.

Mendoza Gives Torre Reason to Be Proud

Before the season, the Yankees and Twins swung a four-for-one deal that brought second baseman Chuck Knoblauch to the Yankees in exchange for pitcher Eric Milton, shortstop Cristian Guzman, and two other players.

There were rumors that Ramiro Mendoza was to be part of the deal, but Yankees manager Joe Torre pleaded with the New York front office to keep the 26-year-old right-hander.

On this day, Torre was vindicated as Mendoza went the distance on a five-hit shutout and the Yankees coasted to a 7–0 win over the Twins at the Metrodome.

Milton was the Twins starter and he struggled, giving up four runs on nine hits in five innings pitched.

The Yanks built an early 3–0 lead thanks to Knoblauch, who doubled and scored in the first inning and drove in the third run with a sacrifice fly in the second.

Mendoza was in total command as he retired the side in three of the first four innings. The Panamanian-born righty did not walk a batter and struck out five in his gem.

"The sinker was the key," said Mendoza, who threw a total of 96 pitches.

"I couldn't be more pleased," Torre said.

Knoblauch combined with Derek Jeter to go 5-for-9 with two runs scored and an RBI to pace the Yankees' 16-hit attack. ~m~

Yankees	AB	R	H	RBI
Knoblauch 2b	4	1	2	1
Jeter ss	5	1	3	0
O'Neill rf	3	0	0	2
Williams cf	4	0	2	0
Martinez 1b	4	1	2	2
Sveum ph,1b	1	0	0	0
Raines dh	4	1	2	0
Curtis lf	5	0	1	0
Posada c	5	1	2	0
Brosius 3b	3	2	2	1
Totals	38	7	16	6

Twins	AB	R	H	RBI
Walker 2b	4	0	1	0
Gates 3b	4	0	0	0
Molitor dh	4	0	0	0
Lawton cf	3	0	0	0
Coomer 1b	3	0	1	0
Merced rf	3	0	1	0
Steinbach c	3	0	1	0
Meares ss	2	0	1	0
Latham lf	3	0	0	0
Totals	29	0	5	0

NY 2 1 0 1 0 1 2 0 0 - 7 16 1
MIN 0 0 0 0 0 0 0 0 0 - 0 5 2

Yankees	IP	H	R	ER	BB	SO
Mendoza W(2–1)	9	5	0	0	0	2

Twins	IP	H	R	ER	BB	SO
Milton L(2–4)	5	9	4	4	2	2
Naulty	0.1	2	1	1	1	1
Guardado	0.2	2	2	1	0	0
Carrasco	2	1	0	0	2	3
Aguilera	1	2	0	0	0	2
Totals	9	16	7	6	5	8

E—New York Jeter; Minnesota Gates, Lawton. DP—New York 4; Minnesota 1. 2B—New York Knoblauch, Posada; Minnesota Steinbach. 3B—New York Jeter. HR—New York Brosius (1), Martinez (6). SH—New York Brosius. SF—New York O'Neill 2, Knoblauch. HBP—Minnesota Meares. LOB— New York 13; Minnesota 3. Attendance: 12,444.

Stottlemyre, White Too Much for Red Sox

Roy White's solo home run proved to be enough for Mel Stottlemyre in the Yankees' 1–0 win over the Red Sox at Yankee Stadium.

Stottlemyre walked two and struck out 10 in going the distance on a seven-hit shutout. Boston had numerous runners on base throughout the game, but Stottlemyre made the big pitches when he needed to.

Stottlemyre gave up two-out singles in four straight innings, but he constantly got out of it by using his arm and his savvy.

P Mel Stottlemyre

One of the most under-rated pitchers to ever wear a Yankees uniform, Mel Stottlemyre acquitted himself very well during his 11-year career in pinstripes.

Stottlemyre came to the big leagues in August 1964 and made an immediate impact as he led the Yankees to rally from behind and win the 1964 American League pennant.

The Hazelton, Missouri, native bested Bob Gibson in Game 2 of the 1964 World Series but lost to the Hall of Famer in Game 7.

Stottlemyre went on to become a successful pitching coach for the Yankees, where he guided the staff that won four of five World Series from 1996 to 2000.

Stottlemyre was up against a tough mound opponent in Boston's Jose Santiago. The 28-year old Puerto Rican pitcher had not lost in nearly a year and he was tough on the entire New York lineup, except for one hitter.

With the game scoreless, White led off the bottom of the seventh inning with a solo shot into the New York bullpen in right-center field for the 1–0 lead.

Santiago probably deserved a better fate, but Stottlemyre had enough to hold down a potent Red Sox lineup that featured Hall of Famer Carl Yastrzemski.

In the eighth inning, the Red Sox had two on and two out but Stottlemyre struck out Joe Foy to end Boston's last threat.

The Yankees ace retired the side in order in the ninth inning to wrap up a very satisfying win for the Bombers. —⁓—

Randolph's Clutch Single Ends Back-and-Forth 13-Inning Thriller

Four hours after the game began, Willie Randolph's walk-off single in the bottom of the 13th gave the Yankees an exciting 5–4 win over the White Sox.

This game had a number of twists and turns.

The Yankees took a 3–1 lead in the fifth inning on a 423-foot home run by third baseman Mike Pagliarulo.

The White Sox rallied in the eighth inning to tie the game on Gary Redus' two-run homer off of Dave Righetti. That prompted a chorus of boos from the 20,634 who were on hand.

The White Sox took a 4–3 lead in the top of the 10th inning on a sacrifice fly, but Pagliarulo smashed his second home run of the game, a solo shot, which tied it at four.

With two out and Wayne Tolleson at second base, Randolph lined a shot over the head of the left fielder Redus for the win. —m—

White Sox	AB	R	H	RBI
Boston cf	5	2	2	0
Redus lf	6	2	4	2
Baines dh	5	0	2	0
Manrique pr,dh	0	0	0	0
Hassey ph,dh	1	0	0	0
Calderon rf	6	0	1	1
Walker 1b	5	0	1	1
Hill 2b	5	0	0	0
Hulett 3b	4	0	0	0
Guillen ss	4	0	0	0
Karkovice c	2	0	0	0
Hairston ph	0	0	0	0
Fisk c	1	0	0	0
Totals	44	4	10	4

Yankees	AB	R	H	RBI
Henderson cf	6	0	1	0
Randolph 2b	6	0	2	1
Mattingly 1b	5	0	0	0
Pasqua lf	3	0	0	0
Kittle ph	1	0	0	0
Cotto lf	1	0	0	0
Winfield rf	4	1	1	0
Ward dh	5	1	1	2
Pagliarulo 3b	5	2	2	2
Tolleson ss	5	1	2	0
Cerone c	3	0	0	0
Washington ph	1	0	0	0
Skinner c	0	0	0	0
Totals	45	5	9	5

```
CHI 1 0 0 0 0 0 2 0 1 0 0 0 - 4 10 0
NY  0 2 0 0 1 0 0 0 1 0 0 1 - 5  9 1
```

White Sox	IP	H	R	ER	BB	SO
Long	7.2	6	3	3	1	1
Searage	0.1	0	0	0	0	0
James	3.2	1	1	1	0	2
McKeon	0.1	0	0	0	0	1
Thigpen L(1–2)	0.2	2	1	1	0	0
Totals	12.2	9	5	5	1	4

Yankees	IP	H	R	ER	BB	SO
Niekro	7	6	2	2	1	4
Righetti	3	3	2	1	2	2
Guante W(3–1)	3	1	0	0	0	1
Totals	13	10	4	3	3	7

E—New York Randolph. DP—New York 1. 2B—Chicago Boston; New York Henderson. 3B—Chicago Redus. HR—Chicago Redus (2); New York Ward (4), Pagliarulo 2 (4,5). SH—Chicago Hulett; New York Skinner. SF—Chicago Walker. HBP—Chicago Karkovice, Guillen. LOB—Chicago 8; New York 4. SB—Chicago Boston, Redus. Attendance: 20,634.

Mattingly's 3-Run Blast Caps Stunning Comeback

What began as a disaster turned into one of the more memorable comebacks in Yankees history.

Don Mattingly slammed a three-run walk-off home run in the bottom of the ninth inning to lead the Yankees to a stunning 9–8 come-from-behind win over the Minnesota Twins.

The Yankees trailed 8–0 in the second inning, but they chipped away, scoring five runs in the sixth inning to set up Mattingly's game-winner.

Twins closer Ron Davis, who entered the game with two outs in the seventh inning, walked pinch-hitter Ron Hassey to start the ninth. Rex Hudler ran for Hassey, but Davis got the next two outs before walking Ken Griffey to bring Mattingly to the plate.

"Donnie Baseball" took some advice into that at-bat from hitting coach Lou Piniella.

"I told him to put all that weight on his back foot," Piniella said, "even if it looks funny."

"I'm not afraid to let Lou tinker," the Yankees first baseman said. "He makes my body do things I can't get it to do."

Mattingly took the first pitch low and outside for ball one from Davis. The next pitch was a fastball, waist high, and Mattingly did not miss it as he drove it into the right-field stands.

Mattingly's clutch blow took starting pitcher Ed Whitson off the hook. Whitson was not living up to the five-year, $4.25 million deal that he signed as a free agent during the offseason. Coming into the game, he had a 1–4 record and only two times had he lasted more than 1 2/3 innings.

The right-hander was absolutely awful. In the first inning, he loaded the bases with nobody out and gave up two runs. In the second, Whitson loaded the bases again before being lifted for reliever Don Cooper.

Twins	AB	R	H	RBI
Puckett cf	5	2	1	0
Hatcher lf	5	2	3	1
Hrbek 1b	5	0	2	1
Brunansky rf	4	1	0	1
Bush dh	4	1	2	3
Smalley ss	4	0	0	0
Gaetti 3b	3	1	1	0
Teufel 2b	4	1	1	0
Salas c	4	0	3	1
Totals	**38**	**8**	**13**	**7**

Yankees	AB	R	H	RBI
Henderson cf	0	0	0	0
Moreno cf	2	1	1	0
Cotto ph,cf	2	0	1	0
Griffey lf	4	1	1	0
Mattingly 1b	4	2	2	4
Winfield rf	4	1	2	2
Baylor dh	4	1	0	0
Wynegar c	4	1	1	3
Randolph 2b	3	0	0	0
Pagliarulo 3b	2	0	0	0
Berra ph,3b	1	0	0	0
Hassey ph	0	0	0	0
Hudler pr	0	1	0	0
Meacham ss	4	1	1	0
Totals	**34**	**9**	**9**	**9**

MIN	2	6	0	0	0	0	0	0	0	-	8	13 1
NY	0	0	0	1	0	5	0	0	3	-	9	9 0

Twins	IP	H	R	ER	BB	SO
Smithson	5.2	7	6	6	1	3
Filson	1	1	0	0	0	1
Davis L(1–4)	2	1	3	3	2	2
Totals	**8.2**	**9**	**9**	**9**	**3**	**6**

Yankees	IP	H	R	ER	BB	SO
Whitson	1	6	5	5	0	0
Cooper	1	2	3	3	1	1
Cowley W(1–2)	7	5	0	0	0	6
Totals	**9**	**13**	**8**	**8**	**1**	**7**

E—Minnesota Gaetti. DP—Minnesota 1; New York 2. 2B—New York Mattingly. HR—Minnesota Bush (3); New York Wynegar (3), Mattingly (2). SF—New York Mattingly. HBP—Minnesota Gaetti; New York Henderson. LOB—Minnesota 5; New York 4. SB—Minnesota Gaetti; New York Henderson. Attendance: 15,136.

Whitson was booed off the mound, accompanied by "Let's Go Mets!" chants from the frustrated crowd of 15,136.

"We heard them," Mattingly said.

Thanks to a grand slam by Twins designated hitter Randy Bush, Minnesota led 8–0.

The rough start wasn't the only bad news for the Yankees. In the bottom of the first inning, future Hall of Famer Rickey Henderson was hit on the elbow by Twins pitcher Mike Smithson. Henderson actually stole second before leaving the game.

Dave Winfield's RBI single in the fourth inning made it 8–1. The Yankees narrowed the gap to 8–6 when they scored five times in the sixth, keyed by a three-run homer from catcher Butch Wynegar.

Joe Cowley relieved Cooper to start the third inning and picked up the win with seven scoreless innings in relief.

The Yankees had a chance in the seventh inning. Bobby Meacham reached on an error and pinch-hitter Henry Cotto singled to put two on with none out, but Griffey was called out on strikes for the first out. Mattingly followed with a ground out to push runners to second and third, but Winfield struck out against Davis, who relieved lefty Pete Filson. ⁓

Did You Know?

The Yankees have won the clinching game of the World Series 10 times at home. The Yankees wrapped up a Series sweep at home four times. Five times they won the Series in six games at home and, in 1947, they won the seventh game at Yankee Stadium.

Gooden's No-Hitter Just What the Doctor Ordered

After bursting onto the baseball scene as a 19-year-old pitching phenom in 1984, Dwight "Doc" Gooden was attempting to resurrect a career that was debilitated by substance abuse.

Making only his seventh start for the Yankees, Gooden no-hit the Seattle Mariners in a 2–0 win.

It was the eighth no-hitter in Yankees history. For the former NL Cy Young Award winner, it was an emotional game in more ways than one.

Gooden's father, Dan, was scheduled to have open-heart surgery the following day.

"I'm dedicating this to my father," the 31 year old said afterwards.

In his previous six starts, Gooden worked 33 1/3 innings and gave up 21 runs. On the advice of pitching coach Mel Stottlemyre, Gooden altered his delivery to go without a windup, similar to the delivery Don Larsen had adopted shortly before throwing his perfect game in the 1956 World Series.

The change worked, but most times it still takes a little luck to throw a no-hitter. Gooden received that good fortune in the top of the first inning.

Seattle's Darren Bragg walked to start the game. Alex Rodriguez then lined a shot into dead center field. Gerald Williams went directly back on the ball and reached up to rob Rodriguez of a sure extra-base hit. Williams, in center field, turned the catch into a double play when he nailed Bragg trying to get back to first base.

After Paul O'Neill snagged Edgar Martinez's line drive near the foul line to end the first inning, Gooden retired the next 12 Mariner hitters.

The zeros were mounting on Seattle's line—no runs, no hits through five innings.

Bragg led off the sixth inning with a bouncer off the chest of first baseman Tino Martinez that was ruled an error, but Gooden worked out of that

Mariners	AB	R	H	RBI
Bragg lf	3	0	0	0
Rodriguez ss	2	0	0	0
Griffey cf	3	0	0	0
E. Martinez dh	3	0	0	0
Amaral pr,dh	0	0	0	0
Buhner rf	4	0	0	0
Sorrento 1b	3	0	0	0
Wilson c	3	0	0	0
Cora 2b	3	0	0	0
R. Davis 3b	2	0	0	0
Strange ph,3b	1	0	0	0
Totals	**27**	**0**	**0**	**0**

Yankees	AB	R	H	RBI
Boggs 3b	4	1	2	0
Girardi c	3	1	1	0
O'Neill rf	4	0	1	0
Sierra lf	3	0	0	0
Martinez 1b	3	0	0	1
Leyritz dh	4	0	2	1
G. Williams cf	1	0	0	0
Eenhoorn 2b	1	0	0	0
Fox ph,2b	1	0	0	0
Jeter ss	3	0	1	0
Totals	**27**	**2**	**7**	**2**

SEA	0	0	0	0	0	0	0	0	0	-	0 0 1
NY	0	0	0	0	0	2	0	0	X	-	2 7 1

Mariners	IP	H	R	ER	BB	SO
Hitchcock L(3–2)	5.2	6	2	2	4	3
Jackson	1	1	0	0	1	0
T. Davis	1	0	0	0	0	0
Hurtado	0.1	0	0	0	0	1
Totals	**8**	**7**	**2**	**2**	**5**	**4**

Yankees	IP	H	R	ER	BB	SO
Gooden W(2–3)	9	0	0	0	6	5

E—Seattle Wilson; New York Martinez. DP— Seattle 1; New York 1. SF—New York Martinez. LOB—Seattle 6; New York 7. SB—New York Leyritz. Attendance: 20,786.

inning. The game remained scoreless until the Yankees' sixth, when they scored the only two runs of the game.

Martinez's sacrifice fly plated the first run and Jim Leyritz's RBI single made it 2–0. Gooden retired the side in order in the seventh and eighth innings, so the stage was set.

Doc took the mound in the ninth inning with 109 pitches thrown and walked A-Rod. Ken Griffey Jr. hit a shot toward first base that Tino Martinez speared. Martinez used a head-first dive to the bag to nail the speedy center fielder as Rodriguez took second.

Gooden was beginning to labor as he walked Edgar Martinez to put runners on first and second.

With Jay Buhner batting, Gooden uncorked a wild pitch and the runners moved to second and third.

The count was 2–2 when Gooden reached back and fed Buhner a rising fastball that the former Yankee outfielder could never catch up to.

With two outs, the crowd of 20,786 was going berserk. Left-handed-hitting first baseman Paul Sorrento was all that stood in the way of a spot in the record books.

The crowd noise headed to a crescendo when Sorrento lifted a pop-up to Derek Jeter. The rookie shortstop grabbed the final out to preserve the gem as the Yankees hoisted Gooden on their shoulders and carried him triumphantly off the field. —⚶—

Posada's Walk-Off Blast Caps Unlikely Comeback

Jorge Posada's walk-off two-run homer led the Yankees to a stunning come-from-behind 14–13 win over the Texas Rangers.

Rangers	AB	R	H	RBI
Matthews cf	5	2	1	0
M. Young ss	6	1	1	2
Teixeira 1b	5	2	4	3
Nevin dh	5	2	3	0
Blalock 3b	4	1	3	4
Mench rf	4	1	2	0
Brown pr,rf	0	1	0	0
Wilkerson lf	3	2	1	2
DeRosa 2b	4	0	1	0
Barajas c	4	1	1	1
Totals	40	13	17	12

Yankees	AB	R	H	RBI
Damon cf	5	4	3	0
Jeter ss	5	3	4	4
Rodriguez 3b	5	2	1	0
Posada c	3	2	2	5
Cano 2b	3	0	0	1
Williams rf	4	2	1	1
Phillips dh	5	0	2	0
Cairo 1b	5	0	2	3
Cabrera lf	4	1	2	0
Crosby lf	1	0	0	0
Totals	40	14	17	14

TEX	2	7	1	0	0	0	2	0	1	-	13	17 1
NY	0	1	2	0	2	6	1	0	2	-	14	17 1

Rangers	IP	H	R	ER	BB	SO
Koronka	4.2	8	5	5	2	2
Feldman	0.1	3	3	3	1	1
Benoit	1	2	3	3	2	2
Bauer	0.2	2	1	1	0	0
Mahay	1.1	0	0	0	1	0
Otsuka L(0–1)	0.2	2	2	2	0	0
Totals	8.2	17	14	14	6	5

Yankees	IP	H	R	ER	BB	SO
Chacon	1.1	6	8	7	2	0
Small	4.1	6	2	2	1	2
Villone	0.1	1	0	0	0	0
Proctor	1	2	2	2	1	1
Farnsworth	1	0	0	0	0	2
Rivera W(1–2)	1	2	1	1	1	0
Totals	9	17	13	12	5	5

E—Texas Barajas; New York Damon. DP—Texas 1; New York 1. 2B—Texas Teixeira 2, Matthews, Blalock, Barajas; New York Phillips 2, Jeter, Rodriguez, Williams. HR— Texas Blalock (8), Wilkerson (5); New York Jeter (5), Posada (6). SH—Texas Wilkerson. SF—New York Posada 2. HBP—Texas Barajas; New York Cano. LOB—Texas 7; New York 9. SB—New York Jeter. Attendance: 40,757.

The Yankees trailed 9–0 in the second, but they kept hacking away to take an 11–10 lead thanks to a six-run rally in the sixth inning.

Derek Jeter's three-run homer cut the deficit to 10–8. Bernie Williams' RBI double made it a one-run game and after Miguel Cairo drove in two with a two-out single, the Yankees led 11–10.

Scott Proctor gave up a two-run homer—and the lead—to the Rangers' Brad Wilkerson in the seventh inning, but the Yankees tied the game at 12 on Posada's sacrifice fly in the bottom half.

Texas took the lead one more time in the ninth off Mariano Rivera on two broken-bat hits.

Kevin Mench led off the inning with a bloop single to center. After a successful sacrifice bunt put Mench on second, he scored on a Rod Barajas double that snuck down the third-base line.

In the bottom of the ninth, Texas went with its closer, Akinori Otsuka, and he promptly gave up a bad-hop single to Johnny Damon. Jeter bounced back to the mound, but Damon took second.

Alex Rodriguez lined to center for the second out.

Posada worked the count to 3–1 and then unloaded on a fastball from Otsuka into the right-center-field bleachers for the dramatic victory.

"I was just hoping it was out of the park so we wouldn't have to keep playing," Posada said. "I didn't want to play anymore. As soon as I hit it, I knew it was gone."

Despite trailing 9–0, the Yankees won, matching the biggest deficit they have ever overcome in franchise history. That occurred three other times, in 1950, 1953, and 1987. "When we were down 9–0, 10–1, I'm just trying to keep from using my whole bullpen," manager Joe Torre said. "That's what my thought process is. I can't really be thinking about winning a game until we can stop them from scoring."

The switch-hitting Yankee catcher finished with five RBIs, but his offense wasn't the only contribution he made.

In the Texas half of the fifth inning, future Yankee Mark Teixeira was on first base with two outs when Hank Blalock lined a shot into the left-field corner. Melky Cabrera retrieved the ball and threw it to Jeter, who was the cutoff man. The Yankee captain fired a two-hopper to the plate as Teixeira came barreling home. Posada held on to the throw and took a vicious hit from his future teammate for the final out of the inning in what proved to be a big play in the game.

"It was pretty tough," said Posada, a 12-year veteran. "That was probably the hardest I've ever been hit."

Jeter finished with four hits while Damon scored four times.

The Yankees were without left fielder Hideki Matsui, who was recovering from a broken wrist, an injury that ended his consecutive games streak at 1,768 (1,250 with Yomuri Giants and 518 with the Yankees). —⁓—

Perfecto in Pinstripes as Wells Makes History

The Bronx had not seen perfection in nearly 42 years, but David Wells ended that streak as he tossed the 15th perfect game in baseball history, a 4–0 masterpiece, to beat the Minnesota Twins.

If you looked at the Twins box score under at-bats, there were 27. If you looked at the column marked hits, there were none. If you looked at the column marked walks, there were none, and if you looked for an error that allowed a runner to reach base, there was none.

There was some irony to Wells pitching a perfecto in pinstripes. When the 35-year-old southpaw was growing up in San Diego, he attended the same high school as Don Larsen, who had pitched a perfect game in the 1956 World Series. Larsen was a member of the Class of 1947 at Point Loma High School; Wells was Class of 1982.

Wells struck out 11 in his gem but he didn't record his first K until he struck out the fifth batter of the game, Ron Coomer, in the second inning.

Boomer struck out the side in the third inning and added one more in the fourth. Meanwhile, the Yankees took a 1–0 lead in the second as Bernie Williams scored from third on a wild pitch by Minnesota starter LaTroy Hawkins.

The Yankees added a run in the fourth on a solo home run by Williams and completed the scoring with two runs in the seventh inning. Darryl Strawberry had an RBI triple, and he scored on a single by Chad Curtis.

Wells faced his first problem of the game in the seventh inning. With two out, he fell behind in the count to Paul Molitor, 3–1. Wells came back with two straight fastballs to strike out the Hall of Famer.

The "Beanie Baby" crowd (fans received free a "Beanie Babies" toy as part of a promotion) of 49,820 was going "ga-ga."

Twins left fielder Marty Cordova led off the seventh inning with a grounder to short that was bobbled momentarily by Derek Jeter, but he completed the play.

In almost any no-hit game, there are always one or two defensive gems that preserve the pitcher's bid for the record books. The defensive gem that preserved this one came with one out in the eighth inning. The batter was Coomer,

David Wells jumps for joy to celebrate throwing a perfect game against the Minnesota Twins on May 17, 1998, at Yankee Stadium. It was just the 15th perfect game in baseball history.

who laced a ball toward the middle of the diamond. New York second baseman Chuck Knoblauch knocked it down with a backhand stab, picked it up, and fired a strike to Tino Martinez at first to nail Coomer.

What made this play even more lucky was that Knoblauch had been having problems making routine throws to first.

Four outs to go. During the bottom of the seventh inning, Wells was consoled by his teammate, David Cone, in the dugout. That broke an old baseball superstition that teammates do not talk to a pitcher who's working on a no-hitter.

Cone, a fellow pitcher and a friend, understood that Wells needed conversation, and while the Yankees batted in the seventh, he made a suggestion about using a knuckleball.

"I can't tell you how much that helped me," Wells said.

The Yankee lefty retired Alex Ochoa on a pop-up to first and the stage was set for the ninth. Wells dropped his glove down in the clubhouse after the eighth.

Twins	AB	R	H	RBI
Lawton cf	3	0	0	0
Gates 2b	3	0	0	0
Molitor dh	3	0	0	0
Cordova lf	3	0	0	0
Coomer 1b	3	0	0	0
Ochoa rf	3	0	0	0
Shave 3b	3	0	0	0
Valentin c	3	0	0	0
Meares ss	3	0	0	0
Totals	27	0	0	0

Yankees	AB	R	H	RBI
Knoblauch 2b	4	0	0	0
Jeter ss	3	0	1	0
O'Neill rf	4	0	0	0
Martinez 1b	4	0	0	0
Williams cf	3	3	3	1
Strawberry dh	3	1	1	1
Curtis lf	3	0	1	1
Posada c	3	0	0	0
Brosius 3b	3	0	0	0
Totals	30	4	6	3

MIN 0 0 0 0 0 0 0 0 0 - 0 0 0
NY   0 1 0 1 0 0 2 0 X - 4 6 0

Twins	IP	H	R	ER	BB	SO
Hawkins L(2–4)	7	6	4	4	0	5
Naulty	0.1	0	0	0	1	0
Swindell	0.2	0	0	0	0	1
Totals	8	6	4	4	1	6

Yankees	IP	H	R	ER	BB	SO
Wells W(5–1)	9	0	0	0	0	11

2B—New York, Williams 2. 3B—New York, Strawberry. HR—New York, Williams (3). LOB—New York 3; Minnesota 0. SB—New York, Jeter, Curtis. Attendance—49,820.

"It's getting a little hairy out there," he said to Cone, who complained, in response, that Wells still had not thrown a knuckler.

The Yankees went out quietly in their half of the eighth inning, so Wells proceeded to get up, grab his glove from the dugout bench, and head toward the Yankee Stadium mound and a place in history.

The crowd acknowledged Wells' walk with destiny as they were roaring, awaiting the first batter of the inning, Jon Shave. Wells retired the Twins' third baseman on a high fly to Paul O'Neill in right.

Two outs to go. Javier Valentin struck out on a nifty curveball from Wells and it was all up to Pat Meares, the Twins' shortstop who had flied to center and struck out in his previous two at-bats.

On the first pitch, Meares swung at a fastball and fouled it back. With the count 0–1, Wells delivered a pitch for the ages. Meares lifted a fly ball that was heading toward the corner in right field.

When Meares' soft fly dropped into O'Neill's glove, the burly and balding Wells bent down and thrust his left fist into the air, and then again.

"This is great, Jorge, this is great," he yelled to catcher Jorge Posada, over and over. ⸻

Tresh's Walk-Off Triple a Unique Way to Finish Off Red Sox

It's not all that common for a ballgame to end on a "walk-off" triple, but Tom Tresh secured that distinction when his three-bagger led the Yankees to a 4–3, 12-inning win over the Boston Red Sox.

The Yankees trailed 3–1 in the bottom of the ninth inning, but tied the game thanks to Ray Barker's first major league home run and a clutch two-out RBI single by Bobby Richardson.

The Yankees had never beaten Red Sox pitcher Dick "The Monster" Radatz, who entered the game after Barker's home run.

The 6-foot-5 reliever struck out six consecutive Yankees over the 10th and 11th innings.

In the top of the 12th, Radatz led off with a single and spent the entire inning on base, which may have caused him to walk Phil Linz to start the bottom of the 12th.

After Richardson popped out trying to advance Linz, Tresh drove the first pitch from Radatz off the right-field auxiliary scoreboard to score Linz with the winning run.

Pedro Ramos was brilliant in relief for the Yankees and earned the win.

Boston starting pitcher Dave Morehead did not allow a hit until Barker led off the seventh inning with a bloop single over second base.

The Yankees scored their first run in the second inning without the benefit of a hit. Morehead lost the plate and walked three batters before giving up a game-tying sacrifice fly to Yankees starter Bill Stafford. —

Red Sox	AB	R	H	RBI
Green lf	6	2	2	1
Jones 3b	4	1	3	0
Mantilla 2b	3	0	0	0
Conigliaro rf	5	0	1	0
Thomas 1b	3	0	0	1
Geiger cf	4	0	0	0
Bressoud ss	5	0	0	0
Tillman c	5	0	0	0
Morehead p	4	0	0	0
Radatz p	1	0	1	0
Totals	**40**	**3**	**7**	**2**

Yankees	AB	R	H	RBI
Linz ss	4	1	0	0
Richardson 2b	5	0	1	1
Tresh cf,lf	6	0	1	1
Mantle lf	4	0	0	0
Moschitto cf	0	0	0	0
Pepitone rf	5	0	0	0
Barker 1b	3	2	2	1
Boyer 3b	4	0	0	0
Edwards c	1	0	0	0
H. Lopez ph	1	0	1	0
Clarke ph	1	1	1	0
Ramos p	1	0	0	0
Stafford p	1	0	0	1
A. Lopez ph	1	0	0	0
Schmidt c	2	0	1	0
Totals	**39**	**4**	**7**	**4**

```
BOS  1 0 0 0 0 2 0 0 0 0 0 0 - 3 7 0
NY   0 1 0 0 0 0 0 0 2 0 0 1 - 4 7 1
```

Red Sox	IP	H	R	ER	BB	SO
Morehead	8	3	2	2	7	4
Radatz L(2–3)	3.1	4	2	2	1	6
Totals	**11.1**	**7**	**4**	**4**	**8**	**10**

Yankees	IP	H	R	ER	BB	SO
Stafford	7	5	3	3	2	4
Hamilton	2	1	0	0	1	3
Reniff	0.1	0	0	0	2	0
Ramos W(2–1)	2.2	1	0	0	1	2
Totals	**12**	**7**	**3**	**3**	**6**	**9**

E—New York Stafford. DP—Boston 1. 3B—New York Tresh. HR—Boston Green (4); New York Barker (1). SH—Boston Mantilla 2. SF—Boston Thomas; New York Stafford. LOB—Boston 10; New York 10. Attendance: 12,371.

Gator Baits Tigers into Efficient 6-Hitter

Ron Guidry came up with a vintage performance as he went the distance on a six-hitter in shutting out the Tigers at Tiger Stadium 1–0.

Guidry used his arm, his savvy, and his experience to negotiate his way through some jams, including one with the bases loaded and nobody out in the sixth.

"That's when Guidry was awesome," said the Tigers' Kirk Gibson.

With the Yankees leading 1–0, the Tigers loaded the bases with no one out. The American League's leading hitter was Alan Trammell, and Guidry struck him out.

"Did you know that before tonight Trammell had struck out only six times?" Gibson said.

Steve Kemp then hit a sharp grounder to first that was fielded by Jim Spencer, who threw to second for the force. Guidry covered first for the return throw. The double play was completed and so was the Tigers' rally, which did not produce a run.

Guidry dodged some bullets in the seventh, eighth, and ninth innings, but Detroit left five men on in those innings. "Gator" ended the contest by getting Dave Stegman on a come-backer to the mound.

Guidry struck out seven, walked three, and saw his ERA drop to 2.80. —

Yankees	AB	R	H	RBI
Randolph 2b	3	0	1	0
Murcer lf	3	0	1	0
Jones cf	4	0	1	0
Jackson dh	4	1	1	0
Spencer 1b	4	0	0	0
Nettles 3b	4	0	1	1
Brown rf	3	0	0	0
Dent ss	3	0	1	0
Cerone c	3	0	0	0
Totals	31	1	6	1

Tigers	AB	R	H	RBI
Whitaker 2b	3	0	1	0
Trammell ss	2	0	0	0
Kemp dh	4	0	0	0
Parrish rf,c	4	0	0	0
Wockenfuss lf	4	0	1	0
Hebner 1b	4	0	1	0
Peters pr	0	0	0	0
Brookens 3b	3	0	1	0
Stegman cf,rf	4	0	1	0
Dyer c	2	0	1	0
Gibson pr,cf	1	0	0	0
Totals	31	0	6	0

NY 0 1 0 0 0 0 0 0 0 - 1 6 2
DET 0 0 0 0 0 0 0 0 0 - 0 6 0

Yankees	IP	H	R	ER	BB	SO
Guidry W(4–0)	9	6	0	0	3	7

Tigers	IP	H	R	ER	BB	SO
Wilcox L(2–3)	9	6	1	1	3	5

E—New York Randolph, Guidry. DP—New York 1; Detroit 1. 2B—New York Murcer, Jackson, Nettles. SH—Detroit Whitaker. LOB—New York 6; Detroit 8. SB—New York Randolph, Brown. Attendance: 27,715.

Shea Crowd Leaves Disappointed in Subway Series Comeback

A memorable comeback in the Subway Series saw the Yankees rally to nip the Mets 5–4 in 11 innings.

The Yankees trailed 4–0 entering the ninth inning, but scored four times off Mets closer Billy Wagner to tie it and frustrate many of the 56,185 on hand at Shea Stadium.

Andy Phillips' RBI single with two outs in the 11th gave the Yankees the lead. Winning pitcher Mariano Rivera struck out the side in the bottom half to wrap up a very satisfying victory.

The ninth inning rally began with a Jason Giambi single and a walk to Alex Rodriguez. Robinson Cano singled in a run to make it 4–1 and bring the tying run to the plate.

After Miguel Cairo flied out, Melky Cabrera produced the key at-bat of the inning. The 21-year-old switch-hitting outfielder was down 0–2 against Wagner, but he did a great job of fouling off pitches and eventually worked a walk that loaded the bases.

"'That was awesome, against a closer like that, to get up there and be 0–2 and battle back, battle back," Rodriguez said. "I was at second base, and he laid off some pitches that are very hard to lay off. He fouled off some great sliders down and in."

Wagner collapsed after Cabrera's at-bat as he walked Kelly Stinnett to force in a run. The Mets' lefty then hit pinch-hitter Bernie Williams to make it 4–3, and he was done.

"We should have won that game hands down," Wagner said. "They never should have been in the ballgame. I let them back in. I just stunk."

Pedro Feliciano relieved Wagner and got Johnny Damon to hit what looked like a game-ending

Yankees	AB	R	H	RBI
Damon cf	5	0	0	1
Jeter ss	5	0	1	0
Giambi 1b	4	1	1	0
Rivera p	0	0	0	0
Rodriguez 3b	4	1	2	0
Cano 2b	5	1	1	1
Cairo lf	4	1	0	0
Cabrera rf	4	1	1	0
Stinnett c	4	0	0	1
Mussina p	2	0	0	0
Reese ph	1	0	1	0
Williams ph	0	0	0	1
Phillips 1b	1	0	1	1
Totals	39	5	8	5

Mets	AB	R	H	RBI
Reyes ss	5	1	0	0
Matsui 2b	4	0	1	0
Beltran cf	5	1	1	1
Delgado 1b	5	1	1	1
Wright 3b	4	0	1	1
Floyd lf	5	1	1	1
Nady rf	5	0	0	0
Castro c	4	0	0	0
Martinez p	2	0	0	0
Franco ph	1	0	1	0
Valentin ph	1	0	0	0
Totals	41	4	6	4

```
NY A  0 0 0 0 0 0 0 0 4 0 1 - 5 8 4
NY N  2 0 0 1 0 0 1 0 0 0 0 - 4 6 3
```

Yankees	IP	H	R	ER	BB	SO
Mussina	7	5	4	2	0	7
Villone	1	0	0	0	2	1
Proctor	1	0	0	0	0	2
Rivera W(2–3)	2	1	0	0	0	4
Totals	11	6	4	2	2	14

Mets	IP	H	R	ER	BB	SO
Martinez	7	4	0	0	1	8
Sanchez	1	1	0	0	0	0
Wagner	0.1	2	4	4	3	0
Feliciano	0.1	0	0	0	0	0
Bradford	0.1	0	0	0	0	0
Julio L(1–2)	2	1	1	1	2	2
Totals	11	8	5	5	6	10

E—New York Yankees Giambi, Rodriguez, Stinnett, Villone; New York Mets Floyd, Castro, Martinez. DP—New York Mets 3. 2B—New York Mets Beltran, Wright, Franco. HR—New York Mets Delgado (14), Floyd (4). HBP—New York Yankees Williams. LOB—New York Yankees 8; New York Mets 6. SB—New York Yankees Damon, Cabrera, Cairo 2; New York Mets Reyes. Attendance: 56,185.

double-play grounder to short, but Damon beat the relay throw and Cabrera scored to tie the game.

Damon was playing with a chipped bone in his foot so it was remarkable that he was able to beat the throw to first. Damon used a movie quote to assess his hustle.

"Just run—'Run, Forrest, run!'" Damon said, quoting a line from the award-winning movie, *Forrest Gump*.

In the 11th inning, Mets pitcher Jorge Julio issued a leadoff walk to Cairo, who promptly stole second and third but was left there with two outs. Phillips was hitting .174 but he lashed a single to center to score the go-ahead run.

"I just haven't swung the bat well since I've been here, regardless of how many at-bats I've had," Phillips said. "But I do have confidence in myself at the plate."

Despite the win, Yankees manager Joe Torre was not pleased with the way the team played, especially on defense.

"It's been terrible," he said. "Especially if it's going to take a little bit more work to score runs, we certainly can't allow extra outs for the opposition. We're capable of getting better, and we need to do that." —∿—

Did You Know?

In 2009, Andy Pettitte became the second Yankees pitcher to win win four games in a single postseason. David Wells turned the trick in 1998. Overall, Pettitte became the 14th pitcher to win at least four games in a single postseason.

Parker Makes It a Career Day with 10 Strikeouts

Clay Parker had a career day as he led the Yankees to a 6–2 win over the Mariners at the Seattle Kingdome, a place where the Bombers had not been very successful over the years.

Parker went the distance, giving up two runs on five hits and striking out a career-high 10 batters.

The 21-year-old right-hander from Columbia, Louisiana, took a shutout into the ninth inning, but a 19-year-old rookie named Ken Griffey Jr. hit a two-run inside-the-park home run that eluded Roberto Kelly in left field to spoil the bid.

When he was asked if he was upset over losing the shutout, Parker said, "For about three seconds. I wanted it, any pitcher does. But I didn't have good stuff the latter part of the game and they were starting to hit pitches hard in the seventh, eighth, and ninth."

Steve "Bye-Bye" Balboni's home run gave the Yankees a 1–0 lead in the second inning.

Catcher Bob Geren had three hits, including a home run, to boost his batting average to .417. Geren had the big hit of the game, a key two-run single in the sixth inning off Mariners pitcher Mark Langston to up the lead to 4–0. —◇—

Yankees	AB	R	H	RBI
Henderson lf	5	2	3	0
Sax 3b	4	1	1	0
Mattingly 3b	5	1	0	0
Balboni dh	3	1	1	2
Brower rf	5	0	3	1
Brookens 3b	3	0	1	0
Geren c	5	1	3	3
Tolleson ss	4	0	1	0
Kelly cf	4	0	0	0
Totals	38	6	13	6

Mariners	AB	R	H	RBI
Reynolds 2b	3	0	0	0
Bradley dh	4	1	1	0
Griffey cf	4	1	2	2
Coles 1b	4	0	1	0
Presley 3b	4	0	0	0
Valle c	3	0	1	0
Brantley rf	4	0	0	0
Cochrane lf,ss	3	0	0	0
Vizquel ss	2	0	0	0
Cotto ph,lf	1	0	0	0
Totals	32	2	5	2

											R	H	E
NY	0	1	0	0	0	3	1	1	0	-	6	13	0
SEA	0	0	0	0	0	0	0	0	2	-	2	5	0

Yankees	IP	H	R	ER	BB	SO
Parker W(2–0)	9	5	2	2	2	10

Mariners	IP	H	R	ER	BB	SO
Langston L(4–5)	6.2	8	5	5	4	3
Jackson	1	3	1	1	1	0
Powell	1.1	2	0	0	0	1
Totals	9	13	6	6	5	4

DP—Seattle 1. 2B—New York Brower; Seattle Griffey. HR—New York Balboni (5), Geren (2); Seattle Griffey (6). SF—New York Balboni. LOB—New York 11; Seattle 5. SB—New York Henderson. Attendance: 35,524.

'The Hardest Ball I Ever Hit' a Blast for Mantle

Mickey Mantle hit a mammoth walk-off home run in the bottom of the 11th inning off Kansas City's Bill Fischer to give the Yankees an 8–7 win over the Athletics at Yankee Stadium.

The game looked like a laugher early on. The Yankees scored seven times in the second inning to take a 7–0 lead, but the Athletics rallied for six runs in the eighth inning and tied the game in the ninth on a two-out solo home run by third baseman Ed Charles off Ralph Terry.

Mantle was the leadoff batter in the 11th, and he worked the count to 2–2.

Fischer uncorked a fastball and Mantle launched what he would later call "the hardest ball I ever hit."

It was a tremendous blast that was still rising as it crashed off the façade that sat atop the right-field grandstand, some 108 feet above the playing field.

This was the second time that the Hall of Fame switch-hitter nearly hit a ball completely out of Yankee Stadium.

In the second inning, the Yankees took advantage of a shaky Ted Bowsfield, the starter for the A's.

Roger Maris got things started with a bloop double followed by three straight singles by Joe Pepitone, Tony Kubek, and pitcher Bill Stafford that made it 3–0.

The Yankees added four more runs that inning and were sitting pretty until the eighth inning.

> ## At a Glance
>
> **WP:** Hamilton (2–1)
>
> **HR:** Mantle (9)
>
> **Key stats:** Mantle game-winning HR in 11th; Pepitone 3-for-5, RBI

A's left fielder Gino Cimoli hit a two-run homer to narrow the gap to 7–2. A Norm Siebern double and an error by the usually reliable Clete Boyer put two runners on with no one out. Kansas City scored six times (only two runs were earned) to cut the lead to one.

In the ninth inning, Terry got Jerry Lumpe on a ground out and induced Siebern to strike out, but Charles belted the game-tying home run.

There's always been a fascination with hitting a ball completely out of Yankee Stadium because it had never been done at the original ballpark.

Rumors have abounded throughout the years that Josh Gibson, the great Negro League catcher, hit a home run completely out of Yankee Stadium during a Negro League game that was played there. —⁓—

From 'Rags' to Riches: Righetti Earns First Win

Rookie left-hander Dave Righetti tossed seven solid innings to lead the Yankees to a 3–2 win over the Cleveland Indians for his first win in pinstripes.

Righetti, who would be named the 1981 American League Rookie of the Year, gave up two runs on four hits. The 22-year-old southpaw walked two and struck out seven.

It was a nine-player trade with the Texas Rangers in November 1978 that brought Righetti to the Bronx. The Yankees felt "Rags" was the key component of that deal that sent the popular Sparky Lyle to Texas.

Righetti had posted a 5–0 record at the Yankees' AAA affiliate in Columbus, Ohio, before he was recalled for this start.

The young lefty was sent back to the minors at the beginning of the season, despite pitching well in the spring.

"I knew they felt good about me," Righetti said.

Dave Winfield's first-ever home run at Yankee Stadium off "Yankee Killer" Rick Waits gave the Yankees a 3–1 lead in the third inning.

The game included an unusual triple play that was turned by Cleveland in the sixth inning.

With runners at first and second and nobody out, Bucky Dent hit a grounder to third base, where Indians third baseman Toby Harrah fielded the ball and stepped on the bag. Harrah threw to Alan Bannister at second to get a sliding Graig Nettles, but second base umpire John Shulock ruled that Nettles interfered with Bannister on the relay attempt to first so a triple play was called. —m—

Indians	AB	R	H	RBI
Dilone lf	3	0	0	0
Littleton lf	0	1	0	0
Kuiper 2b	0	0	0	0
Bannister 2b	3	0	0	0
Orta ph,rf	1	0	1	0
Hargrove 1b	2	0	0	1
Thornton dh	3	0	1	0
Kelly ph,dh	1	0	0	0
Harrah 3b	3	1	0	0
Diaz c	4	0	2	0
Charboneau rf,lf	4	0	0	0
Manning cf	4	0	1	1
Veryzer ss	3	0	0	0
Totals	31	2	5	2

Yankees	AB	R	H	RBI
Milbourne 2b	4	1	2	1
Murcer dh	4	0	1	0
Winfield cf	4	1	1	2
Jackson rf	4	0	1	0
Piniella lf	4	0	1	0
Foote c	4	0	2	0
Nettles 3b	3	0	0	0
Dent ss	2	0	0	0
Werth 1b	1	1	1	0
Revering 1b	1	0	0	0
Totals	31	3	9	3

										R	H	E
CLE	0	1	0	0	0	0	1	0	-	2	5	0
NY	0	0	3	0	0	0	0	X	-	3	9	0

Indians	IP	H	R	ER	BB	SO
Waits L(4–3)	8	9	3	3	2	5

Yankees	IP	H	R	ER	BB	SO
Righetti W(1–0)	7	4	2	2	3	7
Davis SV(4)	2	1	0	0	0	4
Totals	9	5	2	2	3	11

DP—Cleveland 1. 2B—Cleveland Diaz 2, Thornton, Orta; New York Piniella, Milbourne, Jackson, Foote. HR—New York Winfield (4). SH—New York Nettles. SF—Cleveland Hargrove. LOB—Cleveland 6; New York 7. Attendance: 37,179.

Lazzeri Cranks Out Pair of Grand Slams, Chalks Up 11 RBIs

Tony Lazzeri had a game for the ages.

The Hall of Fame second baseman hit three home runs, including two grand slams, and set an American League record with 11 RBIs as the Yankees slaughtered the Athletics at Philadelphia's Shibe Park 25–2.

The Yankees' offensive barrage featured 19 hits, including six home runs, three triples, three doubles, and seven singles for 46 total bases.

Lazzeri broke Jimmie Foxx's record of nine RBIs in a single game, set in 1933. The National League record for one game is 12 RBIs, set by the Cardinals' Jim Bottomley in 1924 and tied by the Cardinals' Mark Whiten in 1993.

Lazzeri wasn't the only Yankee who had a good day. Joe DiMaggio had three hits, including a home run and a double. Lou Gehrig had two hits, as did future Hall of Famer Bill Dickey. The Yankees' catcher had to settle for a triple when one of his hits hit the top of the fence over the scoreboard and fell back to the field.

Not to be outdone, Frank Crosetti, the Yankees' shortstop and leadoff batter, belted two solo homers of his own.

> ## At a Glance
>
> **WP:** Pearson
>
> **HR:** Lazzeri 3 (6, 7, 8), Crosetti 2 (3, 4), DiMaggio (3)
>
> **Key stats:** Lazzeri 4–5, 3 HR, 11 RBIs

The 25 runs scored by the Yankees were three short of the modern day record. The St. Louis Cardinals scored 28 runs in a game in 1929. In 1897, the Chicago Cubs scored 36 runs in a game.

The Yankees' 46 total bases were four short of their own record from 1932 (see: June 3, 1932). In 1893, the Cincinnati Red Stockings had 55 total bases in one game.

When Lazzeri tripled in the eighth inning to set the AL RBI mark, he was almost mobbed by the crowd. At the end of the game, Lazzeri had to fight his way (without a police escort) through a group of autograph seekers.

Hall of Famer Tony Lazzeri carried quite a wallop despite his less-than-intimidating frame. On May 24, 1936, Lazzeri hit two grand slams in a game and set an American League record with 11 RBIs.

Monte Pearson coasted to the victory, giving up two runs on seven hits in nine innings pitched. The native of Oakland, California, walked three and struck out three.

The Yankees scored five runs in the second inning; five in the fourth; six in the fifth; one in the sixth; two in the seventh and six more in the eighth.

Philadelphia pitchers came up two shy of tying the single-game record for most walks as they passed 16 Yankee hitters.

Lazzeri played second base for the Yankees through 1937. He averaged 79 runs, 14 home runs, 96 RBIs, and 12 stolen bases, including seven seasons with more than 100 RBIs and five seasons batting .300 or higher. In 1929, he batted a career-high .354.

The first great ballplayer of Italian heritage to play in New York, Lazzeri was an excellent fielder at second and displayed natural leadership skills on the field.

Lazzeri helped the Yankees win six American League pennants and five World Championships.

The Yankees released their long-time second baseman in October 1937. Less than two weeks later, he signed with the Chicago Cubs and faced the Yankees in the 1938 World Series, where he was 0-for-2. —m—

2B Tony Lazzeri

Tony Lazzeri joined the Yankees in 1926 and made an immediate splash when he drove in 114 runs in his rookie year.

The San Francisco native played 12 years in pinstripes and drove in over 100 runs seven times.

Lazzeri hit 60 home runs for the Salt Lake City Bees in 1925, but he never hit more than 18 in a big-league season.

Lazzeri is best known for holding the American League record for most RBIs in a single game. On May 24th, 1936, Lazzeri became the first player to smack two grand slams in one game while setting the league mark with 11 RBIs.

The Hall of Fame second baseman wore four different numbers throughout his Yankee career.

Spencer's Pinch-Hit Grand Slam Caps Late Comeback

Jim Spencer came off the bench to pinch-hit a grand slam home run and give the Yankees a 4–3 win over the Toronto Blue Jays at Yankee Stadium.

The Yankees trailed 2–0 entering the seventh inning against Toronto left-hander Jerry Garvin, who had limited the Bombers to only four hits. After Reggie Jackson struck out to start the inning, Lou Piniella and Chris Chambliss stroked back-to-back singles.

Graig Nettles walked to load the bases, and with designated hitter Cliff Johnson scheduled to hit, Blue Jays manager Roy Hartsfield elected to go to the bullpen for righty Tom Murphy.

Yankee skipper Billy Martin countered with the left-handed hitting Spencer, who was already 1-for-2 as a pinch-hitter with two RBIs against lefties in 1978.

"He's a selective hitter," Martin said. "When he gets ahead of a pitcher, he's dangerous."

Spencer sat on a 2–0 fastball and drilled it into the right-center-field bleachers for a crushing blow.

Toronto had taken a 2–0 lead in the sixth inning on a two-run homer by John Mayberry.

In the seventh inning, Sparky Lyle relieved Beattie and induced an inning-ending double play from Rick Bosetti as the Blue Jays left a runner at third.

The Blue Jays narrowed the gap in the eighth inning on Mayberry's second home run of the game, but Lyle pitched a scoreless ninth inning to earn the win. ⸺

Blue Jays	AB	R	H	RBI
Bosetti cf	3	0	0	0
Bailor rf	3	1	0	0
Howell 3b	4	0	0	0
Mayberry 1b	3	2	2	3
Hutton lf	3	0	0	0
Velez ph,lf	1	0	0	0
Upshaw dh	2	0	1	0
Ault ph,dh	1	0	0	0
McKay 2b	4	0	1	0
Gomez ss	2	0	2	0
Cerone ph	1	0	0	0
Ashby c	3	0	1	0
Totals	30	3	7	3

Yankees	AB	R	H	RBI
Rivers cf	4	1	1	0
Randolph 2b	4	0	0	0
Munson c	4	0	0	0
Jackson rf	4	0	1	0
Piniella lf	3	1	1	0
Chambliss 1b	3	1	2	0
Nettles 3b	2	1	1	0
Johnson dh	2	0	0	0
Spencer ph,dh	1	1	1	4
Dent ss	3	0	0	0
Totals	30	4	7	4

```
TOR  0 0 0 0 0 2 0 1 0 - 3 7 0
NY   0 0 0 0 0 0 4 0 X - 4 7 1
```

Blue Jays	IP	H	R	ER	BB	SO
Garvin L(2–3)	6.1	6	3	3	1	1
Murphy	1.2	1	1	1	0	0
Totals	8	7	4	4	1	1

Yankees	IP	H	R	ER	BB	SO
Beattie	6.1	6	2	1	5	0
Lyle W(3–1)	2.2	1	1	1	0	0
Totals	9	7	3	2	5	0

E—New York Randolph. DP—New York 3. 2B—Toronto McKay. HR—Toronto Mayberry 2 (8,9); New York Spencer (5). LOB—Toronto 5; New York 3. Attendance: 24,171.

Big Rally Stops Red Sox

The Yankees used an eight-run seventh-inning rally to drub the Red Sox at Fenway Park 17–8.

The Yankees trailed 6–4 when they exploded for eight runs on only four hits. Hank Bauer was the hitting star with three doubles, including two in that seventh-inning barrage.

The Yankees added five more runs in the eighth inning to blow the game wide open.

Mickey Mantle drew one of his four walks to lead off. Bill Skowron and Elston Howard singled for the first run. Andy Carey and Tony Kubek doubled, and before an out was recorded, the Yankees had scored five times to take a 17–6 lead.

One of the story lines from the game was when Boston Hall of Famer Ted Williams was replaced by Gene Stephens to start the eighth inning because Williams had "run and thrown himself into a state of fatigue" in that long seventh inning.

Pitching seemed to be non-existent as both teams walked a total of 20 batters.

Johnny Kucks got the win despite giving up six runs in six innings of work. Bob Grim worked the final three innings and gave up two runs of his own but still earned the save. ⁓

Yankees	AB	R	H	RBI
Bauer rf	6	3	3	2
McDougald ss	4	1	1	1
Martin 2b	6	1	1	1
Mantle cf	2	3	0	0
Skowron 1b	6	3	3	4
Howard c	4	2	2	1
Carey 3b	4	1	1	2
Kubek lf	4	2	2	3
Kucks p	2	0	0	0
Collins ph	0	1	0	0
Totals	38	17	13	14

Red Sox	AB	R	H	RBI
Piersall cf	3	1	1	2
Mauch 2b	3	1	1	1
Williams lf	3	0	1	0
Stephens lf	0	1	0	0
Vernon 1b	4	1	1	0
Lepcio pr	0	1	0	0
Jensen rf	3	0	0	1
Malzone 3b	4	1	2	1
Consolo ss	4	0	1	2
Daley c	4	1	0	0
Brewer p	3	1	2	1
Chakales p	1	0	1	0
Goodman ph	1	0	0	0
Totals	33	8	10	8

NY	0	2	0	0	2	0	8	5	0	-	17 13 2
BOS	0	1	3	0	0	2	0	0	2	-	8 10 2

Yankees	IP	H	R	ER	BB	SO
Kucks W(2–4)	6	8	6	5	5	2
Grim SV(1)	3	2	2	2	4	2
Totals	9	10	8	7	9	4

Red Sox	IP	H	R	ER	BB	SO
Brewer L(6–3)	6	6	7	7	6	5
Porterfield	0	1	3	3	2	0
Minarcin	1	5	7	4	2	0
Chakales	2	1	0	0	1	1
Totals	9	13	17	14	11	6

E—New York Mantle, Kubek; Boston Malzone, Chakales. DP—New York 2. 2B—New York Bauer 3, McDougald, Carey, Kubek, Howard; Boston Malzone. HR—New York Skowron (6); Boston Piersall (3). SH—New York Carey, Grim. SF—New York Carey, Kubek; Boston Jensen, Consolo. HBP—Boston Mauch. LOB—New York 9; Boston 10. Attendance: 29,865.

Nettles Provides the Heroics in Victory over White Sox in 10th Inning

Graig Nettles hit a walk-off double in the bottom of the 10th inning to give the Yankees a 3–2 win over the White Sox at Shea Stadium.

Bobby Murcer, who was starting in right field for the first time, led off the 10th inning with a single.

Yankees manager Bill Virdon, much to the dismay of the 9,075 fans on hand, decided to send up Horace Clarke to pinch-hit for the Yankees' leading hitter, Ron Blomberg.

The crowd booed, but Virdon was asking Clarke to lay down a sacrifice bunt, which he did successfully. White Sox pitcher Terry Forster fielded the bunt and threw it past Ron Santo at first base, putting runners at first and second with no one out.

The next batter was Nettles, who tried to put down a bunt on a 1–1 pitch, but it went foul. The count was full when Nettles lined a double down the right-field line to score the winning run.

Murcer learned of his move to right field before the game when Virdon came over to him and said, "You're playing right field."

Murcer didn't protest the decision.

"I would say it's a surprise to me," Murcer said. "I'm dissapointed in it, but it's not going to affect me." —⚘—

On November 27th, 1972, the Yankees swung a six-player trade with the Cleveland Indians that would net them a great third baseman.

Graig Nettles played 11 seasons with the Yankees and quickly developed a reputation as one of the best defensive third basemen of his era.

Nettles also had a left-handed power stroke that was perfect for Yankee Stadium. He led the American League with 32 home runs in 1976.

The slick-fielding third baseman is credited with helping to spark the Yankees comeback in the 1978 World Series. The Yankees trailed the Los Angeles Dodgers two games to none, but in Game 3, Nettles made some spectacular "series-turning" defensive plays and the Yankees rallied for four straight wins to capture their second straight World Championship.

3B Graig Nettles

Yogi's Grand Slam, 6 RBIs Top Hit Parade

The Yankees pounded out 17 hits en route to a 10–2 whuppin' of the Red Sox at Fenway Park.

Yogi Berra had the biggest day, with a grand slam and six RBIs, while Mickey Mantle added a monster home run off Boston's Sid Hudson.

One of Boston's runs came off the bat of Ted Williams, who slugged a mammoth home run of his own. The ball landed approximately 27 rows up in the right-center-field bleachers at Fenway.

The Yankees broke the game open in the eighth inning by scoring five times.

With the bases loaded, Red Sox manager Lou Boudreau called for Bill Werle, a lefty, to face Berra. On Werle's second pitch, Berra smacked the ball into the right-center-field bleachers for his seventh home run of the season and a 10–2 lead.

Harry Byrd was the beneficiary of all the offense as he went six innings for the win.

Mantle and Andy Carey had three hits each, while pitcher Johnny Sain, who tossed the final three innings for the save, was 2-for-2 with an RBI and a run scored.

The Yankees took a 1–0 lead in the second inning on Carey's RBI single. Mantle's homer made it 2–0 in the third. —

Yankees	AB	R	H	RBI
Bauer rf	6	2	2	0
Coleman ss	5	1	1	0
Mantle cf	4	3	3	2
Berra c	4	1	2	6
Woodling lf	5	0	2	0
Collins 1b	3	0	0	0
Skowron ph,1b	1	0	0	0
McDougald 2b	4	1	2	0
Carey 3b	5	1	3	1
Byrd p	3	0	0	0
Sain p	2	1	2	1
Totals	42	10	17	10

Red Sox	AB	R	H	RBI
Agganis 1b	4	0	0	0
Piersall rf	4	0	0	0
Williams lf	3	1	1	1
Jensen cf	3	1	0	0
Goodman 3b	4	0	0	0
White c	4	0	1	1
Lepcio 2b	3	0	0	0
Bolling ss	2	0	0	0
Hudson p	1	0	0	0
Maxwell ph	1	0	0	0
Lenhardt ph	1	0	0	0
Totals	30	2	2	2

NY	0	1	1	0	3	0	0	5	0	-	10 17 1
BOS	0	0	0	1	0	1	0	0	0	-	2 2 0

Yankees	IP	H	R	ER	BB	SO
Byrd W(2–3)	6	2	2	2	3	4
Sain SV(8)	3	0	0	0	0	0
Totals	9	2	2	2	3	4

Red Sox	IP	H	R	ER	BB	SO
Hudson L(0–2)	5	9	5	5	1	2
Kiely	2	2	0	0	2	2
Brown	0.1	3	4	4	1	0
Werle	1.2	3	1	1	0	1
Totals	9	17	10	10	4	5

E—New York Coleman. DP—Boston 1. 2B—New York McDougald 2, Carey 2, Mantle. HR—New York Mantle (8), Berra (7); Boston Williams (3). SH—New York Coleman. LOB—New York 10; Boston 4. SB—Boston Jensen. Attendance: 21,992.

The Mick Not Done Yet with 2 Homers, 5 RBIs

It was one of the last great games of Mickey Mantle's illustrious career.

The Mick hit two home runs, went 5-for-5, and drove in five runs to lead the Yankees to a memorable 13–4 win over the Senators on Memorial Day at Yankee Stadium.

At a Glance

WP: Bahnsen (5–1)

HR: Mantle 2 (6)

Key stats: Bahnsen 8-hitter, 7 Ks; Mantle 5-for-5, 5 RBIs, 3 runs; Pepitone 2-for-4, 2 RBIs; Gibbs 2-for-5, 2 RBIs

At 36 years of age, Mantle was now an everyday first baseman, but he brought back memories of his peak seasons when he roamed baseball's holyland—center field at Yankee Stadium.

The Hall of Famer got things going right away with a two-run homer in the first inning off Washington's Joe Coleman.

The Mick singled and scored in the third; smacked his second homer of the game in the fifth; doubled in a run in the sixth; and capped off the day with an RBI single in the eighth.

It turned into the single most productive game in the storied 18-year career of the Yankee slugger.

The game marked the third time that Mantle had five hits in a game. The first came in 1955 at Washington and the other time was in a 1956 game in Detroit.

It would also be the 45th and penultimate time that Mantle would hit two home runs in a single game in his career.

MANTLE HITS STADIUM FAÇADE FOR FIRST TIME

On May 30, 1956, Mickey Mantle came within 18 inches of becoming the first player to hit a home run completely out of Yankee Stadium as the Yankees beat the Washington Senators 4–3.

The switch-hitter's prestigious blast came in the fifth inning on a 2–2 pitch from Washington right-hander Pedro Ramos.

According to eyewitness reports, the ball was descending when it hit the façade. The blast was measured at 370 feet from home plate and 117 feet high.

Following the game, Mantle said, "It was the best I ever hit a ball left-handed."

Mantle would later hit another ball that struck the facade and almost left the Stadium (see: May 22, 1963). —⚊—

Spec Hits His Marks, Throws Two-Hitter

A Memorial Day crowd of 62,626 fans was on hand to watch Frank "Spec" Shea toss his best game as a Yankee.

The native of Naugatuck, Connecticut, allowed two Senator singles as the Yankees coasted to a 10–0 win.

The Yankees took a 3–0 lead in the third inning on a two-run homer from Tommy Henrich that landed in the upper deck in right field.

Yogi Berra, Charlie "King Kong" Keller, Bobby Brown, and George McQuinn, who also homered, had three hits apiece to pace a 16-hit attack. McQuinn, a journeyman first baseman who spent the previous 10 years of his career with Cincinnati, the St. Louis Browns, and the Philadelphia Athletics, totaled four RBIs.

Joe DiMaggio had an RBI single and a great catch in center field.

Shea pitched four years for the Yankees. Ironically, he was dealt to the Senators as part of a six-player trade.

Brown started at second base for the injured George "Stuffy" Stirnweiss, who was on the bench with a mild concussion.

> ### At a Glance
>
> **WP:** Shea
>
> **HR:** McQuinn (5), Henrich (5)
>
> **Key stats:** Shea throws 2-hitter; Henrich 2-run homer; Berra, Keller, Brown, McQuinn 3 hits apiece; McQuinn 4 RBIs

In a precursor to the tumultuous 1970s, there were rumors of "internal dissension" within the Yankees clubhouse but the club "strenuously" denied those rumors. ―〰―

Soderholm Hitches a Ride, Then Lets It Ride at the Plate

Eric Soderholm nearly missed out on the best game of his career with the Yankees.

The designated hitter overcame car problems to make it to the ballpark, where he went 5-for-5 to lead the Bombers to an 11–7 win over the Toronto Blue Jays.

Soderholm and teammate Jim Spencer were both stuck on the Major Deegan Expressway (which goes past Yankee Stadium), but they were able to hitch a ride with a man who was taking his son to the game.

Soderholm, a Cortland, New York, native, had four singles and a triple to pace a 13-hit attack.

Toronto grabbed a 3–0 lead in the fourth inning against Tom Underwood, but the Yankees got two back to make it a one-run game.

The Yankees scored four runs in the fifth inning to grab a 6–3 lead. Lou Piniella's RBI single tied the game and Bobby Brown gave the Yankees the lead with a three-run homer off Blue Jays reliever Tom Buskey.

Soderholm was in the lineup because Reggie Jackson was involved in a shooting incident Saturday night after the game. A man reportedly fired three shots at the Yankees slugger after the two exchanged angry words on E. 83rd Street in Manhattan.

Piniella had three hits while Brown drove in four to give Underwood the victory. —⁓—

Blue Jays	AB	R	H	RBI
Griffin ss	5	0	1	1
Bosetti cf	4	1	0	0
Howell 3b	5	1	2	0
Velez dh	4	0	0	0
Bonnell rf	3	0	0	1
Woods lf	3	2	1	0
Mayberry 1b	4	2	3	4
Garcia 2b	4	1	2	0
Whitt c	4	0	1	0
Totals	36	7	10	6

Yankees	AB	R	H	RBI
Randolph 2b	4	2	2	0
Werth rf	2	0	0	0
Lefebvre rf	1	1	0	0
Watson 1b	4	0	0	1
Soderholm dh	5	2	5	2
Piniella lf	4	2	3	1
Blair pr,lf	1	0	0	0
Brown cf	4	1	1	4
Cerone c	4	0	0	1
Oates c	0	0	0	0
Dent ss	2	1	1	0
Stanley 3b	2	0	0	0
Nettles ph,3b	2	2	1	2
Totals	35	11	13	11

```
TOR   0 0 0 3 0 0 1 0 3 - 7 10 2
NY    0 0 0 2 4 2 0 3 X - 11 13 0
```

Blue Jays	IP	H	R	ER	BB	SO
Mirabella L(4–4)	4.2	8	5	5	2	3
Buskey	2.2	4	5	5	2	1
Moore	0.2	1	1	1	1	0
Totals	8	13	11	11	5	4

Yankees	IP	H	R	ER	BB	SO
Underwood W(5–3)	7	5	4	4	3	4
Gossage	2	5	3	3	0	1
Totals	9	10	7	7	3	5

E—Toronto Bonnell, Mayberry. DP—New York 1. 2B—Toronto Howell; New York Piniella. 3B—Toronto Griffin; New York Soderholm. HR—Toronto Mayberry 2 (9,10); New York Brown (5), Nettles (7). SF—New York Watson. LOB—Toronto 5; New York 6. Attendance: 52,049.

Gehrig Supplants Pipp at First Base, Settles In for a Long Run

When the Yankees beat the Washington Senators 8–5 in this Tuesday afternoon game at Yankee Stadium, it seemed like just another win. However, this game carried a lot of meaning.

It marked the second game of Lou Gehrig's incredible streak of 2,130 consecutive games played, a streak that would last until 1939.

Yankees manager Miller Huggins made the historic change when he started Gehrig at first base in place of the incumbent, Wally Pipp. The 32-year-old Pipp was reportedly taken out of the lineup because of a headache, but according to the *New York Times* account of June 3, 1925, "Wally Pipp, after more than ten years as a regular first-baseman, was benched in favor of Lou Gehrig, the former Columbia University fence wrecker."

Gehrig was not the only change made by Huggins. Second baseman Aaron Ward was replaced with Howard Shanks and Benny Bengough started at catcher.

Huggins' maneuvers looked good as Gehrig stroked three hits (including a double), Shanks had a key single that led to the Yanks' first run, and Bengough also contributed three hits.

The Yankees trailed 5–4 in the eighth inning when pinch-hitter Bobby Veach singled to start the inning. Ernie Johnson ran for Veach and took second base on a sacrifice bunt. Earle Combs walked, bringing up Babe Ruth with runners on first and third.

Ruth took an Allan Russell pitch and drove it to deep right-center field beyond the reach of Sam Rice and Joe Harris. The ball bounced into the stands for a double that tied the game and put runners at second and third.

Senators	AB	R	H	RBI
Rice cf	5	0	2	1
B. Harris 2b	5	1	2	0
Judge 1b	4	1	1	2
Goslin lf	4	0	0	0
J. Harris rf	4	1	1	0
Bluege 3b	3	1	1	0
Peckinpaugh ss	4	0	3	2
Ruel c	4	1	2	0
Leibold ph	1	0	0	0
Russell p	1	0	0	0
Ruether ph	1	0	0	0
Totals	36	5	12	5

Yankees	AB	R	H	RBI
Wanninger ss	4	0	1	0
Veach ph	1	0	1	0
E. Johnson ss	0	1	0	0
Dugan 3b	2	0	2	1
Combs cf	4	1	0	0
Ruth rf	4	0	2	1
Witt pr	0	1	0	0
Paschal rf	0	0	0	0
Meusel lf	5	2	2	4
Gehrig 1b	5	1	3	0
Shanks 2b	4	1	1	0
Bengough c	4	1	3	1
Shocker p	2	0	1	1
Ferguson p	2	0	0	0
Totals	37	8	16	8

WAS	0	1	2	0	1	1	0	0	0	-	5	12 0
NY	0	3	1	0	0	0	0	4	X	-	8	16 0

Senators	IP	H	R	ER	BB	SO
Mogridge	2	6	3	3	0	1
Russell L(0–2)	6	10	5	5	3	4
Totals	8	16	8	8	3	5

Yankees	IP	H	R	ER	BB	SO
Shocker	4.1	8	4	4	0	1
Ferguson W(2–2)	4.2	4	1	1	0	3
Totals	9	12	5	5	0	4

2B—Washington Peckinpaugh; New York Ruth, Gehrig. 3B—Washington Peckinpaugh. HR—Washington Judge (5); New York Meusel 2 (13,14). SH— Washington Bluege, Russell; New York Dugan 2. HBP—New York Ruth. LOB—Washington 6; New York 11. Attendance: NA.

Bob Meusel followed with a tremendous blast to left-center field that scored Combs and Ruth as he rounded the bases for an inside-the-park home run and an 8–4 lead. It was the second of two home runs for Meusel, who gave the Yankees a 4–3 lead with his first round-tripper of the game in the third inning.

It was only Ruth's second game of the season as he had missed the first two months with stomach problems (see: April 14, 1925), but the Yankees were pleased to see him get his first hit and first RBI of the season.

Urban Shocker could not last five innings so he did not qualify for the win. Alex Ferguson gave up a run over the final 4 2/3 innings to pick up the victory in relief.

The Yankees greeted their old teammate, George Mogridge (see: April 24, 1917, first no-hitter for the Yankees), with three runs on six hits in two innings pitched.

Prior to starting his first game, Gehrig appeared in 35 games. Gehrig hit his first major league home run at Fenway Park on September 27, 1923. The irony of the blow was that it was the first time that Gehrig started a game hitting fourth behind Ruth.

In his first full season as a starting first baseman, Gehrig batted .295 with 20 home runs, 68 RBIs, 23 doubles, and 10 triples. —∾—

1B Lou Gehrig

One of the greatest players of all time, Lou Gehrig set a major league record by playing in 2,130 consecutive games.

The Hall of Famer made his major league debut on June 15, 1923, as a pinch hitter, and on June 1, 1925, he began his record-setting streak when Yankee manager Miller Huggins put him in the starting lineup to replace the incumbent Wally Pipp.

Gehrig's 17-year career was cut short by ALS (Amyotrophic Lateral Sclerosis), which is now commonly referred to as "Lou Gehrig's Disease."

The numbers that Gehrig accumulated during his career are staggering.

The "Iron Horse" posted a career batting average of .340. He had 2,721 hits, 493 home runs, and 1,995 RBIs, not to mention a lifetime on-base percentage of .447 and a career slugging percentage of .632.

On July 4th, 1939, Gehrig put forth one of the great speeches in American history, where he delivered his famous quote, "I consider myself the luckiest man on the face of the Earth."

Iron Horse's Four Home Runs Tie Big-League Record; Yanks Score 20

Lou Gehrig tied a major league record by hitting four home runs to key a record-setting power surge as the Yankees outslugged the A's 20–13.

Gehrig became the third player (Bobby Lowe and Ed Delahanty were the first two) to smack four round trippers in a single game. (Twelve additional players would go on to hit four home runs in a game.)

The game featured nine home runs that were all hit by future Hall of Fame players. Gehrig's four highlighted the barrage, but homers by Babe Ruth, Earle Combs, and Tony Lazzeri's grand slam made it a record seven in the game for the Yankees. Philadelphia's Mickey Cochrane (whom Mickey Mantle was named after) and Jimmie Foxx rounded out the souvenir frenzy.

"The Iron Horse" tied another record by hitting a home run in his first four at-bats. Gehrig had two chances to hit a record fifth home run in the game.

In the eighth, the Yankees slugger grounded out, but in the ninth, he made a strong bid for home run No. 5.

Gehrig faced 34-year-old right-hander Eddie Rommel and drove a ball into the

> ## At a Glance
>
> **WP:** Brown (1–1)
>
> **S:** Gomez (1)
>
> **HR:** Combs (5), Ruth (15), Gehrig 4 (11), Lazzeri (3)
>
> **Key stats:** Gehrig 4-for-6, 4 HR, 6 RBIs; Lazzeri 5-for-6, 6 RBIs

deepest part of center field, some 470 feet away from home plate. A's center fielder Al Simmons made a terrific catch with his back to the plate. Reportedly, writers who saw the game said that if the ball went over Simmons' head in center, Gehrig would've had an inside-the-park home run for his fifth of the game.

Gehrig had six RBIs and 16 total bases, but he was just the lead in this eye-opening display of offense. Lazzeri, who hit for the cycle, had five hits in all and, like Gehrig, drove in six runs. Combs had three hits while Ruth added a double to his four-bagger. The Yankees pounded out 23 hits and set a club and American League record with 50 total bases.

Gehrig, who always seemed to be overshadowed by Ruth, managed to be one-upped on this day by a bigger New York baseball story. Across the Harlem River, the legendary John McGraw chose this day to offer up his surprise resignation, turning the New York Giants over to Bill Terry, and leaving Gehrig's batting feat as the second-biggest story in the morning papers. —⁓—

Niekro Comes Close to No-Hitter at Age 41

Joe Niekro came within four outs of a no-hitter to lead the Yankees to an 11–0 thrashing of the Angels in Anaheim.

Niekro's bid for history was spoiled in the eighth when Gary Pettis stroked a two-out double into the right-field corner.

"It was a knuckleball down and in," the 41-year-old Niekro said. "You could second-guess yourself on that and say he was looking for the knuckleball because that's all I was really throwing, but I wanted to go with my best pitch."

Niekro went eight innings, allowing the one hit while walking three and striking out five. Reliever Al Holland tossed a perfect ninth inning to wrap up an impressive win.

Dave Winfield paced an 18-hit attack with a pair of home runs, while Dan Pasqua and Willie Randolph had three hits apiece.

At a Glance

WP: Niekro (6–3)

HR: Winfield 2 (10), Easler (5)

Key stats: Niekro 8 IP, 1 H, 5 Ks, 3 BB; Winfield 2-for-5; 3 RBIs; Mattingly 3-for-6, 2 RBIs; Easler 2-for-5, 2 RBIs; Pasqua 3-for-5, RBI; Randolph 3-for-5, RBI

Niekro did not face trouble until the fifth inning. Reggie Jackson drew a lead-off walk but was forced at second base by Ruppert Jones. The former Yankee stole second but was left stranded when Jack Howell flied out and Rob Wilfong struck out.

In the sixth inning, a controversial scoring call enabled Niekro to continue to pursue the record book.

Dick Schofield hit a bouncer toward the mound that Niekro deflected before it was bobbled slightly by shortstop Mike Fischlin. Official scorer Ed Munson ruled an error on the play.

Ironically, this game for Niekro came nearly 16 years to the day after his no-hit bid against the Yankees. While pitching for the Detroit Tigers, Niekro saw his attempt at the record books broken up by Horace Clarke in the ninth inning. It was one of three no-hit bids spoiled by Clarke in the ninth inning in the period of one month during that 1970 season. ﹘

Giambi's Pinch-Hit Two-Run Homer Ends a Long One

Blue Jays	AB	R	H	RBI
Stewart lf	3	0	0	0
Scutaro 2b	1	0	0	0
Eckstein ss	5	1	1	0
Rios cf	4	2	1	0
Rolen 3b	3	2	2	0
Stairs dh	5	2	3	5
Overbay 1b	5	0	1	2
Mench rf	3	0	0	0
Wilkerson rf	0	0	0	0
Barajas c	0	0	0	0
Inglett 2b,lf	3	1	1	0
Totals	**35**	**8**	**9**	**7**

Yankees	AB	R	H	RBI
Damon dh	3	2	2	0
Jeter ss	4	1	1	0
Abreu rf	5	0	2	2
A. Rodriguez 3b	3	1	1	2
Matsui lf	5	1	1	1
Posada c	3	0	1	0
Duncan pr	0	0	0	0
Molina c	0	0	0	0
Giambi ph	1	1	1	2
Cano 2b	4	1	2	0
Betemit 1b	4	1	2	2
Cabrera cf	3	1	1	0
Totals	**35**	**9**	**14**	**9**

TOR	0 0 0	2 5 0	0 0 1	-	8	9	0
NY	2 0 0	0 2 2	0 0 3	-	9	14	1

Blue Jays	IP	H	R	ER	BB	SO
McGowan	5.1	7	5	5	2	5
Carlson	0.1	2	1	1	0	1
Frasor	0.2	1	0	0	0	0
Downs	1.2	1	0	0	2	1
Ryan L(1–2)	0.2	3	3	3	0	0
Totals	**8.2**	**14**	**9**	**9**	**4**	**7**

Yankees	IP	H	R	ER	BB	SO
Wang	4.1	5	7	6	4	4
Ohlendorf	0.2	0	0	0	0	1
Hawkins	1	1	0	0	1	0
Veras	2	0	0	0	1	1
Farnsworth W(1–2)	1	3	1	1	1	1
Totals	**9**	**9**	**8**	**7**	**7**	**7**

E—New York Cabrera. DP—Toronto 2; New York 1. 2B—Toronto Overbay; Stairs; New York Jeter, Abreu. HR—Toronto Stairs (7); New York Betemit (3), Giambi (12). SH—Toronto Inglett. SF—New York A. Rodriguez 2. HBP—Toronto Rolen; New York Jeter. LOB—Toronto 10; New York 7. SB—Toronto Wilkerson; New York Damon. Attendance: 53,571.

It was a long day's journey into night, but Jason Giambi's two-out, two-run, pinch-hit homer off Toronto closer B. J. Ryan gave the Yankees a dramatic 9–8 win over the Blue Jays at Yankee Stadium.

The Jays led 8–6, and the Yankees were down to their last out. Alex Rodriguez singled and took second on defensive indifference. Hideki Matsui's RBI single scored A-Rod to cut the lead to 8–7.

Even though Giambi is a left-handed hitter, manager Joe Girardi used him to hit for Jose Molina against the hard-throwing southpaw Ryan.

Giambi was down in the count 0–2 when he launched a hanging slider high and far toward the right-field corner. The only question was whether it would be fair or foul.

"I was just talking it fair," Giambi said. "It straightened out."

The ball landed fair, and the Yankees turned defeat into victory.

The game lasted 3 hours and 53 minutes, so many of the 53,571 fans were gone by the time Giambi smacked his memorable blow.

The Yankees had numerous chances to bounce back, including in the bottom of the eighth inning, when they had designated hitter Johnny Damon at the plate with two on and two out.

Damon hit a ball toward right-center field that looked like it was going to go for extra bases and give the Yankees the lead, but Blue Jays right fielder Brad Wilkerson made an outstanding grab to kill the rally. —⁓—

Ruth's Day of Rest Lets Hoag Shine with Record Six Hits

Replacing Babe Ruth in the lineup would not be easy, but Myril Hoag passed the test with flying colors.

Hoag tied an American League record with six singles in six at-bats as the Yankees walloped the Red Sox at Fenway Park 15–3.

Johnny Murphy, a 28-year-old New York native, was the beneficiary of all the offense as he went the distance while adding two hits of his own.

The Yanks banged out 25 hits in all, led by Hoag's record day, and they nearly tied another record by scoring at least one run in every inning except the ninth.

Hoag hit seventh in the lineup because Ruth was given the day off, but the first four Yankee batters were a combined 13-for-24 with nine runs scored and 10 RBIs.

Hoag, a 13-year veteran, was a utility outfielder who played left, center, and right field. From 1903 to 2007, Hoag was the only Yankee to go 6-for-6 in a nine-inning game. —⁓—

At a Glance

WP: Murphy (4–2)

HR: Chapman (4)

Key stats: Murphy 7-hitter; Hoag 6-for-6; Chapman 3-for-6, 4 RBIs; Gehrig 3-for-5, 4 RBIs

Damon Matches Hoag with Six-Hit Performance

It had been exactly 74 years and one day since a Yankee batter was 6-for-6 in a nine-inning game, but no one in the stands at Yankee Stadium would've guessed that gap would come to an end.

Royals	AB	R	H	RBI
DeJesus lf	4	2	2	1
Aviles ss,3b	4	2	1	1
Teahen 1b,rf	4	2	1	0
Guillen lf	4	2	3	7
Gload 1b	1	0	0	0
Olivo dh	4	0	0	0
Buck c	3	0	1	1
Callaspo 2b	4	1	2	0
German 3b	4	1	1	0
Pena ss	0	0	0	0
Gathright cf	4	1	1	1
Totals	36	11	12	11

Yankees	AB	R	H	RBI
Damon lf	6	1	6	4
Jeter ss	4	0	1	0
Abreu rf	5	1	1	0
A. Rodriguez 3b	4	2	2	2
Giambi dh	4	2	2	2
Posada c	4	2	2	2
Cano 2b	5	2	2	1
Betemit 1b	3	1	0	1
Cabrera cf	5	1	3	0
Totals	40	12	19	12

KC	2	0	3	0	0	0	5	0	1	-	11	12	0
NY	1	0	0	4	1	0	2	2	2	-	12	19	0

Royals	IP	H	R	ER	BB	SO
Bannister	3.1	8	5	5	2	1
Peralta	1.1	1	1	1	1	1
Tomko	1.2	3	2	2	0	0
R. Ramirez	1	3	2	2	0	2
Gobble	0.1	1	0	0	0	0
Yabuta	0.1	0	0	0	0	0
Soria L(0–1)	0.2	3	2	2	1	0
Totals	8.2	19	12	12	4	4

Yankees	IP	H	R	ER	BB	SO
Pettitte	6.2	10	10	10	2	3
Veras	1.1	1	0	0	0	2
Rivera W(2–1)	1	1	1	1	0	1
Totals	9	12	11	11	2	6

DP—Kansas City 2; New York 1. 2B—Kansas City Teahen, Callaspo; New York Damon, Posada. 3B—Kansas City Aviles. HR—Kansas City Guillen 2 (8,9), DeJesus (5); New York Giambi (13), A. Rodriguez (9), Posada (2). SH—Kansas City DeJesus; New York Jeter. SF—New York Betemit. HBP—Kansas City Teahen. LOB—Kansas City 2; New York 8. SB—Kansas City Callaspo; New York Damon. Attendance: 53,611.

Johnny Damon went 6-for-6, including a walk-off RBI single in the bottom of the ninth inning, to give the Yankees a thrilling 12–11 win over the Kansas City Royals.

On a day when Royals right fielder Jose Guillen drove in seven runs, Yankees starting pitcher Andy Pettitte allowed a career-high 10 earned runs, and Mariano Rivera gave up a tie-breaking home run in the ninth inning, it was Damon who stole the show.

It was a wacky game in which the lead changed hands in dramatic fashion.

The Yankees trailed 5–1 in the fourth inning, but Damon's third hit—an RBI single—tied the game at five. After Damon stole second base to put runners on second and third, Guillen threw out Melky Cabrera at the plate. Cabrera was trying to score on Derek Jeter's fly ball.

Jason Giambi's solo home run in the fifth inning gave the Yankees a 6–5 lead.

A grand slam by Guillen keyed a five-run seventh inning, and the Royals knocked out Pettitte by taking a 10–6 lead.

Alex Rodriguez's two-run homer made it a 10–8 deficit, and the Yankees rallied with two runs in the eighth inning to tie the game again thanks to Damon's record-setting afternoon.

Damon stroked his fifth hit of the game, a two-run single, and a crowd of 53,611 was on its feet, showing much appreciation for what they were witnessing.

Rivera came in to pitch the ninth inning, and his first pitch was deposited in the right-center-field bleachers by David DeJesus for an 11–10 lead.

The Royals went to their closer, Joakim Soria, who was looking to record his 14th consecutive save.

Giambi lined out to center to start the bottom of the inning, but Jorge Posada stroked a game-tying home run, setting up one more chance for Damon to shine.

"A day like this, it seemed like anything could happen," Posada said.

After a Robinson Cano grounded out, Wilson Betemit drew a two-out walk. Cabrera reached on an infield single, putting runners on first and second base.

The crowd was standing and cheering as Damon stepped to the plate.

Soria threw a pitch on the inside part of the plate, and Damon stroked it down the right-field line. The ball fell a few feet on the fair side of the line, Betemit scored, and Damon had his sixth hit of the game—a walk-off RBI single that gave the Yankees an exciting win. ―⁓―

Doubleheader Sweep Caps Memorable Day to Honor Mickey Mantle

One of the most historic days in Yankees history couldn't have been scripted any better.

It was Mickey Mantle Day at Yankee Stadium, and a packed house of 61,157 fans came out on this Sunday afternoon to honor No. 7 between games of a doubleheader against the White Sox.

The current Yankees did their part in paying tribute to their retired teammate and all-time great. They went out and swept the twin bill from the Chisox, 3–1 in the opener and 11–2 in the nightcap.

In the first game, Mel Stottlemyre went the distance on a three-hitter for his 10th complete game. The right-hander walked four, struck out six, and got all the runs he would need when Joe Pepitone clubbed a three-run homer in the fourth inning.

Bobby Murcer and Roy White singled off White Sox losing pitcher Gerry Nyman in the fourth before Pepitone hit a shot into the right-field seats, bringing the enormous crowd to its feet.

In the ninth inning, the crowd, anticipating the Mantle ceremonies, started chanting, "We Want Mick!"

Stottlemyre got the White Sox's Bobby Knoop to ground into a game-ending double play, and then it was time to fete one of the greatest players of all time.

Yankees broadcaster Mel Allen, who was making his first appearance at Yankee Stadium since he shockingly was fired after the 1964 season, was

Mel Stottlemyre, looking at home at Yankee Stadium in this 1970 photo, used his magic to get the Yankees off to a solid start on Mickey Mantle Day (June 8, 1969). Stottlemyre pitched a three-hitter with six strikeouts in a 3–1 victory over the White Sox in Game 1 of a doubleheader sweep.

GAME 1

White Sox	AB	R	H	RBI
Williams rf	4	0	0	0
Aparicio ss	3	0	0	0
May lf	4	0	1	0
Ward 1b	2	1	1	0
Berry pr	0	0	0	0
Herrmann c	4	0	0	0
Knoop 2b	4	0	1	1
Melton 3b	2	0	0	0
Bradford cf	3	0	0	0
Nyman p	2	0	0	0
Bravo ph	1	0	0	0
Totals	29	1	3	1

Yankees	AB	R	H	RBI
Clarke 2b	2	0	0	0
Cox 3b	4	0	0	0
Murcer rf	3	1	1	0
White lf	3	1	1	0
Pepitone 1b	3	1	1	3
Ellis c	3	0	1	0
Robinson cf	3	0	0	0
Michael ss	3	0	0	0
Stottlemyre p	3	0	1	0
Totals	27	3	5	3

CHI 0 1 0 0 0 0 0 0 - 1 3 0
NY   0 0 0 3 0 0 0 0 X - 3 5 1

White Sox	IP	H	R	ER	BB	SO
Nyman L(2–2)	6	4	3	3	2	3
Osinski	2	1	0	0	0	1
Totals	8	5	3	3	2	4

Yankees	IP	H	R	ER	BB	SO
Stottlemyre W(9–4)	9	3	1	1	4	6

E—New York, Michael. DP—Chicago 1; New York 2. 2B—Chicago, Ward; New York, Ellis. HR—New York, Pepitone (16). SH—New York, Clarke. LOB—Chicago 5; New York 3. SB—Chicago, Knoop, Aparicio; New York, Clarke.

brought out to introduce Mantle. With the crowd going wild, Allen introduced Mantle.

"The great number seven . . . Mickey Mantle," said Allen, who was trying to be heard above the crowd.

Mantle walked toward the infield where former teammates, including Joe DiMaggio and Whitey Ford, and other invited guests gathered to honor the switch-hitting legend.

Some of those invited guests included his former manager, Ralph Houk, and his former teammate and manager, Yogi Berra. The scout who signed Mantle, Tom Greenwade, was there, along with a "Who's Who" of former teammates, including Phil Rizzuto, Jerry Coleman, Gil McDougald, Bobby Richardson, Elston Howard, and Tom Tresh.

The fans stood and cheered and cheered and cheered and kept on cheering for a reported 15-minute standing ovation. Mantle tried to calm the crowd himself by hoisting his hands into the air.

Finally, the noise settled down, and Mantle was able to accept a plaque that was presented by DiMaggio, while Ford gave the Mick his uniform with the retired No. 7.

After that brief respite, the crowd roared again as Mantle took the microphone for a few choice words.

"When I walked into the Stadium 18 years ago, I guess I felt the same way I do now. I can't describe it," Mantle said. "I just want to say that playing 18 years in Yankee Stadium for you folks is the best thing that could ever happen to a ballplayer. Now having my number [7] join 3, 4, and 5 kind of tops everything."

The crowd roared again.

Mantle went on to say, "I never knew how a man who was going to die [Lou Gehrig] could say he was the luckiest man in the world. But now I can understand how Lou Gehrig felt."

Mantle finished his speech by referring to his family and his late father, Mutt Mantle, who groomed him to be a big-league ballplayer. "I just wish my father could have been here," Mantle said. "I'll never forget this. Thank you all. God bless you and thank you very much."

GAME 2

White Sox	AB	R	H	RBI
Bravo cf	5	1	2	0
Aparicio ss	2	0	0	0
May lf	4	0	1	1
Hopkins 1b	2	0	0	0
Melton 3b	3	0	0	0
Hansen ph	1	0	0	0
Knoop 2b	4	0	0	0
Herrmann c	4	1	2	1
Williams rf	4	0	1	0
Carlos p	1	0	0	0
Ward 3b	2	0	0	0
Totals	32	2	6	2

Yankees	AB	R	H	RBI
Clarke 2b	4	2	2	3
Kenney 3b	3	2	3	2
Murcer rf	4	1	0	0
White lf	4	1	2	3
Pepitone 1b	4	1	2	2
Tresh ss	4	0	0	0
Lyttle cf	4	1	2	1
Gibbs c	4	1	1	0
Burbach p	4	2	1	0
Totals	35	11	13	11

CHI	0 0 1 0 0 0 0 1 0 -	2 6 3
NY	0 1 1 0 5 4 0 0 X -	11 13 0

White Sox	IP	H	R	ER	BB	SO
Carlos L(2–2)	4.1	7	6	6	3	4
Peters	0.2	4	4	4	0	0
Wood	2	2	1	1	0	0
Ellis	1	0	0	0	1	1
Totals	8	13	11	11	4	5

Yankees	IP	H	R	ER	BB	SO
Burbach W(3–4)	9	6	2	2	5	6

DP—Chicago 1; New York 1. 2B—Chicago, Bravo; New York, Burbach, White, Kenney. 3B—Chicago, Bravo; New York, Clarke. HR—Chicago, Herrmann. LOB—Chicago 8; New York 4. SB—New York, Clarke 2, Pepitone, Kenney. Attendance—60,096.

The crowd was going crazy at this point. Mantle moved to the final stage of the ceremony when he entered a golf cart for a ride around the perimeter of the stadium to acknowledge the fans.

It was quite a scene as Mantle rode around the ballpark, thanking fans along the way. Some overzealous rooters, including one attractive young woman, took it upon themselves to enter the field and shake Mantle's hand while he was riding in the cart.

The ceremonies lasted approximately 45 minutes, and then it was time for the second game.

Rookie Bill Burbach started the nightcap for the Yankees, and like Stottlemyre in the opener, went the distance.

The Yankees led 2–1 but broke the game open in the fifth inning by scoring five runs, including a two-run double by White and a two-run single from Pepitone.

After the ceremonies, Mantle was down in the Yankee Stadium press room, where he felt a need to unwind.

"That last ride around the park, that gave me goose pimples," he said. "But I didn't cry. I felt like it. Maybe tonight when I go to bed, I'll think about it." —⚋—

First Pitch Thames Sees in Bigs Is One to Remember

It was the first game between the teams since the seventh game of the 2001 World Series, so the payback would not be as sweet, but it was payback nonetheless.

The Yankees beat the Arizona Diamondbacks and Randy Johnson 7–5 at Yankee Stadium in a game that featured a rare accomplishment for someone who was making his major league debut.

At a Glance

WP: Stanton (3–0)

HR: Thames (1), Jeter (8), Spencer (3)

Key stats: Spencer 3-for-4, 4 RBIs; Thames 2 RBIs

Yankees right fielder Marcus Thames homered off Johnson on the first pitch that he ever saw in the big leagues, becoming the 16th player to do so, according to the Elias Sports Bureau. Thames was the second Yankee to homer in his first big-league at-bat. John Miller turned the trick in 1966.

Shane Spencer led off the inning with a double and was at second with no one out when Thames stepped into the batter's box.

A 30th-round pick in the 1996 amateur player draft who was recalled the day before, Thames swung at the first pitch he ever saw in the major leagues and drove it over the left-field fence for his first major league home run, hit, and RBIs.

Johnson was stunned, to say the least.

"It was a fastball up and away," the tall southpaw said. "You throw your best pitch and if he hits it, he hits it. I threw a fastball, which is my best pitch. The location wasn't the greatest. I'm not going to lose any sleep over it."

Thames' blast gave the Yankees a 2–0 lead, but Arizona rallied to grab a 4–2 advantage in the fifth inning.

In the eighth inning, Bret Prinz relieved Johnson with runners on second and third base and two out. Robin Ventura was intentionally walked, but the move backfired when Spencer connected for a grand slam and a 7–4 lead. —∾—

Routine Pop-Up Leads to a Gift Thanks to Castillo

The Yankees snatched victory from the jaws of defeat.

In one of the most improbable endings in Yankees history, Mets second baseman Luis Castillo dropped a routine pop-up with two out in the ninth inning to allow two runs to score and give the Bombers a gift of a 9–8 victory.

In a game in which the lead changed hands five times, the Yankees were trailing 8–7 in the bottom of the ninth and had runners at first and third with Alex Rodriguez at the plate against Mets closer Frankie Rodriguez.

K-Rod was always tough on the Yankees when he was a member of the Angels, and it appeared things would be no different when he switched uniforms and went to the National League.

On a 3–1 pitch, A-Rod lifted a pop toward the right side. Castillo drifted toward short right field and put one hand up to catch it but dropped the ball. Derek Jeter, who had singled and stole second, scored the tying run. Mark Teixeira, who was intentionally walked in front of A-Rod, hustled all the way around from first to score the winning run as Castillo, for some ungodly reason, threw the ball to second base instead of trying to get the winning run out at the plate.

"I just put my head down—I was just running," Teixeira said. "I picked up 'Topper' [third base coach Rob Thomson] at third base, and I could tell he was really looking intently, like something was going on, so I kept on running, running."

"Then when he started waving me, I put it into second gear," the Yankees' first baseman said. "I don't have a third, fourth, or fifth [gear], so I just tried to run as hard as I could and get home."

After the game, Castillo stood by his locker and faced the music.

Mets	AB	R	H	RBI
Cora ss	3	1	0	0
F. Martinez lf	4	0	0	0
Beltran cf	2	2	1	1
D. Wright 3b	4	1	2	1
Church rf	4	1	1	3
Sheffield dh	5	2	2	2
Dn. Murphy 1b	5	0	1	0
Schneider c	2	0	0	0
Tatis ph	1	0	0	0
O. Santos c	1	0	0	0
L. Castillo 2b	2	1	0	0
Totals	**33**	**8**	**7**	**7**

Yankees	AB	R	H	RBI
Jeter ss	5	2	2	1
Swisher rf	3	0	0	0
Damon ph	1	0	0	0
Teixeira 1b	3	2	1	2
A. Rodriguez 3b	5	0	1	0
Cano 2b	4	2	2	1
Posada c	3	1	1	0
H. Matsui dh	4	1	1	3
Me. Cabrera lf	4	0	0	0
Gardner cf	4	1	1	0
Totals	**36**	**9**	**9**	**7**

											R	H	E
NYM	0	0	2	0	4	0	1	1	0	–	8	7	1
NYY	0	1	2	0	1	3	0	0	2	–	9	9	1

Mets	IP	H	R	ER	BB	SO
L. Hernandez	5.1	7	6	6	1	1
Switzer	0.2	1	1	1	0	0
S. Green	1.1	0	0	0	2	1
P. Feliciano	0.2	0	0	0	0	0
F. Rodriguez L(1–1)	0.2	1	2	0	1	1
Totals	**8.2**	**9**	**9**	**7**	**4**	**3**

Yankees	IP	H	R	ER	BB	SO
Chamberlain	4.0	1	2	2	5	3
Tomko	0.2	3	4	4	2	1
D. Robertson	1.1	1	1	1	1	3
Coke	1.2	1	0	0	0	0
Ma. Rivera W(1–2)	1.1	1	1	1	1	2
Totals	**9**	**7**	**8**	**8**	**9**	**9**

E—New York Mets L. Castillo; New York Yankees Cano. DP—New York Yankees 1. 2B—New York Mets Beltran, Church, Sheffield, D. Wright; New York Yankees Posada, A. Rodriguez. HR—New York Mets Sheffield (6); New York Yankees Cano (10), Teixeira (20), Jeter (9), H. Matsui (9). HBP—New York Mets F. Martinez, Church. LOB—New York Mets 9; New York Yankees 5. SB—New York Mets Church, L. Castillo, Beltran; New York Yankees Jeter. Attendance: 47,967.

"I have to catch that ball," the veteran second baseman said. "I didn't get it, I feel bad. It was a routine fly ball. I need to get it."

"That's why you play for nine innings," A-Rod said. "That's why you play hard. The lesson we take from here is to play all 27 [outs] and hustle all the time."

There were five home runs in the game, including a three-run shot from Hideki Matsui off Mets left-hander Jon Switzer that gave the Yankees a 7–6 lead in the sixth inning.

The Mets rallied to take the lead in the eighth on an RBI double by David Wright off Mariano Rivera. There was some controversy surrounding Rivera's appearance, as he was brought in during the eighth inning of a tie game. Usually, Rivera is only brought in during the eighth when the Yankees have a lead. Manager Joe Girardi elected to go to his closer only to see it backfire.

The Mets went with K-Rod to close it out. Brett Gardner popped out to start the inning but Jeter singled. Johnny Damon pinch hit for Nick Swisher but struck out as Jeter stole second.

"Tex" was intentionally passed, and the rest is history. —∞—

Friday the 13th Brings on a Melee, Forfeit Victory in Detroit

It was Friday the 13th. If you suffer from "triskaidekaphobia" (a fear of the number 13), or even if you don't, you knew something screwy was going to happen at Detroit's Navin Field when the Yankees met the Tigers.

For the third time in their history, the Yankees won a game by forfeit.

The Yankees were leading 10–6 in the top of the ninth inning when "Babe Ruth told Bob Meusel he saw Ty Cobb give Bert Cole the sign to hit Meusel with a pitch," according to an account in Marshall Smelser's *The Life That Ruth Built.*

Ruth took some chin music from Cole during his at-bat, avoiding a high, hard one, and eventually fouled out to Tigers first baseman Lu Blue.

The next hitter was Meusel, who took a pitch in the ribs. The 6-foot-3 outfielder dropped his bat, and went to the mound to fight the 6-foot-1 Cole.

Ruth rushed out while Cobb and the umps converged on the hill. Both dugouts emptied, and Ruth had a tough time getting to Cobb because of all the traffic.

Police in the stands came out on the field to try to restore order among the participants.

Home plate umpire Billy Evans threw Ruth and Meusel out of the game, and the two had to be escorted from the field through the Detroit dugout.

As this was taking place, a riot ensued as a crowd of fans rushed onto the field. Some other rowdies took to tearing up the seats in the stands and throwing those broken pieces on the field.

After it became apparent that the police could not clear the field, Evans ordered the game forfeited to the Yankees. The authorities reportedly arrested a half dozen perpetrators, and the melee began to die down.

Yankees	AB	R	H	RBI
Johnson 2b	3	1	1	0
McNally 2b	1	1	0	0
Combs cf	5	2	2	0
Ruth lf	3	1	0	1
Meusel rf	3	1	2	2
Pipp 1b	4	2	0	1
Schang c	3	1	2	3
Dugan 3b	4	0	0	1
Scott ss	4	0	2	2
Jones p	2	0	0	0
Gaston p	2	1	1	0
Totals	34	10	10	10

Tigers	AB	R	H	RBI
Blue 1b	3	0	1	2
Cobb cf	4	0	0	0
Manush lf	4	0	1	0
Heilmann rf	4	0	0	0
Pratt 2b	4	2	2	0
Rigney ss	4	2	1	1
B. Jones 3b	3	1	1	0
Bassler c	2	1	2	3
Stoner p	1	0	0	0
Cole p	3	0	0	0
Totals	32	6	8	6

```
NY   0 3 3 0 0 0 4 0 0 - 10 10 2
DET  0 2 0 0 2 2 0 0 X -  6 8 1
```

Yankees	IP	H	R	ER	BB	SO
Jones	5	7	6	5	1	0
Gaston W(1–0)	3	1	0	0	2	1
Totals	8	8	6	5	3	1

Tigers	IP	H	R	ER	BB	SO
Stoner	2	6	6	4	1	1
Cole (2–7)	6.1	4	4	4	3	3
Totals	8.1	10	10	8	4	4

E—New York Johnson, Scott; Detroit Pratt. DP—New York 1; Detroit 1. 2B—New York Combs, Meusel, Schang; Detroit Pratt, B. Jones. SH—New York Schang; Detroit B. Jones. HBP—New York Meusel. LOB—New York 5; Detroit 6. SB—Detroit Cobb. Attendance: 18,000.

Even though the game was won by forfeit, the score did not change to the standard 9–0 forfeit score. Major league rules dictate that if a game is forfeited by the losing team while still in progress, the score shall be what it was at the time of the forfeit.

The Yankees jumped on Tigers starter Ulysses Simpson Grant "Lil" Stoner for three runs in the second and third innings for a 6–2 lead.

Detroit battled back to score two in the fifth inning and two in the sixth off Yankees pitcher "Sad Sam" Jones to tie the game at six.

In the seventh inning, the Yankees rocked Cole for four runs on three hits, so he decided to get even by plunking the hitters in the later innings.

The fallout from the incident was felt the next day when commissioner Ban Johnson suspended Meusel and Cole for 10 days. Johnson fined Meusel $50 and gave Ruth a $100 fine.

The Bambino also had to find a new glove. Reportedly, his was stolen during the riot.

Cobb was 37 years old when this game was played. Even after he went 0-for-4, he was still batting .349. He finished the 1924 season with 211 hits and a .338 batting average. —⁄⁄⁄⁄—

Did You Know?

Mariano Rivera has been the finishing pitcher in the final game of each of the Yankees' last six World Series appearances and in 15 overall playoff series through the end of the 2009 season. The 2009 season marked the fourth time that Rivera was on the mound in the final game of three postseason series in a single year.

Martin Bids Farewell to Yankees as a Player

It was the last hurrah for Yankees infielder Billy Martin, who played his final game as a Yankee in their 10–1 win over the Athletics at Kansas City's Municipal Stadium.

Before the game, American League president Will Harridge announced a number of fines resulting from a nasty incident in Chicago, when the White Sox's Larry Doby got into a brawl with Yankees pitcher Art Ditmar. Martin got involved with Doby after things had settled down, so he was fined $150, along with Doby and the Yankees' Enos Slaughter. Ditmar and Walt Dropo of the White Sox were hit with $100 fines.

Martin was 1-for-4 in the game with a big two-run single in the fifth inning that gave the Yankees a 6–0 lead.

The name of Billy Martin began to surface in trade rumors. The Yankees grew tired of the fiery Martin's act and particularly what they felt was a bad influence on the young Mickey Mantle.

It had been less than a month since the infamous incident at the Copacabana night club, where Martin and several other members of the Yankees got into a brawl with a group of drunken bowlers. Mantle, Whitey Ford, Hank Bauer, Johnny Kucks, and Yogi Berra were there with their wives to celebrate Martin's birthday and see a performance by Sammy Davis Jr.

Martin, Mantle, Ford, Berra, and Bauer were each fined $1,000 by the Yankees for their part in the fracas. Kucks was fined $500.

The 29-year-old Martin had a history of getting into fights with other players, including Boston's Jimmy Piersall and Baltimore's Clint Courtney.

This latest incident with the White Sox seemed to be the last straw. An hour and nine minutes before the June 15 trade deadline expired, the Yankees completed a seven-player trade with Kansas City.

Yankees	AB	R	H	RBI
Richardson 2b	6	2	3	1
McDougald ss	4	0	0	0
Mantle cf	3	2	1	2
Berra lf	2	2	1	0
Bauer rf	5	1	3	3
Skowron 1b	3	2	3	1
Martin 3b	4	0	1	2
Johnson c	5	1	1	1
Sturdivant p	5	0	1	0
Totals	**37**	**10**	**14**	**10**

Athletics	AB	R	H	RBI
Power 1b	4	0	0	0
Cerv cf	4	0	2	0
Zernial lf	4	0	1	0
Simpson rf	4	0	1	0
Smith c	4	0	0	0
Lopez 3b	3	1	0	0
DeMaestri ss	2	0	1	0
Hunter pr	0	0	0	0
Burnette p	1	0	0	0
Skizas ph	1	0	0	0
McDermott p	1	0	0	0
Noren ph	1	0	0	0
Graff 2b	3	0	0	0
Totals	**32**	**1**	**8**	**0**

NY	0	0	0	1	5	0	0	2	2 -	10	14	0
KC	0	0	0	0	0	0	1	0	0 -	1	8	0

Yankees	IP	H	R	ER	BB	SO
Sturdivant W(5–3)	9	8	1	1	2	5

Athletics	IP	H	R	ER	BB	SO
Burnette L(4–4)	4.2	5	6	6	6	4
Gorman	0.1	1	0	0	0	0
McDermott	2.2	1	1	1	4	2
Host	1.1	7	3	3	0	1
Totals	**9**	**14**	**10**	**10**	**10**	**7**

DP—New York 3; Kansas City 2. 2B—New York Skowron. HR—New York Mantle (19). SH—New York McDougald. HBP—Kansas City DeMaestri. LOB—New York 11; Kansas City 7. Attendance: 24,369.

Billy Martin, Woodie Held, Bob Martyn, and Ralph Terry were sent to the Athletics in exchange for outfielders Jim Pisoni and Harry Simpson, plus pitcher Ryne Duren.

Simpson drove in 105 runs for Kansas City in 1956, so the Yankees felt they were adding a little more pop to the lineup. But Simpson never panned out and was traded back to the A's exactly one year later in 1958.

Martin played his first game as a member of the A's against the Yankees and was 2-for-5, including a solo home run off Kucks, but the Bombers prevailed in that game 8–6.

The trade fractured Martin's relationship with manager Casey Stengel. "The Ol' Perfessor" was Martin's mentor. Martin was devastated and didn't speak to Stengel for years.

In 1975, Martin was managing his third team, the Texas Rangers, and wanted to bury the hatchet with Stengel, so he wrote him a note on Rangers stationary.

When Charles Dillon Stengel died on September 29, 1975, Martin went to the funeral and was inconsolable. The night before the funeral, Martin slept in Stengel's bed. ─⚊─

Boxing Bout Forces Extended Road Trip

The Yankees began a grueling 16-game road trip in style as they beat the Orioles 6–4 before a crowd of 29,840 at Memorial Stadium.

One of the reasons for the extended stay away from home was that a championship boxing match was scheduled to be held at Yankee Stadium on June 17 between Rocky Marciano and Ezzard Charles.

The fight was slated to be televised in 61 movie theatres in 45 cities. Rain could have caused a problem, because a postponement due to weather would push the bout back a week.

The Yankees and the boxing promoters reportedly worked a deal to have the team play away from home for an extended period so the boxing match could take place.

The Yankees took a 6–2 lead in the fifth inning thanks to a triple from Yogi Berra on a ball that was lost in the lights by Orioles right fielder Cal Abrams.

The O's scored two runs in the ninth inning off Allie Reynolds to cut the lead and had runners on first and third base when Yankees manager Casey Stengel called for Johnny Sain out of the bullpen.

The four-time 20-game winner was the closer in 1954 and he got Baltimore's Bob Kennedy to strike out on a 2–2 pitch that ended the game. —\~—

Yankees	AB	R	H	RBI
Rizzuto ss	2	1	0	0
Collins 1b	4	2	3	4
Mantle cf	3	1	1	1
Berra c	4	0	1	1
Woodling lf	4	0	0	0
Noren rf	4	0	1	0
Brown 3b	4	0	0	0
McDougald 3b	0	0	0	0
Coleman 2b	4	1	1	0
Reynolds p	3	1	0	0
Totals	32	6	7	6

Orioles	AB	R	H	RBI
Abrams rf	5	1	2	0
Hunter ss	3	0	0	0
Moss ph	1	0	1	1
Garcia pr	0	0	0	0
Kryhoski 1b	5	0	1	1
Kennedy 3b	4	0	1	0
Courtney c	3	0	1	0
Fridley lf	4	0	0	0
Coan cf	4	1	1	0
Young 2b	4	1	1	0
Coleman p	2	1	1	2
Mele ph	1	0	0	0
Diering ph	0	0	0	0
Totals	36	4	9	4

NY	0	0	2	0	4	0	0	0	0	–	6	7	1
BAL	0	0	2	0	0	0	0	0	2	–	4	9	0

Yankees	IP	H	R	ER	BB	SO
Reynolds W(8–1)	8.2	9	4	4	3	7
Sain SV(12)	0.1	0	0	0	0	1
Totals	9	9	4	4	3	8

Orioles	IP	H	R	ER	BB	SO
Coleman L(7–5)	7	6	6	6	2	3
Fox	2	1	0	0	0	3
Totals	9	7	6	6	2	6

E—New York Rizzuto. 2B—Baltimore Courtney. 3B—New York Mantle. HR—New York Collins (3); Baltimore Coleman (2). SH—New York Reynolds, Rizzuto; Baltimore Hunter. LOB—New York 3; Baltimore 9. SB—New York Rizzuto. Attendance: 29,840.

Shirley Puts on a Show for the Ages, Tosses Four-Hitter vs. Tigers

Dave Winfield's simple walk-off single ended the Yankees' thrilling 2–1 win over the Detroit Tigers. Pitcher Bob Shirley won it by throwing his best game ever as a Yankee.

The beleaguered southpaw made this a Father's Day to remember by limiting the defending World Champions to one run on four hits.

Shirley's lone mistake was a big one as the Tigers' Kirk Gibson unloaded a tremendous blast that hit the back wall in the right-center-field bleachers, an estimated 450 feet.

"It was the only mistake we made today," said Shirley's catcher, Butch Wynegar. "He can blame it on me. I called that pitch."

Future Hall of Famer Rickey Henderson's impact on the game was front and center in the bottom of the ninth after he walked on a 3–2 pitch to start the inning.

Tigers pitcher Randy O'Neal, who had limited the Yankees to a run on two hits to that point, tried a pick-off at first base but threw it away, allowing Henderson to take second.

Ken Griffey was intentionally walked, and after an O'Neal wild pitch put runners on second and third, Winfield ended the game with a hard single to center. —

Tigers	AB	R	H	RBI
Whitaker 2b	4	0	0	0
Trammell ss	4	0	0	0
Gibson cf	4	1	2	1
Parrish dh	4	0	0	0
Herndon lf	2	0	0	0
Sanchez rf	3	0	2	0
Evans 1b	3	0	0	0
Melvin c	3	0	0	0
Brookens 3b	3	0	0	0
Totals	**30**	**1**	**4**	**1**

Yankees	AB	R	H	RBI
Henderson cf	3	1	0	0
Griffey lf	3	0	0	0
Winfield rf	4	0	1	1
Mattingly 1b	3	0	0	0
Baylor dh	3	0	0	0
Wynegar c	2	0	0	0
Randolph 2b	2	0	0	0
Pagliarulo 3b	3	1	2	1
Meacham ss	3	0	0	0
Totals	**26**	**2**	**3**	**2**

										R	H	E
DET	0	0	0	1	0	0	0	0	0	1	4	1
NY	0	0	1	0	0	0	0	0	1	2	3	0

Tigers	IP	H	R	ER	BB	SO
O'Neal L(1–1)	8	3	2	2	4	7

Yankees	IP	H	R	ER	BB	SO
Shirley W(2–1)	9	4	1	1	2	5

E—Detroit O'Neal. DP—New York 1. 2B—Detroit Sanchez. HR—Detroit Gibson (12); New York Pagliarulo (4). LOB—Detroit 4; New York 4. Attendance: 36,036.

Guidry Mows Down Record 18 Via Strikeout

Ron Guidry put his name alongside the all-time great Yankee pitchers when he set a franchise record by striking out 18 California hitters in the Yankees' 4–0 win at Yankee Stadium.

The win gave Gator an 11–0 record during his phenomenal 1978 season, when he finished 25–3. The four-hit shutout lowered his ERA to 1.45.

Rick Miller led off the game with a double, but Guidry got out of the first inning with two strikeouts. Don Baylor walked to lead off the second but was left on base when Guidry fanned Brian Downing to end the inning.

Ron Guidry needed the 1–2 punch of ice and nourishment following his memorable performance on June 17, 1978. Guidry set a franchise record with 18 strikeouts in a 4–0 win over the Angels at Yankee Stadium. Guidry, boosted by the four-hit shutout, went on to finish the season 25–3.

The Yankees gave Guidry all the offense he would need with a run in the first inning and three more in the third, keyed by a run-scoring triple from Gary Thomasson. Thomasson was in the lineup because Mickey Rivers was nursing a swollen left hand.

The strikeouts began to accumulate in the third inning when Guidry whiffed the side, sandwiched around singles by Miller and Dave Chalk.

Six Ks in three innings got the crowd going and prompted Yankee announcer Phil Rizzuto to coin a moniker for Guidry that stuck throughout his career, "Louisiana Lightning."

The crowd of 33,162 sensed something special was going on and they wanted to be a big part of it. When Guidry would get two strikes on a batter, the fans would start cheering and clapping, trying to help Guidry get that third strike.

"When they start hollering and screaming," Guidry said, "you just get pumped up that much higher. You try harder."

Three more strikeouts in the fourth inning and then two more in the fifth gave Gator a total of 11 through five innings.

Angels	AB	R	H	RBI
Grich 2b	4	0	1	0
R. Miller cf	4	0	1	0
Chalk ss	4	0	1	0
Rudi 1b	4	0	0	0
Baylor lf	3	0	1	0
Jackson 3b	4	0	0	0
Rettenmund rf	3	0	0	0
Downing c	2	0	0	0
Hampton dh	3	0	0	0
Totals				

Yankees	AB	R	H	RBI
White lf	4	1	1	0
Munson c	4	1	2	0
Thomasson cf	4	1	2	2
Blair cf	0	0	0	0
Jackson rf	4	1	1	1
Chambliss 1b	4	0	1	0
Nettles 3b	4	0	1	1
Spencer dh	4	0	1	0
Stanley ss	3	0	0	0
Doyle 2b	3	0	2	0
Totals	34	4	11	4

CAL 0 0 0 0 0 0 0 0 0 - 0 4 0
NY 1 0 3 0 0 0 0 X - 4 11 0

Angels	IP	H	R	ER	BB	SO
Hartzell L(1–5)	2.1	8	4	4	0	1
Brett	5.2	3	0	0	0	4
Totals	8	11	4	4	0	5

Yankees	IP	H	R	ER	BB	SO
Guidry W(11–0)	9	4	0	0	2	18

2B—California, Grich. 3B—New York, Thomasson. LOB—California 6; New York 6. SB—California, Baylor 7. Attendance—33,162.

The Yankee record of 15 (Bob Shawkey, 1919) for a nine-inning game was certainly within reach and the major league record of 19 was in striking distance.

Guidry made it 14 strikeouts through six innings as he fanned the side in order. In the seventh, Ron Jackson flied out and Merv Rettenmund grounded out but Brian Downing struck out for No. 15 to end the inning.

Angels designated hitter Ike Hampton was Gator's 16th strikeout victim, a Yankees record, but that was all he would get in the eighth inning.

The Angels could only watch in awe at what the lanky left-hander was doing to their bats.

Angels first baseman Joe Rudi, who fanned four times, said, "If you saw that pitching too often, there would be a lot of guys doing different jobs."

In the ninth inning, Chalk and Rudi struck out, so Guidry needed one more K to tie the all-time mark.

The crowd was going bonkers as Gator set down 14 Angels in a row, but Baylor singled with two out to end that streak. There was still a chance at the strikeout record, but Jackson put an end to that when he forced Baylor at second to end the game.

After it had witnessed 18 strikeouts, not to mention a four-hit shutout, the crowd would not leave. The fans wanted Guidry to come out of the dugout for a curtain call. They kept cheering until he emerged and acknowledged their applause by lifting his cap overhead.

"I didn't know I had that many strikeouts," Guidry said in the clubhouse after the game. "I knew I had several but I didn't think I was up that high."

When it was all said and done, Guidry threw 138 pitches, 65 percent of which he estimated were sliders. "Louisiana Lightning" struck out every Angels batter at least once. He got all nine outs in the middle innings by strikeouts.

Guidry took time to laud his catcher, Thurman Munson. According to manager Billy Martin, Munson could have used a day off, but he wanted to be in the lineup simply because Guidry was pitching.

"Thurman makes a whole lot of difference," Guidry said. "Most of the pitchers depend on him so much because of his knowledge of the hitters."

Guidry averaged 4.5 strikeouts per game in his first eight starts, but he had struck out 10 or more in five of his last six.

"In those early games, I didn't feel strong because I had a bad case of flu in the spring," Guidry said. "I didn't have that extra foot on my fastball."

To this day, fans will stand and applaud when the home team needs one more strike to end a game, or, if a pitcher is having a big strikeout game, they'll be on their feet with two strikes. ―∾―

P Ron Guidry

Ron Guidry pitched for the Yankees for 14 years and recorded the greatest single season by a pitcher in franchise history.

In 1978, Guidry was a remarkable 25–3 with a 1.74 ERA. "Louisiana Lightning" (a nickname given to him by Yankee icon Phil Rizzuto) tossed nine shutouts and struck out 248 batters to capture the 1978 Cy Young Award. He finished second in the MVP voting to Red Sox Jim Rice that season, but many felt he should have won that award as well for leading the Yankees to their historic comeback.

Guidry was a three-time 20-game winner and a five-time Gold Glove winner.

On June 17, 1978, Guidry set a Yankee record for the most strikeouts in a single game when he fanned 18 California Angels.

Mantle Makes a Winner of Scoreless Reliever Shantz with Solo Blast

Mickey Mantle led off the bottom of the 10th inning with a line-drive solo home run deep into the right-field stands to give the Yankees a 5–4 win over the White Sox.

Mantle connected on a 1–0 pitch from White Sox losing pitcher Gerry Staley to make a winner of Bobby Shantz, who tossed three scoreless innings in relief.

The Yankees trailed 4–2 in the eighth inning when a Yogi Berra RBI double and an RBI single from Hector Lopez tied the game at four.

The Yankees had a chance to win the game in the eighth inning, but Gil McDougald lined to right and Bill Skowron was nailed at home on a great throw from Chicago right fielder Jim Rivera.

The game featured intriguing matchups between the two managers. White Sox skipper Al Lopez and Yankees manager Casey Stengel pulled out all the stops in the bottom of the eighth inning.

At one point, Stengel put up left-handed hitting Johnny Blanchard to face right-hander Turk Lown, but Lopez went to Rudy Arias, a lefty. Stengel countered by putting up right-handed hitting Elston Howard for Blanchard. Howard was intentionally walked to load the bases and Staley was brought on to face the pinch-hitter McDougald. ⎯

White Sox	AB	R	H	RBI
Aparicio ss	5	1	2	1
Fox 2b	5	0	2	2
Torgeson 1b	2	0	0	1
Lollar c	5	0	1	0
Rivera rf	5	0	1	0
Goodman 3b	4	0	1	0
Phillips 3b	1	0	0	0
Smith lf	4	0	1	0
Landis cf	4	1	1	0
Shaw p	4	2	1	0
Totals	39	4	10	4

Yankees	AB	R	H	RBI
Bauer rf	5	0	1	2
Pisoni rf	0	0	0	0
Siebern lf	5	1	1	0
Mantle cf	4	1	2	1
Berra c	4	1	1	1
Skowron 1b	3	0	0	0
Lopez 3b	4	0	1	1
Richardson 2b	3	1	1	0
Blanchard ph	0	0	0	0
Howard ph	0	0	0	0
Brickell pr,ss	0	0	0	0
Kubek ss	3	1	2	0
McDougald ph,2b	1	0	0	0
Bronstad p	1	0	0	0
Slaughter ph	1	0	0	0
Shantz p	1	0	0	0
Totals	35	5	9	5

											R	H	E
CHI	0	0	0	2	0	2	0	0	0	-	4	10	0
NY	0	0	2	0	0	0	2	0	1	-	5	9	2

White Sox	IP	H	R	ER	BB	SO
Shaw	7.1	7	4	4	2	2
Lown	0	1	0	0	0	0
Arias	0	0	0	0	1	0
Staley L(2–3)	1.2	1	1	1	0	3
Totals	9	9	5	5	3	5

Yankees	IP	H	R	ER	BB	SO
Bronstad	4.2	5	2	0	3	2
Terry	2.1	5	2	2	0	2
Shantz W(1–2)	3	0	0	0	0	1
Totals	10	10	4	2	3	5

E—New York Richardson, Kubek. DP—Chicago 1; New York 1. 2B—Chicago Shaw, Fox; New York Berra. HR—New York Mantle (15). HBP—New York Bronstad. LOB—Chicago 8; New York 7. SB—Chicago Aparicio. Attendance: 17,882.

Coors Field Provides a Wild Night for Yanks

Since the inception of interleague play in 1997, the Yankees have played some "wild" interleague games, but this one at Colorado's Coors Field goes right to the top of the list.

In a typical Coors game, one that ended with a football-like score, the Yankees beat the Colorado Rockies 20–10.

The Yankees pounded out 18 hits and scored in six of the nine innings.

Bernie Williams and Jorge Posada led the way with three hits apiece, while Robin Ventura and John Vander Wal each drove in four runs.

The Yankees scored three or more runs in four consecutive innings, capped off by the seventh, when four runs scored on three walks, two errors, and a double by Vander Wal that just missed being a grand slam.

Starting pitching was nonexistent for both teams. Yankee lefthander Andy Pettitte gave up eight runs (five earned) in 3 2/3 innings of work. "I wasn't able to get the balls in when I wanted to," Pettitte said. "I gave up a lot hits on four-seamers that I was trying get in and left over the plate."

The Rockies' Mike Hampton was no better, as the southpaw gave up seven earned runs in five innings pitched.

The Yankees grabbed a 4–1 lead in the fourth but Colorado scored seven times in their half to grab an 8–4 lead.

At a Glance

W: Mendoza (4–2)

HR: Soriano (16), Giambi (18), Ventura (18)

Key Stats: Posada 3-for-6, 4 R; Williams 3-for-5, 3 R; Ventura 4 RBIs; Vander Wal 4 RBIs

New York made it an 8–7 game with three in the fifth before rain forced a 38-minute delay. Once the storm passed, the Yankees stormed back and took control.

With one out, Alfonso Soriano hit a solo home run off reliever Rick White to tie the game at eight.

After Derek Jeter singled, Jason Giambi went deep for a two-run blow and a 10–8 advantage. The Yankees would put up a six spot in the sixth to take a 13–8 lead.

"Their line looked like a zip code," Colorado manager Clint Hurdle said. "It wasn't pretty. I don't know of many games I've been involved in where the team I've been associated with scored seven runs in an inning and lost."

The Yankee bullpen was superb as they worked 5 1/3 innings, giving up two unearned runs. Ramiro Mendoza was awarded the win as he worked 1 2/3 innings and essentially settled the game down, despite giving up those two un-earned runs.

The game became part of the second-highest scoring three-game series in the history of the franchise. The Yankees had 54 hits and scored 41 runs in the three games played at Coors Field, but they gave up 29. In 1951, the Yankees scored 42 runs in a three game series vs. the St. Louis Browns.

"You get to the point where, unlike in other ballparks, you just relax and let things happen because there is nothing you can do about it," Yankees manager Joe Torre said. "It is fun because everybody comes in and just sort of shakes their heads."

The Rockies went quietly in the ninth against Steve Karsay in what was an emotionally draining affair.

"I'm exhausted right now, but you have to keep running and going around the bases, and you can't quit," Giambi said. "You can't even let down when you get a big lead here because like what happened tonight, you can score quite a few runs and get right back in the ball game." —ᴡᴡ—

Did You Know?

The center-field wall at the original Yankee Stadium was 490 feet from home plate from 1923–1936. Beginning in 1937, center field was 461 feet from home plate and it was increased to 463 feet in 1967. It was 417 feet to dead center at the remodeled stadium but that eventually was decreased to 410 feet and then 408 feet from 1988–2008.

Sultan of Swat Makes a Winner of Durable Mays

How about a game that featured 13 runs on 21 hits yet both pitchers went 10 innings?

That happened at Fenway Park when the Yankees' Carl Mays and the Red Sox's Elmer Myers hooked up in what could not be described as a pitchers' duel.

Mays gave up six runs on 11 hits during his stint but got the win when Babe Ruth homered off Myers in the top of the 10th inning to provide the winning margin in a 7–6 victory.

Ruth had a big game in his old stomping grounds. In addition to hitting the game-winning home run, Ruth gave the Yankees a 1–0 lead with a run-scoring double in the first inning and was 3-for-5 with two RBIs and two runs scored.

The right-handed Myers was victimized by shoddy defense as he gave up three unearned runs.

Myers faced Ruth as the first batter in the 10th inning. Ruth wasted no time as he smacked Myers' first pitch of the inning over the wall in left field for the lead. (The left-field wall at Fenway was not called the "Green Monster" in 1921. It was not painted green until 1947.)

Mays sat the Red Sox down in order in the 10th inning to wrap up the win.

Yankees manager Miller Huggins felt the lineup needed a slight adjustment so he put Frank "Home Run" Baker in the cleanup spot behind Ruth and moved Wally Pipp from fourth to sixth in the order.

Pipp had a pair of doubles while Baker was hitless in five at-bats.

Yankees	AB	R	H	RBI
Hawks lf	4	1	0	0
Peckinpaugh ss	4	0	0	0
Ruth cf	5	2	3	2
Baker 3b	5	0	0	0
Meusel rf	4	2	2	0
Pipp 1b	4	2	2	1
Ward 2b	4	0	3	2
Schang c	3	0	0	1
Mays p	4	0	0	0
Totals	37	7	10	6

Red Sox	AB	R	H	RBI
Vitt 3b	5	1	2	0
Menosky lf	4	1	1	0
Pratt 2b	5	0	0	1
Hendryx rf	0	0	0	0
Leibold cf	5	1	1	1
McInnis 1b	5	1	4	0
Collins cf	5	1	1	1
Scott ss	5	1	1	2
Ruel c	2	0	1	1
Myers p	4	0	0	0
Totals	40	6	11	6

```
NY   4 0 0 0 0 1 0 1 0 1 - 7 10 1
BOS  3 0 0 0 0 0 0 3 0 0 - 6 11 2
```

Yankees	IP	H	R	ER	BB	SO
Mays W(10–5)	10	11	6	6	2	5

Red Sox	IP	H	R	ER	BB	SO
Myers L(5–3)	10	10	7	4	3	1

E—New York Ruth; Boston Hendryx, Ruel. DP—Boston 1. 2B—New York Ruth, Meusel, Pipp 2; Boston McInnis, Ruel. 3B—New York Ward; Boston Scott. HR—New York Ruth (24). SH—New York Peckinpaugh, Schang; Boston Ruel. LOB—New York 5; Boston 7. SB—New York Meusel. Attendance: 8,000.

Ford, Mantle Too Much for Yankee-Killer Lary

The combination of Whitey Ford pitching and Mickey Mantle hitting served the Yankees well as they beat noted Yankee-killer Frank Lary with a 6–0 win.

Ford gave up four hits, all singles, while Mantle clubbed two home runs off Lary, who usually had his way with the Yankees.

The 5-foot-11 right-hander was 28–13 in his career vs. the Yankees, including 7–1 in 1958, but in this game he did not have it. Lary lasted into the seventh inning but yielded five runs on 11 hits.

The Yankees took a 1–0 lead in the fourth inning. Roger Maris tripled and scored on Lary's wild pitch.

Mantle led off the sixth inning with his first home run, a solo shot into the right-field stands for a 2–0 lead. The Mick reached the left-field seats with his second home run in the seventh inning, a two-run shot to make it 5–0.

Lary was so tough on the Yankees that he prompted manager Casey Stengel to ponder delaying the appearance of his ace, Ford, by one day so he wouldn't have to face Lary.

"If Lary is going to beat us anyway, why should I waste my best pitcher?" Stengel questioned.

Mantle actually hit .297 in his career vs. Lary, with nine home runs in 138 career at-bats. Maris batted .330 in his career against Lary with eight lifetime home runs vs. the righty. —⁓—

Yankees	AB	R	H	RBI
Kubek ss	4	0	2	0
Cerv lf	5	0	1	0
Mantle cf	5	3	3	3
Maris rf	4	1	2	0
Berra c	4	1	1	0
Howard c	1	0	0	0
Skowron 1b	3	0	2	0
Hadley 1b	2	0	0	0
Boyer 3b	4	0	0	1
Richardson 2b	4	0	2	0
Ford p	4	1	1	0
Totals	40	6	14	4

Tigers	AB	R	H	RBI
Yost 3b	3	0	0	0
Fernandez ss	4	0	1	0
Maxwell lf	4	0	0	0
Bilko 1b	4	0	1	0
Kaline cf	3	0	1	0
Colavito rf	3	0	0	0
Wilson c	0	0	0	0
Berberet c	3	0	0	0
Bolling 2b	3	0	0	0
Lary p	2	0	1	0
Groth ph	1	0	0	0
Totals	30	0	4	0

```
NY   0 0 0 1 0 2 2 0 1 - 6 14 1
DET  0 0 0 0 0 0 0 0 0 - 0 4 2
```

Yankees	IP	H	R	ER	BB	SO
Ford W(5–3)	9	4	0	0	1	1

Tigers	IP	H	R	ER	BB	SO
Lary L(6–7)	6.2	11	5	5	1	3
Sisler	1.1	1	0	0	0	1
Morgan	1	2	1	0	0	1
Totals	9	14	6	5	1	5

E—New York Skowron; Detroit Fernandez 2. DP—New York 2; Detroit 1. 3B—New York Maris. HR—New York Mantle 2 (15,16). SH—New York Kubek. LOB—New York 9; Detroit 4. SB—New York Mantle. Attendance: 39,311.

Berra's Walk-Off Homer Gives Byrne a Victory

Yogi Berra hit a walk-off home run and Tommy Byrne tossed nine scoreless innings in relief to lead the Yankees to a 6–5 13-inning win over the Chicago White Sox at Yankee Stadium.

Berra took an 0–1 pitch from White Sox losing pitcher Paul LaPalme and drove it deep into the right-field seats, thus ending this 4 hour, 13 minute marathon.

Byrne entered the game in the fifth inning and allowed only one hit (an eighth-inning single by White Sox outfielder Jim Rivera) the rest of the way.

Art Ditmar started for the Yankees but was relieved in the second inning by Don Larsen, who gave the Yankees three innings.

Mickey Mantle got the Yankees jump-started in the first inning with a two-run home run into the right-field stands off White Sox starter Jack Harshman, but Chicago rallied to take a 5–2 lead in the third inning.

In the sixth inning, Bill Skowron hit a long home run into the Yankees' bullpen in right-center field to make it a one-run deficit. The Yankees tied the game in the seventh inning on an RBI single by Harry Simpson.

The Yankees nearly broke the tie in the eighth inning. Elston Howard hit a shot to center field, but Bubba Phillips misjudged it. Howard was off to the races. He tried to complete an inside-the-park home run but was thrown out at the plate on a nifty four-man relay. —⁓—

White Sox	AB	R	H	RBI
Aparicio ss	7	0	0	0
Fox 2b	6	0	1	0
Torgeson 1b	2	0	1	1
Moss c	1	0	0	0
Minoso lf	6	0	0	0
Rivera rf	6	2	2	0
Battey c	4	1	0	0
Dropo ph,1b	3	0	0	0
Phillips 3b,cf	6	2	2	1
Landis cf	0	0	0	1
Northey ph	0	0	0	0
Esposito pr,3b	2	0	0	0
Harsham p	1	0	0	2
Howell p	2	0	0	0
Wilson ph	1	0	0	0
LaPalme p	0	0	0	0
Totals	47	5	6	5

Yankees	AB	R	H	RBI
Richardson 2b	6	2	3	0
McDougald ss	3	0	0	0
Mantle cf	6	1	2	2
Bauer rf	1	0	0	0
Simpson ph,rf	4	1	1	1
Skowron 1b	5	1	1	2
Berra c	6	1	1	1
Howard lf	4	0	1	0
Carey 3b	4	0	2	0
Larsen p	1	0	0	0
Slaughter ph	1	0	0	0
Byrne p	2	0	0	0
Totals	43	6	11	6

```
CHI  0 3 2 0 0 0 0 0 0 0 0 0 0 - 5 6 0
NY   2 0 0 0 2 1 0 0 0 0 0 0 1 - 6 11 2
```

White Sox	IP	H	R	ER	BB	SO
Harsham	2.1	3	2	2	2	1
Howell	5.2	5	3	3	3	4
LaPalme L(0–1)	4	3	1	1	2	2
Totals	12	11	6	6	7	7

Yankees	IP	H	R	ER	BB	SO
Ditmar	1	3	3	1	2	0
Larsen	3	2	2	2	3	3
Byrne W(2–2)	9	1	0	0	7	7
Totals	13	6	5	3	12	10

E—New York Howard, Ditmar. DP—Chicago 2. 2B—Chicago Rivera; New York Richardson. 3B—Chicago Phillips; New York Howard. HR—New York Mantle (20), Skowron (12), Berra (9). SH—New York McDougald. HBP—Chicago Fox. LOB—Chicago 16; New York 9. SB—Chicago Rivera; New York Carey. Attendance: 33,130.

Kelly Shows His Promise with 5-for-5 Effort

Ever since he was signed as an undrafted free agent in 1982, Roberto Kelly was being touted as the Yankees' next great center fielder. Against the Twins at Yankee Stadium, Kelly began to display some of that potential as he went a career-high 5-for-5 to lead the Yankees to an 11–2 rout.

Coming into the game, the 26-year-old Kelly was struggling, but four singles and a home run put a nice end to a frustrating slump.

"You just have to say to yourself sooner of later you're out of it," Kelly said.

Kelly's home run was part of a six-run second-inning outburst that sent the Yankees on their way.

Meanwhile, rookie Scott Kamieniecki was limiting a red-hot Twins team (they had won 19 of 20 coming in) to two runs on six hits through 7 2/3 innings of work.

"When you jump on a team early," Kamieniecki said, "you have to bury them."

Kelly played one more season for the Yankees before being involved in one of the franchise's most significant trades. Following the 1992 season, the Yankees sent Kelly to the Cincinnati Reds for pitcher Joe DeBerry and an outfielder named Paul O'Neill.

The move also opened up the center field spot for an up-and-coming young player named Bernie Williams. —

Twins	AB	R	H	RBI
Gladden lf	5	0	2	0
Knoblauch 2b	5	0	1	0
Bush 1b	4	2	2	2
Davis dh	4	0	0	0
Harper c	3	0	1	0
Oritz c	0	0	0	0
Larkin rf	4	0	1	0
Mack cf	3	0	0	0
Leius 3b	4	0	0	0
Gagne ss	4	0	0	0
Totals	**36**	**2**	**7**	**2**

Yankees	AB	R	H	RBI
Sax 2b	3	0	2	1
Sheridan rf	1	0	0	1
Mattingly dh	5	2	1	0
R. Kelly cf	5	2	5	3
Maas 1b	3	1	0	0
Barfield lf	4	0	0	0
Rodriguez 2b	1	0	1	1
Meulens lf	5	2	3	2
Espinoza ss	4	1	1	0
Geren c	4	1	2	2
P. Kelly 3b	3	2	1	0
Totals	**38**	**11**	**16**	**9**

MIN	0	0	1	0	0	0	0	1	0	-	2 7 2
NY	0	6	0	1	0	0	3	1	X	-	11 16 2

Twins	IP	H	R	ER	BB	SO
Anderson L(4–5)	1.2	6	6	2	1	0
Abbott	5.1	7	4	4	2	7
Leach	1	3	1	1	0	1
Totals	**8**	**16**	**11**	**7**	**3**	**8**

Yankees	IP	H	R	ER	BB	SO
Kamieniecki W(2–0)	7.2	6	2	2	1	3
Howe	0.1	0	0	0	0	0
Farr	1	1	0	0	0	2
Totals	**9**	**7**	**2**	**2**	**1**	**5**

E—Minnesota Bush, Harper; New York Maas 2. DP—Minnesota 2. 2B—Minnesota Harper; New York Meulens, Geren. HR—Minnesota Bush 2 (1,2); New York R. Kelly (8). HBP—Minnesota Harper; New York P. Kelly. LOB—Minnesota 9; New York 7. SB—Minnesota Gladden; New York R. Kelly 3, Maas, P. Kelly. Attendance: 36,952.

Reed's First—and Only—Homer Ends Game in 22nd Inning

The Yankees have played some long games in their glorious history, but none as long as this one.

Seven hours and 22 innings after this game began, the Yankees beat the Tigers 9–7 in what turned into, at the time, the longest game—in terms of minutes—in major league history.

Jack Reed's first, and only, major league home run into the left-field stands off Tigers losing pitcher Phil Regan in the top of the 22nd inning turned out to be the deciding blow. The Yankees smacked around Frank Lary for six runs

As part of a seven-hour, 22-minute game on June 24, 1962, Yogi Berra went 3-for-10 before the Yankees won it 9–7 over the Tigers in the 22nd inning. Playing catcher, Berra helped the Yankees win the longest game in baseball history.

<table>
</table>

Yankees	AB	R	H	RBI
Tresh ss	9	0	2	0
Richardson 2b	11	2	3	0
Maris cf	9	2	2	0
Mantle rf	3	1	1	2
Pepitone rf	1	0	0	0
Linz ph	0	0	0	0
Reed rf	4	1	1	2
Blanchard lf	10	1	1	0
Berra c	10	0	3	1
Skowron 1b	10	1	2	1
Boyer 3b	9	1	3	3
Turley p	1	0	0	0
Lopez ph	1	0	1	0
Howard ph	1	0	0	0
Clevenger p	2	0	0	0
Daley p	1	0	0	0
Cerv ph	1	0	0	0
Bouton p	2	0	1	0
Totals	**85**	**9**	**20**	**9**

Tigers	AB	R	H	RBI
Boros 3b, 2b	10	1	1	0
Bruton cf	9	2	2	0
Goldy rf	10	1	1	3
Colavito lf	10	1	7	1
Cash 1b	8	1	2	0
McAuliffe 2b	5	0	1	0
Morton ph	1	0	0	0
Osborne 3b	1	0	0	0
Fernandez ss	10	1	1	1
Roarke c	5	0	2	2
Wood pr	0	0	0	0
Brown c	4	0	1	0
Maxwell ph	1	0	1	0
Casale p	1	0	0	0
Wertz ph	1	0	0	0
Kline p	1	0	0	0
Aguirre p	2	0	0	0
Fox p	2	0	0	0
Mossi ph	1	0	0	0
Totals	**82**	**7**	**19**	**7**

NY 610000000000000000002—9194
DET 303001000000000000000—7203

Yankees	IP	H	R	ER	BB	SO
Turley	0.1	1	3	3	3	0
Coates	2.2	4	3	3	1	6
Stafford	2.2	4	1	1	1	3
Bridges	0.1	0	0	0	0	0
Clevenger	6.1	5	0	0	3	1
Daley	2.2	2	0	0	0	2
Bouton W(2–1)	7	3	0	0	2	6
Totals	**22**	**19**	**7**	**7**	**10**	**18**

Tigers	IP	H	R	ER	BB	SO
Lary	2	7	7	7	1	1
Casale	3	1	0	0	2	0
Nischwitz	1.2	2	0	0	2	0
Kline	1	0	0	0	2	0
Aguirre	5.1	2	0	0	1	8
Fox	8	7	0	0	0	2
Regan L(4–7)	1	1	2	2	1	1
Totals	**22**	**20**	**9**	**9**	**9**	**12**

E—New York, Tresh, Berra, Boyer, Daley. Detroit, Goldy, McAuliffe, Fernandez. DP—New York 4. 2B—New York, Richardson; Detroit, Roarke. 3B—Detroit, Colavito. HR—New York, Boyer (10), Reed (1); Detroit, Goldy (3). SH—New York, Tresh; Detroit Fox, Brown. SF—New York, Berra. HBP—Detroit Goldy. LOB—New York 21; Detroit 22. SB—New York, Tresh; Detroit, Bruton. Attendance—35,368.

in the first inning. With three runs already across the plate, third baseman Clete Boyer hit a three-run homer off the Yankees' nemesis.

Yankees starter Bob Turley couldn't stand prosperity as he gave up a three-run homer to Purnal Goldy in the first inning to cut the lead in half.

The Tigers came all the way back to tie the game at seven on Rocky Colavito's RBI single in the sixth inning.

From that point on, the bullpens dominated the game as they kept the teams from scoring for the next 15 innings.

Regan (a.k.a. "The Vulture") was brought on to start the 22nd inning, but with one out, he walked Roger Maris. Reed entered the game in the 13th, replacing Joe Pepitone, who had replaced Mickey Mantle. (A total of 43 players were used in the game; 21 by the Yankees.)

Mantle was playing hurt, but he drove in a run in the first inning, another in the second and then was benched after fouling out in the seventh.

John "Jack" Burwell Reed hit one major league home run in his career and it came off Regan in the 22nd inning of the longest Yankee game in history.

If you like numbers, you've got plenty to salivate over from this marathon affair.

Start with 14 pitchers used, seven from each side.

Yankee rookie pitcher Jim Bouton pitched the final seven and earned the win. Journeyman reliever Tex Clevenger pitched 6 1/3 scoreless innings for the Yankees, while Detroit's Terry Fox pitched eight scoreless innings before Regan came on to take the loss.

Bobby Richardson was 3-for-11, while Yogi Berra was 3-for-10. Johnny Blanchard played left field the entire game and was 1-for-10. Roger Maris played the entire game in center field and was 2-for-9 with 10 putouts, while Boyer had a home run and three RBIs.

Colavito, who would later play and actually pitch for the Yankees, was 7-for-10. Tiger starters Steve

Boros, Goldy, and Chico Fernandez were each 1-for-10.

The Tigers threatened to take the lead in the 11th inning, when Colavito opened the inning with a triple. The Yankees elected to walk the next two hitters to load the bases. Fernandez's line drive to left was not deep enough to score Colavito, so Detroit chose to go with a squeeze bunt to try to win the game. The maneuver backfired when Dick Brown bunted the ball into the air. Berra caught it in foul territory and then doubled up Colavito, who had been rushing for the plate.

The previous longest game by time was just under five hours, when Baltimore beat Boston in 17 innings in a 1954 game.

The longest game by innings is 26, when Brooklyn and Boston played to a 1–1 deadlock in 1920. That game only lasted 3 hours and 50 minutes.

The AL record for most innings is 25 between Chicago and Milwaukee in 1984, which took eight hours and six minutes, but was suspended after 17 innings and finished the next day.

Reed played fewer than 250 games in his big-league career. After his baseball career ended in 1963, he coached minor league teams in Virginia, Florida, Georgia, and New York.

He was inducted into the Mississippi Athletic Hall of Fame in 1999. He is one of only four people to have played in a World Series game as well as a major college football bowl game, the Sugar Bowl of 1953. —

June 24, 1970

Murcer Hits Four Homers in a Row in Doubleheader

Yankees icon Bobby Murcer slammed four consecutive home runs as the Yankees and Indians split a doubleheader on June 24, 1970.

In his final at-bat of the first game, Murcer homered off hard-throwing lefty Sam McDowell.

Murcer began the nightcap with a solo home run in the first inning off Indians pitcher Mike Paul.

After drawing a walk in the fourth, Murcer hit a two-run shot in the fifth inning for his third in a row.

Murcer faced Indians reliever Fred Lasher in the eighth inning and hit his fourth home run in a row to complete quite a day.

In his next game, Murcer walked in the first inning, but the streak ended in the fifth when he lined out to second base.

Don't Trade Me Yet; Ellis Dials In with Seven-Hit Shutout

During the winter of 1975–76, the Yankees made a pivotal trade with the Pittsburgh Pirates that helped snap their 12-year drought without an American League pennant.

The Yankees acquired second baseman Willie Randolph and pitchers Ken Brett and Dock Ellis in exchange for pitcher George "Doc" Medich.

Ellis lasted a little over a year in the Bronx, but his best game came at Yankee Stadium when he authored a seven-hit shutout of the Brewers in a 1–0 win.

The enigmatic right-hander shut out a lineup that featured future Hall of Famers Hank Aaron and Robin Yount.

The only run of the game was scored when Mickey Rivers led off the sixth inning with a home run to hand Brewers left-hander Bill Travers a very tough loss.

Less than a month into his second season, Ellis was traded to the Oakland A's as part of a four-player trade that sent Mike Torrez to New York. —⁓—

Brewers	AB	R	H	RBI
Joshua cf	4	0	1	0
Yount ss	4	0	1	0
Money 3b	4	0	0	0
Carbo rf	4	0	2	0
Aaron dh	3	0	1	0
Scott 1b	4	0	1	0
Lezcano lf	4	0	1	0
Porter c	2	0	0	0
Johnson 2b	3	0	0	0
Totals	32	0	7	0

Yankees	AB	R	H	RBI
Rivers cf	4	1	2	1
White lf	4	0	1	0
Maddox rf	3	0	1	0
Gamble rf	1	0	0	0
Piniella dh	3	0	0	0
Chambliss 1b	3	0	2	0
Nettles 3b	3	0	0	0
Healy c	3	0	2	0
Randolph 2b	2	0	0	0
Stanley ss	3	0	0	0
Totals	29	1	8	1

MIL 0 0 0 0 0 0 0 0 0 - 0 7 0
NY 0 0 0 0 0 1 0 0 X - 1 8 0

Brewers	IP	H	R	ER	BB	SO
Travers L(8–5)	8	8	1	1	1	2

Yankees	IP	H	R	ER	BB	SO
Ellis W(8–4)	9	7	0	0	2	2

DP—Milwaukee 2; New York 2. 2B—Milwaukee Carbo. HR—New York Rivers (4). SH—New York Randolph. LOB—Milwaukee 7; New York 6. SB—Milwaukee Joshua. Attendance: 21,389.

Blair's Bases-Loaded Single in Ninth Inning Keeps Red Sox Quiet

The Yankees needed to make a statement against the Red Sox.

Coming into the series, Boston was red hot, having won 16 of 18, but Paul Blair bounced a single over third base with the bases full and the Yankees walked off with a 5–4 win over their archrivals.

The Yankees led 4–1 in the ninth inning, but Boston rallied to tie the game on a two-run single by Tommy Helms and an RBI groundout by Rick Burleson.

The top of the Yankees order did the offensive damage against Red Sox starter Reggie Cleveland. Mickey Rivers, Roy White, and Thurman Munson combined for eight hits in 12 at-bats, with five runs scored and two RBIs.

Don Gullett allowed one run in the first inning after the Red Sox loaded the bases with nobody out. From there, he was solid until the ninth, when manager Billy Martin may have stayed with him a little too long.

After Helms' two-run single, Gullett gave up a hit to Steve Dillard. When Rivers threw wide of the bag at third base, Dillard took second with one out. Dick Tidrow relieved Gullett and got Burleson to ground out. That tied the game and Martin went to Sparky Lyle to get Fred Lynn on a flyout to center.

In the bottom of the ninth inning, White drew a one-out walk. Munson lined a single to left field to put runners on the corners. Chris Chambliss was intentionally walked to load the bases, and Blair delivered off Bill Campbell with the winning hit over a drawn-in infield. —ɯ—

Red Sox	AB	R	H	RBI
Burleson ss	5	1	2	1
Lynn cf	4	0	1	0
Rice rf	3	0	2	0
Yastrzemski lf	4	0	0	0
Fisk c	2	1	0	1
Scott 1b	4	1	1	0
Hobson 3b	4	0	0	0
Helms dh	4	0	1	2
Miller pr,dh	0	1	0	0
Dillard 2b	4	0	1	0
Totals	34	4	8	4

Yankees	AB	R	H	RBI
Rivers cf	5	3	3	0
White lf	3	2	2	0
Munson c	4	0	3	2
Chambliss 1b	3	0	1	2
Jackson rf	4	0	1	0
Blair rf	1	0	1	1
Nettles 3b	3	0	0	0
May dh	3	0	0	0
Johnson ph,dh	0	0	0	0
Zeber 2b	3	0	1	0
Dent ss	4	0	0	0
Totals	33	5	12	5

BOS 1 0 0 0 0 0 0 0 3 - 4 8 0
NY 1 0 2 0 0 0 1 0 1 - 5 12 0

Red Sox	IP	H	R	ER	BB	SO
Cleveland	2.2	8	3	3	0	0
Stanley	3.1	2	1	1	4	0
Hernandez	2	0	0	0	1	2
Campbell L(5–4)	0.1	2	1	1	2	0
Totals	8.1	12	5	5	7	2

Yankees	IP	H	R	ER	BB	SO
Gullett	8.1	8	4	4	3	8
Tidrow	0.1	0	0	0	0	0
Lyle W(5–2)	0.1	0	0	0	0	0
Totals	9	8	4	4	3	8

DP—Boston 2. 2B—Boston Scott; New York Jackson. SF—Boston Fisk; New York Chambliss. LOB—Boston 7; New York 11. SB—New York Rivers, White, Munson. Attendance: 55,039.

Nettles Gives a Preview with Two-Run Walk-Off Home Run vs. Red Sox

In an exciting game that was a harbinger of things to come, the Yankees beat the Red Sox 6–4 on a two-run walk-off home run by Graig Nettles.

Ron Guidry was looking to go 13–0, and he got off to a great start as he sat down the first nine Red Sox hitters, striking out the side in the third inning.

The Yankees had a 3–0 lead but the Sox got two back in the sixth inning on RBI singles from future Hall of Famers Carlton Fisk and Carl Yastrzemski.

This was not Guidry's best game as the Red Sox scored two more runs in the seventh inning to take a 4–3 lead. Boston loaded the bases with nobody out, at which time Yankees manager Billy Martin went to Goose Gossage. Rick Burleson greeted Gossage with a two-run single.

The Yankees tied the game in the bottom of the eighth inning on an RBI single by Reggie Jackson.

Yankees catcher Thurman Munson played a terrific all-around game, just one day before he was to begin serving a three-game suspension for bumping an umpire.

The captain drove in a run and scored a run in the third inning. In the fifth inning, Munson adeptly blocked the plate when Fred Lynn tried to score on Dwight Evans' double.

Then in the eighth inning, Munson singled and dove head first into third base on Lou Piniella's single. He later scored on Jackson's bloop hit.

For good measure, Munson threw out Jerry Remy trying to steal second in the top of the 12th inning.

Red Sox pitcher Dick Drago was working in his fifth inning of relief when he walked Roy White with one out in the bottom of the 14th inning.

Red Sox	AB	R	H	RBI
Burleson ss	7	1	3	2
Remy 2b	7	0	2	0
Rice dh	4	0	1	0
Yastrzemski lf	5	0	1	1
Fisk c	6	0	1	1
Lynn cf	4	0	1	0
Scott 1b	6	1	1	0
Evans rf	6	1	2	0
Hobson 3b	5	1	1	0
Totals	50	4	13	4

Yankees	AB	R	H	RBI
White lf	5	1	1	0
Nettles 3b	6	2	2	2
Munson c	6	2	3	1
Chambliss 1b	6	0	1	1
Piniella dh	6	0	1	0
Jackson rf	4	1	3	1
Thomasson cf	1	0	1	0
Blair ph,cf	4	0	1	0
Stanley ss	5	0	0	0
Garcia 2b	3	0	0	1
Spencer ph	1	0	1	0
Doyle 2b	1	0	0	0
Totals	48	6	14	6

```
BOS 0 0 0 0 0 2 2 0 0 0 0 0 0 0 - 4 13 0
NY  0 1 2 0 0 0 0 1 0 0 0 0 0 2 - 6 14 0
```

Red Sox	IP	H	R	ER	BB	SO
Wright	2.2	5	3	3	3	2
Burgmeier	4.2	3	1	1	0	0
Stanley	0	1	0	0	0	0
Campbell	1.2	1	0	0	0	2
Drago L(2–2)	4.1	4	2	2	3	2
Totals	13.1	14	6	6	6	6

Yankees	IP	H	R	ER	BB	SO
Guidry	6	8	4	4	3	6
Gossage	6	4	0	0	2	4
Lyle W(6–1)	3	1	0	0	1	2
Totals	14	13	4	4	6	12

DP—Boston 3; New York 2. 2B—Boston Evans, Lynn, Rice; New York Jackson, Munson. HR—New York Nettles (13). SH—New York Blair. SF—New York Garcia. LOB—Boston 10; New York 10. Attendance: 55,132.

That brought up Nettles, who was looking to go deep and end this marathon.

"I had a home run on my mind," Nettles said.

Nettles didn't waste any time as he drove Drago's first pitch into the right-field stands to give the Yankees a much-needed victory over their archrivals.

"I hit a fastball over the plate, the same kind I was missing before," Nettles said.

The Yankees had a chance to end the game in the 11th inning. Jackson walked and was sacrificed to second base by Paul Blair. After Fred Stanley struck out, Jim Spencer pinch-hit and singled to right field.

Evans jumped to keep the ball from going over his head and then threw a bullet to the plate, where Fisk grabbed it like an infielder and then applied a sweeping tag to nab Jackson at the plate.

"In a normal situation, he wouldn't have gone on a play like that," Evans said, "but you have to gamble in extra innings. Anybody could've thrown him out."

The win left the Yankees 8½ games behind Boston. The deficit would grow larger in the next month, but the Yankees would complete the greatest single-season comeback in their history later that year (see: October 2, 1978). —⧚—

Tresh's First Grand Slam Completes Comeback

Tom Tresh had never hit a grand slam in his career. He picked the right time for his first.

The Yankees beat the Tigers 8–6 thanks to an eighth-inning slam by Tresh off Tigers losing pitcher Larry Sherry.

Tigers	AB	R	H	RBI
Lumpe 2b	5	0	1	1
Wood 1b	4	1	1	0
Cash ph	0	0	0	0
Kaline rf	4	1	3	0
Freehan c	4	0	2	1
Demeter lf	5	2	3	3
Wert 3b	3	1	1	0
Thomas cf	4	0	1	0
McAuliffe ss	4	1	1	1
Rakow p	3	0	0	0
Fox p	1	0	0	0
Totals	37	6	13	6

Yankees	AB	R	H	RBI
Linz 3b	3	2	1	0
Richardson 2b	2	1	0	1
Maris rf	5	0	1	0
Mantle cf	3	1	1	1
Tresh lf	5	1	2	5
Howard c	5	1	4	0
Pepitone 1b,cf	4	0	0	0
Boyer ss	4	1	2	0
Hamilton p	2	0	1	0
Blanchard ph	1	0	1	1
Lopez ph	1	1	1	0
Totals	35	8	14	8

DET	1	0	0	2	2	1	0	0	0	-	6 13 0
NY	2	0	0	0	0	2	0	4	X	-	8 14 2

Tigers	IP	H	R	ER	BB	SO
Aguirre	0.1	2	2	2	2	1
Rakow	5	7	2	2	2	3
Fox	2	3	2	2	1	1
Sherry L(4–5)	0.2	2	2	2	1	1
Totals	8	14	8	8	6	6

Yankees	IP	H	R	ER	BB	SO
Hamilton	4.1	9	5	4	1	2
Terry	1.2	2	1	1	0	0
Williams W(1–1)	2	0	0	0	1	2
Mikkelsen SV(6)	1	2	0	0	1	0
Totals	9	13	6	5	3	4

E—New York Linz, Pepitone. DP—Detroit 1; New York 3. 2B—New York Tresh. HR—Detroit Demeter 2 (7,8), McAuliffe; New York Tresh (8). SH—Detroit Freehan; New York Richardson. SF—New York Richardson. LOB—Detroit 8; New York 11. Attendance: 35,383.

The Tigers built a 6–2 lead on home run power from Don Demeter, who hit two, and Dick McAuliffe.

Pinch-hitter Hector Lopez got the eighth inning rally started on the right note with a single. Phil Linz singled, and then Bobby Richardson sacrificed the runners to second and third. Sherry was brought in to face Roger Maris, who lined out to first baseman Jake Wood.

Mickey Mantle walked to load the bases to set the stage for the switch-hitting Tresh, who began his career as a shortstop but was now playing left field. The 26 year old took a 3–2 pitch from Sherry and lined it into the right-field stands to rally the Yankees from that four-run deficit.

Tresh drove in five while catcher Elston Howard had four hits to key a 14-hit attack.

Sherry took the loss for Detroit. Stan Williams got the win in relief while Pete Mikkelsen pitched a scoreless ninth for the save. ⁓

Pair of Grand Slams Part of 5-Homer Barrage

For the second time in their history, the Yankees hit two grand slams to score a wild 15–14 win over the Blue Jays at Toronto's Exhibition Stadium.

Don Mattingly hit a grand slam in the second inning off Jays lefty John Cerutti to give the Yankees an 8–3 lead.

It was quite an exhibition of power as the teams combined for eight home runs—five by the Yankees, including two by Dave Winfield.

The Yankees led 11–4 in the seventh inning when Dave Righetti entered the game with bases loaded and no one out. Two infield errors led to a six-run inning, including three unearned runs, and Toronto stole the momentum. The Yankees, however, came right back in the eighth inning.

Toronto reliever Jeff Musselman walked Mike Pagliarulo to start the inning. Wayne Tolleson forced Pags at second base, but Rickey Henderson lined a ball off Musselman's knee for a hit that forced the left-hander out of the game.

Tom Henke, Toronto's closer, was brought in to relieve. He struck out Willie Randolph for the second out but walked Mattingly to load the bases for Winfield.

During his Yankees tenure, Winfield took some criticism from Yankees owner George Steinbrenner for his lack of hits in the clutch, but there was no argument in this game as the 6-foot-6 outfielder delivered a huge hit.

"Everyone got excited," said Righetti, who picked up the win after blowing the save. "You've got to carry that reaction over. If I give up a hit, it's here we go again. I've got to do my job."

After the game, Winfield addressed those critiques. "I'm not justifying this to anybody," Winfield said. "I'm not going to say this is a backlash. I'm just cruising along."

Yankees	AB	R	H	RBI
Henderson lf	5	1	1	0
Randolph 2b	4	2	2	0
Mattingly 1b	4	2	2	5
Winfield rf	5	2	2	6
Ward cf	4	1	0	0
Kittle dh	3	1	1	2
Washington ph-dh	2	0	0	0
Cerone c	4	1	1	0
Pagliarulo 3b	4	2	2	2
Tolleson ss	3	3	0	0
Totals	38	15	11	15

Blue Jays	AB	R	H	RBI
Fernandez ss	5	2	2	2
Moseby cf	6	2	2	3
Barfield rf	6	0	1	2
Bell lf	4	2	3	0
Fielder dh	3	2	2	2
McGriff ph-dh	1	1	0	0
Gruber 3b-2b	4	0	0	0
Upshaw 1b	5	2	2	3
Moore c	2	0	0	0
Whitt ph-c	3	2	1	1
Iorg 2b	2	0	1	0
Mulliniks ph-3b	1	0	1	0
Lee ph-2b	2	1	1	0
Totals	44	14	16	13

```
NY   4 4 0 0 0 3 0 4 0 - 15 11 3
TOR  3 0 0 1 0 4 6 0 0 - 14 16 1
```

Yankees	IP	H	R	ER	BB	SO
Rasmussen	5	7	4	4	1	1
Guante	0.2	4	4	4	0	2
Stoddard	0.1	1	1	1	0	0
Clements	0	0	2	2	2	0
Righetti (W5-3)	3	4	3	0	1	0
Totals	9	16	14	11	4	3

Blue Jays	IP	H	R	ER	BB	SO
Cerutti	1.1	5	8	8	3	0
Nunez	4.1	3	3	2	1	5
Eichhorn	1.1	0	0	0	0	1
Musselman	0.1	1	2	2	1	0
Henke L(0-3)	1.2	2	2	2	1	3
Totals	9	11	15	14	6	9

E—New York, Randolph, Pagliarulo, Rasmussen; Toronto, Gruber. DP—Toronto. 2B—Toronto, Fielder, Upshaw, Fernandez. HR—New York, Winfield 2 (18), Kittle (8), Mattingly (8), Pagliarulo (12). LOB—New York 2; Toronto 7. SB—Toronto, Fernandez. Attendance—42,179.

The win was important because the Yankees took over first place from Toronto.

Mattingly said, "I don't think this is so much a crucial series as it is a matter of setting a tone."

Manager Lou Piniella agreed. "There's still a lot of baseball to be played, but you've got to like this team's chances."

Winfield drove in six runs, and Mattingly had five RBIs. Cecil Fielder, a 23-year-old future Yankee, was the designated hitter for Toronto. He had two hits, including a two-run homer off Yankees starting pitcher Dennis Rasmussen.

When Righetti entered the game in the seventh inning with the bases loaded, it brought back memories of the year before.

It had been 374 days since Righetti entered the game at Exhibition Stadium with two on and no one out in the bottom of the ninth inning with the Yankees leading the Blue Jays 8–2. A few minutes later, George Bell hit a game-tying grand slam home run. Righetti was so frustrated about blowing the lead that he took the baseball given to him for the next pitch and heaved it over the right-field fence.

Don Mattingly wasn't the best first baseman in Yankees history, but he makes a strong argument for being the second best behind Lou Gehrig.

Mattingly won the 1985 American League Most Valuable Player award with an outstanding all-around season. The Evansville, Indiana, native batted .324, with 35 home runs and 145 RBIs that year, not to mention one of his nine Gold Glove awards.

Mattingly had the unfortunate timing of being on a Yankees team that went through a postseason drought until 1995, when the Bombers returned to the playoffs as the AL wild-card team.

Mattingly had developed a chronic back problem that was limiting his production, but in the 1995 American League Divisional Series against Seattle, he acquitted himself very well. In five games, Mattingly batted .417 with a home run and six RBIs.

Game 5 turned out to be Mattingly's swan song, as he never played again.

The Yankees would go on to win that game 10–8, but the sight of Righetti throwing a ball over the right-field fence was the impression that was left with everyone who was there or watching the game on television.

"This time I kept the ball inside the park," the closer joked.

Winfield was carrying the Yankees at that time because of injuries to Mattingly and Henderson. In the 22 games since the duo went down, Winfield was batting .345 with seven home runs and 25 RBIs.

Don Mattingly's smooth stroke was on display on June 29, 1987, when he hit a grand slam and tallied five RBIs in a 15–14 win over the Blue Jays.

The first time the Yankees hit two grand slams in one game was when Tony Lazzeri had the record-setting 11 RBIs in 1936 (see: May 24, 1936).

The Yankees would accomplish the feat one more time in September 1999, when Bernie Williams and Paul O'Neill hit grand slams in consecutive innings.

One of the eight home runs was a first for Ron Kittle. The Yankees designated hitter hit a ball toward right field that was going foul at first, but the wind got it and brought it back into fair territory behind Jays right fielder and future Yankee Jesse Barfield. The ball actually rolled back toward the infield, where it was picked up by Toronto second baseman Garth Iorg, who threw home on a bounce as Kittle crossed the plate.

Winfield put the game in its proper perspective.

"It wasn't pretty and it wasn't a great defensive game," he said, "it was just an offensive show. Obviously, if we didn't have our full team back, we would've lost that game." —⟜—

Did You Know?

Yogi Berra is the Yankees' all-time leader with nine pinch-hit home runs. Johnny Blanchard holds the single season mark with four in 1961.

Johnson Brings the Pop to New Club with Three Home Runs

During the 1977 season, the Yankees acquired Cliff Johnson from Houston to add some right-handed pop to the lineup.

Fifteen days after his acquisition, Johnson delivered more than his share as he blasted three home runs, including two in one inning, to lead the Yankees over the Blue Jays at Exhibition Stadium 11–5.

Johnson's first home run came in the fourth inning off losing pitcher Jerry Garvin, a shot into the left-center-field stands. But the eighth inning is where things got interesting.

The 6-foot-4 Johnson led off with his second home run of the game and his second off Garvin. The Yankees batted around, and Johnson came up again with two out to face ex-teammate and Blue Jays pitcher Jerry Johnson.

Chris Chambliss was at second base after a double. Chambliss was safe on a pop fly that should have been caught, so Jerry Johnson was not too thrilled to see his ex-teammate come to the plate.

Jerry Johnson threw Cliff Johnson some chin music, which knocked the big man off the plate.

Three pitches later, Cliff Johnson took a pitch from Jerry Johnson and smashed it an estimated 450 feet for his third homer of the game and second of the inning.

"Don't ever knock me down," Cliff Johnson said as he crossed the plate in front of Jays catcher Alan Ashby, "because I like it like that."

Cliff Johnson became the first American League player to hit two homers in one inning since the Angels' Rick Reichardt turned the trick in 1966. Cliff Johnson was the third Yankee (Joe DiMaggio and Joe Pepitone were the two previous) to do so. Alex Rodriguez later became the fourth Yankee to accomplish the feat (see: September 5, 2007).

Yankees	AB	R	H	RBI
Randolph 2b	4	2	2	1
Rivers cf	6	1	3	1
Munson c	4	1	1	4
Chambliss 1b	5	1	1	0
Johnson dh	3	3	3	4
Jackson rf	5	0	0	0
Piniella lf	5	2	3	1
Nettles 3b	4	1	1	0
Dent ss	3	0	1	0
Totals	39	11	15	11

Blue Jays	AB	R	H	RBI
Bailor ss	4	0	0	0
Ewing rf	4	0	1	2
A. Woods lf	4	0	2	0
Fairly 1b	4	1	1	0
Rader 3b	4	1	1	1
Velez dh	3	1	1	1
Scott cf	4	0	1	1
Torres 2b	2	1	0	0
Whitt ph	1	0	0	0
Ashby c	3	1	0	0
Totals	33	5	7	4

NY 0 0 1 1 0 0 0 8 1 - 11 15 2
TOR 0 0 0 0 1 0 0 3 1 - 5 7 2

Yankees	IP	H	R	ER	BB	SO
Hunter W(4–3)	9	7	5	3	2	2

Blue Jays	IP	H	R	ER	BB	SO
Garvin L(7–7)	7.1	8	5	5	5	4
Johnson	0.1	5	5	5	0	0
DeBarr	1.1	2	1	1	0	2
Totals	9	15	11	11	5	6

E—New York Chambliss, Jackson; Toronto Torres, Ashby. 2B—New York Randolph, Piniella, Rivers; Toronto Scott. HR—New York Johnson 3 (2,3,4), Munson (11); Toronto Rader (3). SF—New York Munson, Randolph. HBP—New York Johnson; Toronto Torres. LOB—New York 9; Toronto 4. Attendance: 33,283.

After the game, Cliff Johnson downplayed the greatest game of his career.

"It doesn't mean anything if you can't come back the next night and help the ballclub," he said.

When asked about the brushback pitch he received from his former teammate, Johnson remarked, "I hadn't done anything, but I was kind of expecting it, so I wasn't surprised."

So did he have any thoughts of charging the mound?

"I charged the mound one time this year, but you're not going to see that out of me. I'm generally a fun-full type person," Johnson said.

Mickey Rivers and Lou Piniella joined Johnson with three hits apiece while Thurman Munson hit a mammoth three-run homer in the eighth inning that preceded Johnson's third homer.

Catfish Hunter gave up five runs (three earned) and earned the win with a complete-game effort to partially silence the criticism he had been receiving due to a slow start to the season.

Johnson became the 12th Yankee in franchise history to hit three home runs in one game. Several Yankees have done it multiple times, including four times by Lou Gehrig, three by Joe DiMaggio, and twice each by Tony Lazzeri and Bobby Murcer.

After Johnson, six more Yankees would hit three home runs in one game, including Mike Stanley, Paul O'Neill, Darryl Strawberry, Tino Martinez, Tony Clark, and Alex Rodriguez.

Babe Ruth (twice) and Reggie Jackson are the only two Yankees and only players in baseball history to hit three home runs in a World Series game. —⁓—

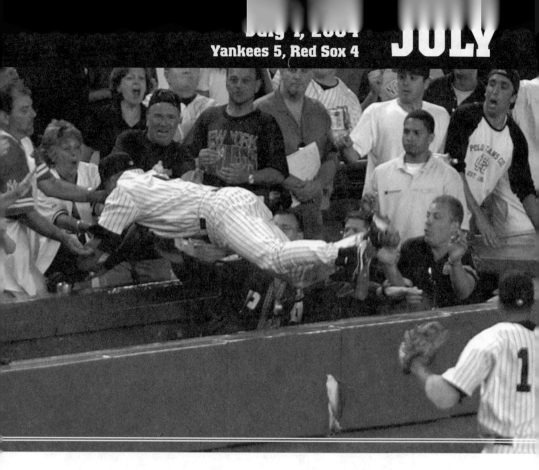

Regular-Season Gem Ends with Flaherty's 13th-Inning Single

Many Yankee historians consider this game to be one of the greatest regular season contests in franchise history.

It was John Flaherty's RBI single in the bottom of the 13th inning that gave the Yankees a thrilling 5–4 win over the Red Sox at Yankee Stadium, but there were many other aspects to this game that made it a memorable one.

"I was so happy I could win a game for the guys here like [Derek] Jeter and [Jorge] Posada," Flaherty said.

In the 12th inning of a July 1, 2004, game that the Yankees won in the 13th, Derek Jeter dives head first into the stands to make a catch. Jeter left the game for a visit to the hospital following the spectacular grab.

Flaherty was the backup catcher, so there wasn't much chance he would even get into the game, but he made a subtle adjustment in his batting style that would pay off later on.

"I went to the cage with [hitting coach Don] Mattingly before the game and changed my stance," Flaherty said.

Red Sox	AB	R	H	RBI
Damon cf	5	0	1	0
Bellhorn 2b-3b	6	0	0	0
Ortiz dh	5	1	3	0
Kapler pr-dh	0	0	0	0
Nixon ph-dh	1	0	0	0
Ramirez lf	6	2	4	3
Varitek c	5	0	0	0
Millar rf	6	0	0	0
McCarty 1b	4	1	1	0
Youkilis 3b	3	0	1	0
Crespo pr-2b	1	0	0	0
Reese ss	4	0	0	0
Totals	46	4	10	3

Yankees	AB	R	H	RBI
Lofton cf	4	0	0	0
Cairo 2b	2	1	2	1
Jeter ss	4	0	1	0
Giambi ph	1	0	0	0
Flaherty ph	1	0	1	1
Sheffield rf-3b	4	0	0	0
Rodriguez 3b-ss	5	0	1	0
Matsui lf	4	0	1	0
Crosby pr-cf-lf	1	0	0	0
Williams dh-cf	6	0	0	0
Posada c	4	2	2	1
Clark 1b	5	1	1	2
Wilson 2b	3	0	1	0
Sierra ph-lf-rf	3	1	1	0
Totals	47	5	11	5

BOS 0 0 0 0 0 2 1 0 0 0 0 1 - 4 10 0
NY 0 2 0 0 1 0 0 0 0 0 0 2 - 5 11 2

Red Sox	IP	H	R	ER	BB	SO
P. Martinez	7	4	3	3	3	8
Foulke	2	2	0	0	1	1
Timlin	0.2	1	0	0	0	0
Embree	1.1	0	0	0	1	0
Leskanic L(0-4)	1.2	4	2	2	1	3
Totals	12.2	11	5	5	6	12

Yankees	IP	H	R	ER	BB	SO
Halsey	5.1	4	2	2	2	5
Quantrill	1.1	2	1	1	0	0
Heredia	0.2	0	0	0	0	0
Gordon	1.2	0	0	0	0	1
Rivera	2	2	0	0	1	2
Sturtze W(3-0)	2	2	1	1	2	1
Totals	13	10	4	4	5	9

E—New York 2. DP—Boston 2; New York 3. 2B—Boston, Ortiz 2, McCarty; New York, Posada, Rodriguez, Cairo. 3B—New York, Cairo. HR—Boston, Ramirez 2 (22); New York, Clark (6), Posada (10). SH—Boston, Reese. HBP—Boston, Damon; New York, Sheffield 2, Jeter. LOB—Boston 10; New York 13. SB—Boston, McCarty; New York, Rodriguez. Attendance—55,265.

In the top of the 12th inning, the Red Sox had a runner on third base with two out. Pinch-hitter Trot Nixon lifted a pop-up toward the third-base side that looked like it would land fair and give Boston the lead.

Jeter came streaking over and caught the ball on the dead run, but he couldn't stop so he dove head-first into the stands.

After being helped up by local authorities, Jeter's face had blood on his chin and right cheek and his jersey was bloodied as well.

Jeter left the stadium and was taken to a local hospital for x-rays. The Yankees announced that the captain had suffered a laceration of his chin, a bruised right cheek, and a bruised right shoulder.

Alex Rodriguez couldn't help but admire the play.

"Greatest catch I've ever seen," said A-Rod, "it was unbelievable. He's just so unselfish. He put his body in a compromising spot."

The Yankees took a 3–0 lead on a two-run homer by Tony Clark in the second inning and a solo shot by Posada in the fifth.

In the sixth inning, David Ortiz doubled and Manny Ramirez hit the first of his two home runs in the game to cut the Yankees' lead to one.

The Red Sox tied the game in the seventh inning, scoring the run on a double-play groundout.

In the 11th inning, the Red Sox had the bases loaded and no one out when Kevin Millar grounded a ball toward the third-base line. Rodriguez began an unusual double play when he fired home for the force out. Posada threw back to third to get Ramirez on the force. David McCarty flied out to left to end the threat.

The Yankees had another golden opportunity to end the game in the 12th. Miguel Cairo led off with a triple but was left stranded. Pinch-hitter Jason Giambi struck out. With the bases loaded and one out, Bubba Crosby forced Cairo at home and Bernie Williams struck out.

The Red Sox took a 4–3 lead in the top of the 13th inning when Ramirez clubbed his second home run of the game off Yankees reliever Tanyon Sturtze.

Jeter's injury forced the Yankees to use Rodriguez at shortstop. Gary Sheffield played third base for the first time in 11 years and committed a throwing error after the Ramirez home run, but a double play ended the inning without any more damage. Williams moved into center field, which meant the Yankees lost their designated hitter, so Sturtze was in the lineup.

"When Alex [Rodriguez] went to short, that was when I started thinking that I may get a chance," Flaherty said.

Boston reliever Curtis Leskanic was looking to close out this classic as he got the first two outs. But Ruben Sierra kept the game alive with a single to center and scored the tying run when Cairo came up with a clutch two-out run-scoring double to right-center field.

The Yankees were down to their final position player in Flaherty, who was sent up to pinch-hit for Sturtze.

Flaherty was mentally preparing himself earlier in the game when he walked into the clubhouse to find pitcher Jon Lieber hitting off a tee. Flaherty said, "If Lieber hits instead of me, then I know it's time to go."

Flaherty worked the count to 3–1.

"He's [Leskanic] gotta come get me because Gary Sheffield is on deck," Flaherty said. "He threw me a slider that sped my bat up."

"Flash" hit the ball to the left-field warning track for the game-winning hit that scored Cairo. —⁓—

Berra Caps Another Clutch Performance with Key Hits

Yogi Berra was always known as a clutch hitter, but in this game, he was even better. Berra tied the game in the ninth inning and then won it with a walk-off RBI single in the 11th to give the Yankees a 6–5 win over the Washington Senators at Yankee Stadium.

The Senators scored twice in the top of the ninth inning to take a 5–4 lead. With two out and runners at second and third base, Washington center fielder Jim Busby singled in one run to tie the game. A second run scored on the first of Yankees shortstop Phil Rizzuto's three errors in the game.

> ### At a Glance
> **WP:** Morgan (6–2)
> **HR:** Carey (6)
> **Key stats:** Skowron 3-for-4, RBI; Berra 2-for-5, 2 RBIs; Noren 3-for-5, RBI

This was most unusual for The Scooter, who in his career never led the league in errors and twice led all shortstops in fielding percentage.

In the bottom of the ninth, the Yankees were down to their final out when pinch-hitter Joe Collins walked. Mickey Mantle singled to put runners at first and third base. Berra tied the game with a two-out RBI single off Senators' reliever Veston Goff "Bunky" Stewart.

Washington pitcher Camilo Pascual walked pinch-hitter Bob Cerv to begin the 11th inning. After a sacrifice bunt by Jerry Coleman put the winning run at second base, Berra connected for a long drive into left-center field ("Death Valley") that would have been a double or triple, except for the fact that Cerv scored the winning run from second base. —∾—

Lawrence Peter "Yogi" Berra was the best catcher to ever wear the pinstripes. The Hall of Famer won 10 World Series championships and 14 pennants overall.

Berra came up in 1946 and played 18 years with the Yankees. In 1964, Berra stepped away from the playing field to manage the Yankees to the American League pennant.

During his illustrious career, Berra won 3 AL Most Valuable Player Awards, was a 15-time All-Star, and established no less than seven World Series records.

Berra was elected to Baseball's Hall of Fame on his first attempt in 1972.

c Yogi Berra

Meusel Becomes Only Yankees Player to Hit for Cycle Twice

Bob Meusel accomplished a first in Yankee history and something that hasn't been duplicated since.

Meusel became the only Yankee to hit for the cycle twice in his career as the Bombers routed the Philadelphia Athletics 12–1 at Shibe Park.

Meusel's RBI single in the first inning gave the Yankees a 1–0 lead. In the fifth, the right fielder tripled off the center-field scoreboard to make it a 6–0 contest.

Not to be outdone, Babe Ruth cracked a solo home run into the left-field bleachers and then Meusel followed with a solo blast against Philadelphia's Charlie Eckert.

With two on in the eighth inning, Meusel completed the feat with a two-run double that gave the Yankees an insurmountable 12–0 advantage.

Carl Mays was the benefactor of this offensive barrage as he went the distance, giving up a run on six hits.

Meusel drove in six runs and scored twice. In addition to becoming the only Yankee to hit for the cycle twice in his career, he did it a third time a little more than six years later. Interestingly, all three cycles came on the road. —

Yankees	AB	R	H	RBI
Witt cf	4	2	2	0
McNally 3b	4	2	1	0
Ruth lf	5	2	2	2
Meusel rf	5	2	4	6
Pipp 1b	5	1	3	1
Ward 2b	4	0	1	0
Scott ss	4	2	2	2
Hofmann c	5	0	2	1
Mays p	4	1	0	0
Totals	40	12	17	12

Athletics	AB	R	H	RBI
Young 2b	4	0	1	0
Hauser 1b	3	1	2	1
Walker lf	4	0	1	0
Perkins c	4	0	0	0
Galloway ss	4	0	0	0
McGowan cf	3	0	1	0
Welch rf	4	0	0	0
Dykes 3b	4	0	1	0
Sullivan p	1	0	0	0
Scheer ph	1	0	0	0
Callaway ph	1	0	0	0
Totals	33	1	6	1

NY	1 2 0 0 3 0 2 4 0 -	12	17	0
PHI	0 0 0 0 0 0 0 1 0 -	1	6	1

Yankees	IP	H	R	ER	BB	SO
Mays W(9–7)	9	6	1	1	2	2

Athletics	IP	H	R	ER	BB	SO
Sullivan L(0–2)	5	9	6	5	2	0
Eckert	3	8	6	6	0	0
Heimach	1	0	0	0	0	1
Totals	9	17	12	11	2	1

E—Philadelphia Dykes. 2B—New York Meusel; Philadelphia Dykes. 3B—New York Meusel. HR—New York Ruth (13), Meusel (6), Scott (2); Philadelphia Hauser (2). SH—New York McNally, Ward. LOB—New York 5; Philadelphia 7. SB—Philadelphia McGowan. Attendance: 13,000.

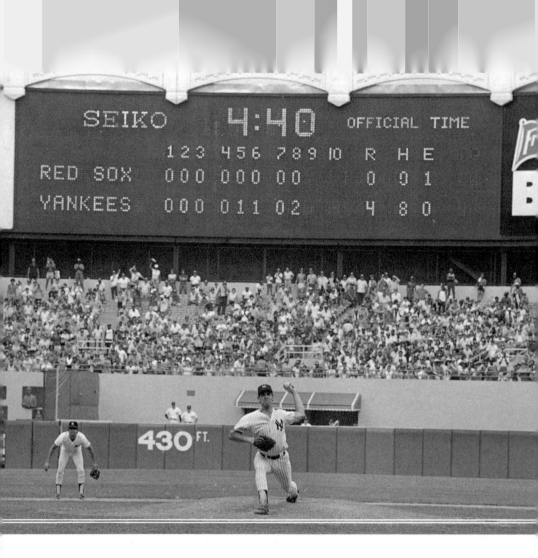

Righetti's No-Hitter the Perfect Way to Celebrate

It was the 44th anniversary of Lou Gehrig's famous speech, it was Yankee owner George Steinbrenner's 53rd birthday, and it became Dave Righetti's signature moment.

Righetti tossed the sixth no-hitter in Yankees history when he turned the trick vs. the Boston Red Sox in a 4–0 win on a hot, sultry day at Yankee Stadium.

The temperature was in the mid-90s at game time, but there were some early signs that this was going to be a special day when Righetti struck out five of the first seven batters he faced. Only Reid Nichols put the ball in play, and he flied out to right field.

Boston's John Tudor was matching Rags zero for zero, but Tudor gave up the first run in the bottom of the fifth inning on an RBI single by Andre Robertson. Don Baylor hit a solo home run in the sixth inning for a 2–0 lead.

The spotlight began to focus on Righetti when he took the mound in the seventh inning.

When Righetti went out for the eighth, he received a standing ovation from the 41,077 fans on hand with the hope of witnessing history.

"I was nervous, definitely, without a doubt," he said.

Righetti got an important defensive play, which is needed to complete most no-hit games, in the top of the eighth.

Boston's Dwight Evans led off with a fly ball toward the right-field corner. Even though the ball was going foul, right fielder Steve Kemp made a leap into the stands and came up with the foul fly for the first out of the inning.

"Even though it couldn't be a hit," Righetti said, "it pumped me up."

Righetti had an otherwise stress-free eighth inning. In the ninth, the scheduled hitters were Jeff Newman, Glenn Hoffman, and Jerry Remy, with Wade Boggs, the league's leading hitter, scheduled to bat fourth.

Nerves may have been a factor because Righetti walked Newman, a .190 hitter, to start the ninth.

Hoffman hit a potential double-play grounder to short, but second baseman Robertson could not complete the relay throw for the twin killing.

With one out, Remy grounded out to second base on the first pitch.

The count on Boggs was 2–2 when catcher Butch Wynegar thought about a fastball. At the last minute, Wynegar changed his mind and called for a slider.

"I got down in my crouch and got ready to flash

Red Sox	AB	R	H	RBI
Remy 2b	4	0	0	0
Boggs 3b	4	0	0	0
Rice lf	1	0	0	0
Armas cf	3	0	0	0
Evans rf	3	0	0	0
Nichols dh	2	0	0	0
Stapleton 1b	3	0	0	0
Newman c	2	0	0	0
Hoffman ss	3	0	0	0
Totals	25	0	0	0

Yankees	AB	R	H	RBI
Campaneris 3b	3	0	2	0
Mattingly 1b	4	0	0	0
Winfield cf	3	1	1	0
Piniella lf	4	0	0	0
Baylor dh	3	1	1	1
Wynegar c	3	0	0	0
Kemp rf	4	1	2	2
Smalley ss	4	0	1	0
Robertson 2b	3	0	1	1
Totals	31	4	8	4

											R	H	E
BOS	0	0	0	0	0	0	0	0	0	-	0	0	1
NY	0	0	0	1	1	0	2	X	-		4	8	0

Red Sox	IP	H	R	ER	BB	SO
Tudor L(5–5)	7.2	8	4	4	4	2
Stanley	0.1	0	0	0	0	0
Totals	8	8	4	4	4	2

Yankees	IP	H	R	ER	BB	SO
Righetti W(10–3)	9	0	0	0	4	9

E—Boston, Boggs. DP—Boston 2; New York. HR—New York, Baylor (9). LOB—Boston 2; New York 7. SB—New York, Campaneris. Attendance—41,077.

the fastball sign," Wynegar said, "and suddenly it just came in my mind to call a slider."

In his two previous at-bats, Boggs had good swings against Righetti but both times he flied out deep to center field.

"He'd [Boggs] hit me hard both times, and in the ninth I saw he was looking to go to left field," Righetti said.

Wynegar added, "All I know if Boggs had gotten a hit, I'd have kicked myself from now to kingdom come."

Boggs admitted that he was anxious to break up the no-hit bid and that he "may have been prone to chase a bad pitch."

"Sure when I came up I was thinking about breaking up the no-hitter," Boggs said. "I wasn't looking for anything in particular, just going with the pitches. I wanted to keep the game going."

Righetti threw an absolutely perfect slider that Boggs swung at and missed badly.

"For one split second, I was blank," Righetti said about his feelings once the game ended. "I just kinda looked at Butch and I saw him coming and I said 'Oh geez.' I just leaned on him and held onto him."

Ever since he was acquired from the Texas Rangers in 1979 in a nine-player deal that included Sparky Lyle, big things were expected of the talented left-hander. Those expectations went even higher after the no-hitter.

Following the 1983 season, Yankee closer Rich "Goose" Gossage signed with the San Diego Padres as a free agent, so the Yankees decided to make Righetti, the American League Rookie of the Year in 1981, the closer for the 1984 campaign.

As the Yankees closer, Righetti set an American League record with 46 saves in 1986. He would total 224 saves in a Yankees uniform before leaving as a free agent to sign with the San Francisco Giants.

Righetti started four games for the Giants during the 1992 season and nine more times as a member of the Chicago White Sox in 1995, his final season. —⁓—

July 4, 1939

Gehrig's Famous Speech Leaves 'Em Speechless

One of the most famous quotes in American history was born at Yankee Stadium between games of a doubleheader against Washington on Lou Gehrig Appreciation Day.

Some 61,808 fans were on hand to honor the "Iron Horse," who was forced to end his consecutive games streak at 2,130 because he was diagnosed with what became known as the disease that was named after him, ALS (Amyotrophic Lateral Sclerosis). "Lou Gehrig's Disease" affects the nerve cells in the brain and spinal cord.

A number of the 1927 World Championship team members were on hand, including Babe Ruth.

The crowd was fixated on Gehrig as he approached the microphone.

"Fans, for the past two weeks you have been reading about the bad break I got. Yet today, I consider myself the luckiest man on the face of the Earth."

Gehrig concluded his famous address in grand style.

"So I close in saying that I may have had a tough break, but I have an awful lot to live for."

Lou Gehrig's storied career ended with his diagnosis of ALS.

Rasmussen Stands Tall with Complete Game

The Yankees always expected big things from their 6-foot-7 left-hander **Dennis Rasmussen.** On this day at Chicago's Comiskey Park, he tossed the best game of his pinstriped career.

The Yankees shut out the White Sox 8–0 behind Rasmussen, who allowed three hits while walking four and striking out seven in a complete-game gem.

Rasmussen allowed one hit after the third inning and got some early help from his defense as the Yankees turned double plays in each of the first two innings.

"I think it's obvious from the way I'm doing my job that I'm pitching with confidence," Rasmussen said. "I'm getting a lot of runs, shutting people down and pitching long enough into games to give myself a chance to win."

The Yankees hit four home runs off White Sox pitching, including solo shots from Dan Pasqua, Mike Pagliarulo, and Ron Hassey, and a two-run blast by Claudell Washington.

Rasmussen was rebounding from an awful 1985 season in which he went 3–5. With this shutout win, he upped his record to 9–2 and lowered his ERA to 3.47.

The tall southpaw would go on to win a career-high 18 games in 1986, but in late August 1987 he was traded to the Cincinnati Reds in exchange for pitcher Bill Gullickson. ─❧─

Yankees	AB	R	H	RBI
Washington cf	5	2	3	1
Mattingly 1b	5	1	2	0
Easler dh	4	2	0	0
Hassey c	4	1	1	2
Winfield rf	4	0	0	0
Pasqua lf	4	1	2	2
Pagliarulo 3b	4	1	2	2
Randolph 2b	4	0	0	0
Zuvella ss	4	0	0	0
Totals	38	8	10	7

White Sox	AB	R	H	RBI
Cangelosi cf	2	0	0	0
Lyons cf	0	0	0	0
Guillen ss	4	0	1	0
Baines rf	4	0	0	0
Kittle dh	3	0	0	0
Bonilla 1b	4	0	0	0
Hulett 2b	3	0	0	0
Nichols lf	3	0	1	0
Tolleson 3b	2	0	1	0
Skinner c	3	0	0	0
Totals	28	0	3	0

NY	0	2	3	0	0	0	3	0	-	8	10	0
CHI	0	0	0	0	0	0	0	0	0	-	0	3	1

Yankees	IP	H	R	ER	BB	SO
Rasmussen W(9–2)	9	3	0	0	4	7

White Sox	IP	H	R	ER	BB	SO
Cowley L(4–4)	3	4	5	2	0	2
McKeon	4	1	0	0	0	2
Nelson	2	5	3	3	1	1
Totals	9	10	8	5	1	5

E—Chicago Cowley. DP—New York 2. 2B—New York Mattingly, Washington; Chicago Guillen. 3B—New York Mattingly. HR—New York Pasqua (6), Pagliarulo (18), Hassey (6), Washington (2). HBP—Chicago Cangelosi. LOB—New York 4; Chicago 6. SB—New York Washington. Attendance: 21,759.

Munson's Final Home Run Part of Yanks' Victory over Oakland

No one would know it at the time, but Thurman Munson's final home run of his career helped the Yankees to a 4–3 road win over Oakland A's.

Munson's final home run came off Oakland right-hander Steve McCatty in the third inning to give the Yankees a 3–0 lead.

Yankees center fielder Bobby Murcer had one of his worst games as he misplayed Mike Heath's line drive for a run-scoring double in the sixth inning. Then in the seventh, Murcer botched Rickey Henderson's sinking liner for a single and a two-base error as Oakland tied the game at three.

In the top of the eighth inning, the Yankees took the lead when A's pitcher Mike Norris walked Willie Randolph on a 3–2 pitch with the bases loaded.

Norris was not happy with the call, feeling that Randolph swung at ball four, but home plate umpire Ted Hendry disagreed.

"He [Hendry] didn't acknowledge the third strike," Norris said. "He was just looking for the swing."

A crowd of 19,538 featured a large portion of Yankee fans, something that didn't go unnoticed by Norris.

"It's disturbing that the fans root for the Yankees, but I can't argue with it," Norris said. "At least they're in the ballpark."

Munson would play his final game on August 1 at Chicago's Comiskey Park. He would perish in a plane crash the very next day in Canton, Ohio. —

Yankees	AB	R	H	RBI
Randolph 2b	4	1	2	1
Murcer cf,lf	3	1	0	0
Munson c	3	1	2	2
Jackson rf	3	0	1	1
Piniella lf	5	0	1	0
Beniquez pr,cf	0	0	0	0
Nettles 3b	5	1	1	0
Chambliss dh	4	0	2	0
Spencer 1b	3	0	0	0
Dent ss	4	0	0	0
Totals	**34**	**4**	**9**	**4**

Athletics	AB	R	H	RBI
Henderson cf	5	1	2	0
Chalk 2b	3	0	0	1
Page dh	4	0	2	0
Newman 1b	4	0	1	0
Gross 3b	4	1	0	0
Heath c	4	1	3	1
Armas rf	4	0	1	1
Picciolo ss	4	0	1	0
Murray lf	0	0	0	0
Edwards ph	1	0	0	0
Bryant lf	0	0	0	0
Essian ph	1	0	0	0
Totals	**34**	**3**	**10**	**3**

NY	1	0	2	0	0	0	0	1	0	-	4	9	1
OAK	0	0	0	0	0	2	1	0	0	-	3	10	1

Yankees	IP	H	R	ER	BB	SO
Hunter	5.2	8	2	2	1	2
Davis W(8–0)	3.1	2	1	0	0	0
Totals	**9**	**10**	**3**	**2**	**1**	**2**

Athletics	IP	H	R	ER	BB	SO
McCatty L(5–3)	7.1	7	4	4	7	1
Norris	1.2	2	0	0	2	1
Totals	**9**	**9**	**4**	**4**	**9**	**2**

E—New York Murcer; Oakland Gross. DP—New York 1. 2B—New York Chambliss; Oakland Heath. 3B—New York Randolph. HR—New York Munson (3). SH—Oakland Murray. SF—New York Jackson. LOB—New York 13; Oakland 7. SB—New York Jackson. Attendance: 19,538.

One City, Two Stadiums, Two Games, One Broom

The most unusual day-night doubleheader in the history of New York baseball saw the Yankees sweep the twin bill by the exact same score—4–2 in the opener at Shea in the daytime and 4–2 in the nightcap at Yankee Stadium.

The first game featured a controversy on the very first pitch of the game. Chuck Knoblauch singled to center but was thrown out trying for second by center fielder Jay Payton. However, Yankees first base coach Lee Mazzilli argued that Knoblauch was obstructed from going to second by Mets first baseman Todd Zeile.

First base umpire Rob Cook agreed and Knoblauch took second on the obstruction call. He later scored on Derek Jeter's double.

The Yankees went on to win behind former Mets pitcher Dwight Gooden. The Yankees signed Doc to a minor league contract after he was released by

Roger Clemens made things interesting in the second game of a doubleheader sweep against the Mets on July 8, 2000. Clemens hit Mets catcher Mike Piazza in the head with a pitch in the second inning, beginning a series of tense meetings between the crosstown rivals.

Tampa Bay in May. The former Cy Young Award winner was in his second go-round with the Yankees and he came through with five solid innings to get the win against his former team.

The nightcap is where things really heated up between the rivals as they boarded charter buses and headed toward the Bronx.

In the top of the second inning, Mets catcher Mike Piazza was hit in the head by a Roger Clemens pitch, sparking a firestorm of emotion between the two intracity rivals.

A portent of things to come occurred in the top of the first inning, when Clemens buzzed a pitch past leadoff batter Lenny Harris' head.

Piazza was 7-for-12 in his career vs. Clemens with three home runs.

"Everybody knows Mike's had success against me," Clemens said. "I wanted to pitch him inside."

Clemens began the at-bat with a first-pitch fastball for a strike. The next pitch was heading right toward the Mets' catcher. He began to duck but the ball caught him solidly on the helmet, just above the bill. Piazza fell onto his back and had a blank stare on his face.

Mets manager Bobby Valentine and Mets coach John Stearns rushed to Piazza's side, along with the training staff, but both kept looking in the direction of Clemens.

Stearns was yelling and holding up two fingers at Clemens to signify that he threw at their hitters twice.

Piazza walked off unsteadily and was replaced by pinch-runner Matt Franco.

When play resumed, many of the Mets players stood at the railing at the front of the dugout looking for payback.

GAME 1

Yankees	AB	R	H	RBI
Knoblauch 2b	4	1	1	0
Vizcaino 2b	0	0	0	0
Jeter ss	5	2	2	1
O'Neill rf	5	0	0	0
Williams cf	2	0	0	0
Martinez 1b	4	1	3	3
Justice lf	2	0	0	0
Nelson p	1	0	0	0
Posada c	3	0	0	0
Brosius 3b	4	0	0	0
Gooden p	2	0	0	0
Spencer lf	1	0	0	0
Totals	33	4	6	4

Mets	AB	R	H	RBI
Mora ss	4	0	0	0
Bell rf	4	0	2	1
Alfonzo 2b	3	0	0	0
Piazza c	4	0	0	0
Ventura 3b	4	0	0	0
Zeile 1b	4	1	2	0
Payton cf	4	0	1	0
Agbayani lf	3	1	1	1
Bobby J. Jones p	1	0	0	0
Harris ph	0	0	0	0
Totals	31	2	6	2

NYY 2 0 0 0 0 1 0 1 0 - 4 6 0
NYM 0 1 0 0 1 0 0 0 0 - 2 6 2

Yankees	IP	H	R	ER	BB	SO
Gooden W(3–3)	5	6	2	2	1	1
Grimsley	1.2	0	0	0	1	0
Nelson	1.1	0	0	0	0	1
Rivera S(20)	1	0	0	0	0	1
Totals	9	6	2	2	2	3

Mets	IP	H	R	ER	BB	SO
Bobby J. Jones L(3–4)	7	4	3	3	3	3
Cook	1	2	1	1	1	1
Wendell	0.2	0	0	0	2	1
J. Franco	0.1	0	0	0	0	1
Totals	9	6	4	4	6	6

E—New York Mets 2. 2B—New York Yankees, Jeter 2. New York Mets, Zeile, Bell. HR—New York Yankees, Martinez (8). SH—New York Mets, Bobby J. Jones, Harris. LOB—New York Yankees 8; New York Mets 6. SB—New York Mets, Bell. Attendance—54,165.

That came in the form of a Glendon Rusch pitch that hit Tino Martinez in his backside when he led off the bottom of the second inning.

At this point, home plate umpire Doug Eddings warned both benches, but the bad blood between the clubs had boiled over and would last as long as Clemens' tenure with the Yankees continued.

Piazza was found to have a concussion but, fortunately, he only missed one game. That didn't temper the anger that the Mets had for the Yankees' ace.

"We've handed his lunch to him every time we've played him, so the first hitter he throws at his head, the third hitter he throws at his head, and the fourth hitter he hits him in the head," Valentine said.

Clemens answered those charges.

"I didn't hit Mike on purpose. I was going to pitch him inside."

Later in the year, The Rocket would face Piazza and the Mets in the World Series, where a famous incident would take place.

It was Game 2 and it was Piazza's first at-bat against Clemens since he was beaned. Clemens sawed off Piazza's bat on a foul dribbler down the first-base line. The barrel of the bat landed at Clemens' feet, where he picked it up and threw it toward Piazza.

Piazza stared at Clemens while both benches emptied. Reportedly, Piazza yelled to Clemens, "What's your problem?"

When order was restored, Piazza grounded to second base to end the inning and the fireworks.

Clemens would not face the Mets in the regular season interleague series until June 2002. The game was at Shea, so Clemens had to bat, and in the third inning, Mets pitcher Shawn Estes threw a pitch behind Clemens' knees, which brought a roar from the crowd. Both benches were warned and Clemens eventually was called out on strikes. —

GAME 2

Mets	AB	R	H	RBI
Harris lf	3	1	0	0
Bell rf	4	0	3	1
Alfonzo dh	4	0	2	1
Piazza dh	0	0	0	0
M. Franco pr-dh	2	0	1	0
Agbayani ph-dh	1	0	0	0
Ventura 3b	4	0	0	0
Zeile 1b	4	0	0	0
Payton cf	4	0	0	0
Pratt c	4	0	0	0
Mora ss	3	1	1	0
Johnson ph	1	0	0	0
Totals	34	2	7	2

Yankees	AB	R	H	RBI
Knoblauch 2b	4	1	1	3
Vizcaino 2b	0	0	0	0
Jeter ss	4	0	0	0
O'Neill rf	4	0	1	0
Williams cf	3	0	0	0
Martinez 1b	2	0	0	0
Justice dh	3	1	1	0
Spencer lf	3	1	1	0
Turner c	2	0	0	0
Brosius 3b	3	1	1	1
Totals	28	4	5	4

NYM 0 0 0 0 2 0 0 0 0 - 2 7 0
NYY 0 0 0 0 4 0 0 0 X - 4 5 1

Mets	IP	H	R	ER	BB	SO
Rusch L(6–7)	8	5	4	4	0	10

Yankees	IP	H	R	ER	BB	SO
Clemens W(6–6)	7.1	7	2	2	1	4
Stanton	0.2	0	0	0	0	1
Rivera SV(21)	1	0	0	0	0	0
Totals	9	7	2	2	1	5

E—New York, Yankees Jeter. DP—New York Yankees. 2B—New York Mets, Bell. HR—New York Yankees, Knoblauch (4). SH—New York Yankees, Turner. HBP—New York Mets, Piazza; New York Yankees, Martinez. LOB—New York Mets 7; New York Yankees 2. SB—New York Mets, Bell. Attendance—55,821.

Bambino Gets Called Out during Intentional Walk

This one had a little bit of everything, including Babe Ruth being called out for stepping out of the batter's box to swing at an intentional walk.

Lou Gehrig's walk-off single in the bottom of the 12th inning gave the Yankees a 4–3 win over the Cleveland Indians at Yankee Stadium. The Iron Horse made a rare blunder in the top of the eighth that allowed Cleveland to take the lead.

Cleveland took a 2–1 lead when Gehrig ran into Yankees right fielder Ben Paschal as Paschal was about to catch a routine fly ball. The play was ruled a double for future Hall of Famer Tris Speaker, who then scored the third Indians' run on an RBI single by George Burns.

In the bottom of the eighth inning, the Yankees tied it on a sacrifice fly by Paschal and a run-scoring triple by Joe Dugan to deep left-center field.

Later in the inning, the Yankees had the bases loaded with one out and threatened to take the lead. Earle Combs lifted a foul fly toward the left-field line. Indians left fielder Charlie Jamieson nailed the catch before he crashed into the stands, then whirled around and threw a strike to catcher Luke Sewell, who put the tag on Dugan, who had tried to tag up and score.

At a Glance

WP: Braxton (3–1)

HR: Lazzeri (12)

Key stats: Braxton 4 shutout IP in relief, 2 H; Lazzeri 3-for-5, RBI; Ward 2-for-5; Paschal 2-for-5, RBI

There were other great plays in the game, including a game-saving catch by Combs in the top of the 10th inning. With two on and two out, Joe Sewell lined a ball to right-center field, but Combs raced back and snared the screaming liner with his back half turned toward home plate.

In the bottom of the sixth, the Yankees had a runner on third base with two out, and Ruth was the scheduled hitter. Indians player/manager Speaker ordered pitcher Joe Shaute to intentionally walk Ruth to pitch to Gehrig. On the second pitch, Ruth stepped across the plate and fouled it off. Home plate umpire Brick Owens properly called Ruth out to end the inning, but not before the fans vented their anger.

The game featured some other interesting side notes. Reportedly, the Yankees staged a raid on the right-field bleachers and arrested 16 men on gambling charges. In the 11th inning, rain became a factor. With Tony Lazzeri at bat, heavy storm clouds emerged while there were terrific blasts of wind that kicked up the dust in the infield. Within a few minutes, it began to pour but the game resumed some 20 minutes later. —⚊—

Sanderson's One-Hitter Lands Him Just Shy of Record Books

A double by the Angels Luis Polonia was all that stood between Scott Sanderson and immortality as the Yankees blanked the California Angels 2–0 in Anaheim.

Sanderson faced one batter over the minimum as he dominated the Angels lineup by changing speeds and keeping the hitters off balance all game long.

Afterward, the Yankees' right-hander was not distraught about coming up short of being in the record books.

"Does it bother me? Not at all," Sanderson said. "Will I replay it in my mind? Yes, I'll go over that hit."

That hit came in the fourth inning. Polonia led off with a shot just inside the first-base line and just out of the reach of first baseman Don Mattingly.

Sanderson sat down the first nine Angels batters of the game before Polonia's hit and followed that by retiring 13 more in a row before Gary Gaetti reached base with one out in the eighth inning on an error by Yankees shortstop Carlos Rodriguez.

The Yankees took a 1–0 lead in the second inning. Bernie Williams, playing in only his second major league game, drove in Jesse Barfield from second base with an RBI single.

The Yankees made it 2–0 in the sixth inning on Matt Nokes' RBI single. From there, it was all Sanderson as he made the slim lead hold up. —⁓—

Yankees	AB	R	H	RBI
Sax 2b	4	0	1	0
Rodriguez ss	4	0	1	0
Mattingly 1b	4	1	3	0
Hall lf	4	0	2	0
Maas dh	4	0	1	0
Nokes c	4	0	2	1
Barfield rf	4	1	0	0
Williams cf	4	0	1	1
P. Kelly 3b	4	0	0	0
Totals	36	2	11	2

Angels	AB	R	H	RBI
Polonia lf	4	0	1	0
Gallagher cf	2	0	0	0
Joyner 1b	3	0	0	0
Winfield rf	3	0	0	0
Parker dh	3	0	0	0
Gaetti 3b	3	0	0	0
Parrish c	3	0	0	0
Sojo 2b	2	0	0	0
Hill ph	1	0	0	0
Schofield ss	3	0	0	0
Totals	27	0	1	0

NY	0	1	0	0	0	1	0	0	0	-	2	11	2
CAL	0	0	0	0	0	0	0	0	0	-	0	1	1

Yankees	IP	H	R	ER	BB	SO
Sanderson W(10–3)	9	1	0	0	0	1

Angels	IP	H	R	ER	BB	SO
McCaskill L(7–11)	7	10	2	2	0	2
Bannister	1	1	0	0	0	1
Eichorn	1	0	0	0	0	0
Totals	9	11	2	2	0	3

E—New York Rodriguez; California McCaskill. DP—New York 1; California 2. 2B—New York Mattingly, Nokes; California Polonia. SH—California Gallagher. LOB—New York 7; California 1. Attendance: 31,218.

Jeter Becomes First Yankee to win All-Star MVP Award

Derek Jeter was 3-for-3 with two runs scored to become the first Yankee to win the All-Star Game Most Valuable Player Award as the American League doubled up the National League 6–3 in Atlanta.

Jeter's two-run single in the fourth inning off the Mets' Al Leiter broke a 1–1 tie, and the Junior Circuit was never threatened.

AL manager Joe Torre named Jeter the starting shortstop after Alex Rodriguez had suffered a concussion four days earlier.

Jeter found it amazing that no Yankee before him had ever won the All-Star MVP Award.

"I wasn't aware that no other Yankee had won this award, and it's kind of hard to believe," Jeter said.

Reynolds' No-Hitter Too Much for Future Hall of Famer Feller

In one of the great regular-season mound duels of all time, Allie Reynolds outpitched Hall of Famer Bob Feller, but not by much.

Reynolds tossed a no-hitter and the Yankees scratched out one run against one of the all-time great pitchers for an impressive 1–0 win at Municipal Stadium in Cleveland. (Reynolds pitched a second no-hitter later that season on September 28.)

The Chief was in total command as he sat down the final 17 Indians batters to sew up his first career gem.

Feller was just as stingy, not allowing a hit for 5 1/3 innings until Mickey Mantle (who hit leadoff) smacked a one-out double. Mantle was left stranded and the scoreless duel continued.

Reynolds was able to navigate through some early hiccups. Phil Rizzuto's first-inning error gave Cleveland a base runner with one out, but Larry Doby hit into an inning-ending 6–4–3 double play.

At a Glance

WP: Reynolds (10–5)

HR: Woodling (6)

Key stat: Reynolds no-hitter

In the second, Reynolds walked two batters, Luke Easter and Harry Simpson, with one out. Ray Boone flied out to deep center field and Easter took third base, but the runners were left on when Jim Hegan grounded out to end the threat.

The Indians got one last runner on base in the fourth inning, but Al Rosen struck out and Doby was picked off first base.

The Yankees broke through in the seventh inning when center fielder Gene Woodling took Feller's lone mistake of the game over the right-field wall for a home run and a 1–0 lead.

Reynolds made that stand up with an assist to left fielder Hank Bauer. In the Cleveland seventh, Indians center fielder Sam Chapman, who replaced Doby in the lineup, sent a long drive to left field that Bauer hauled in with his back against the wall.

Allie Reynolds pitched a game for the ages on July 12, 1951. Facing Cleveland's Bob Feller, Reynolds tossed the first of his two no-hitters of the season in a 1–0 victory.

Reynolds, a former Indian who was acquired in a deal for nine-time All-Star Joe Gordon, dazzled his old team and had the crowd of 39,195 on his side as Cleveland batted in the ninth inning.

The Indians sent up pitcher Bob Lemon as a pinch-hitter to start the ninth inning, and Reynolds struck out the future manager of the Yankees.

Dale Mitchell (who would be the last out of Don Larsen's perfect game in 1956) grounded out to second.

Bobby Avila was Cleveland's last hope. On the eighth pitch of the at-bat, the Indians second baseman went down swinging, and the fans went crazy.

In less than two weeks, Cleveland Stadium had seen two no-hitters. Feller threw a no hitter against the Detroit Tigers and was now on the short end of this latest no-no.

Mantle, Woodling, Yogi Berra, and Gil McDougald were the only four Yankees to get a hit off the Indians' future Hall of Famer.

The Yankees had substitute base coaches for the game. Frank Crosetti, the third base coach, was absent due to a bruised leg he suffered when he was hit by a line drive. The first base coach, Bill Dickey, was given permission to leave the team for a family matter. Jim Turner and Tommy Henrich were the fill-ins, respectively. —⚘—

P Allie Reynolds

Allie Reynolds was known as the "Superchief" because he was one-quarter Creek Indian.

In 1946, the Yankees acquired the 6-foot, 195-pound right-hander from Cleveland in exchange for second baseman Joe Gordon.

In 1951, Reynolds became the first American League pitcher to throw two no-hitters in one season. In 1952, he won 20 games for the only time in his career and led the league in strikeouts with 160.

One of the Yankees' most underrated pitchers, Reynolds was a six-time All-Star and played on six World Series champion teams with the Yankees.

In 1989, the Yankees dedicated a plaque in Reynolds' honor that hangs in Monument Park and reads, "One of the Yankees' greatest right-handed pitchers."

DiMaggio's Hit Streak Reaches 56 Games

The crowd of 15,000 at Cleveland's League Park didn't know it at the time, but they were watching history.

When Joe DiMaggio lined a single through the middle and into center field off Indians starter Al Milnar, it marked the 56th straight game that the Yankee Clipper would reach safely via a hit.

It also marked the last game of the famous streak because the next day, DiMaggio did not get a hit, and the streak ended.

On this day, however, DiMaggio had two singles and a double as the

Joe DiMaggio drives a pitch up the middle off Indians starter Al Milnar to establish a record 56-game hitting streak on July 16, 1941, in Cleveland. The streak ended the next day, but the Yankee Clipper's record still stands and is considered one of most unattainable benchmarks in all of sports.

Yankees whipped the Indians 10–3.

Since Joltin' Joe set this record, no one has really threatened to tie or surpass the mark. In 1978, Pete Rose came close with a National League-record 44-game hitting streak, but that's been it.

Of course, a streak of this magnitude would have to feature a little good fortune along the way.

Back in June, in the 30th game of the streak, DiMaggio's only hit of the game against the White Sox came in the seventh inning. He hit a sharp grounder to White Sox shortstop Luke Appling for what looked to be a routine ground out, but the ball took a funny bounce and hit Appling in the shoulder to give DiMaggio an infield hit, and the streak carried on.

At a Glance

WP: Donald

HR: Keller (20)

Key stats: DiMaggio extends hit streak to 56 games

A 30-game hit streak established a Yankees franchise record, breaking the previous mark held by Roger Peckinpaugh and Earle Combs.

On July 1, DiMaggio singled in his first at-bat against Red Sox starter Jack Wilson to tie Wee Willie Keeler's record of hitting in 44 consecutive games. Another stroke of luck touched DiMaggio in this one, as the game was a rain-shortened, five-inning affair.

The next day, DiMaggio homered off Boston pitcher Dick Newsome to set a new modern-day record by hitting in his 45th straight game.

In game 54 of the streak in Chicago, DiMaggio hit a topper toward third base that White Sox third baseman Bob Kennedy could not make a play on.

On July 17 in Cleveland's huge Municipal Stadium, DiMaggio went hitless for the first time in two months. Indians lefty Al Smith got DiMaggio out twice, thanks to a pair of great defensive plays from Cleveland third baseman Ken Keltner.

DiMaggio had one last shot to

OF Joe DiMaggio

The "Yankee Clipper" was a three-time MVP Award winner but is best known for his 56-game hitting streak in 1941, a record that still stands to this day.

DiMaggio won one of his three MVP Awards in 1941, despite the fact that his rival, Ted Williams, batted .406 that season.

The Yankees center fielder made his big-league debut in 1936 and led the Yankees to nine World Series championships in his 13-year career.

DiMaggio was an all-around player who could make difficult plays in the field look easy.

"Joltin' Joe" lost three years of his career to the war and retired after the 1951 season. He was inducted into the Baseball Hall of Fame in 1955.

extend the record when he batted with the bases loaded and one out in the eighth inning.

Joltin' Joe took a 1–1 pitch from Indians pitcher Jim Bagby and hit a grounder to Lou Boudreau at short, who began a 6–4–3 double play that dramatically put an end to one of baseball's most enduring records.

During the run, DiMaggio had 91 hits, including 56 singles, 16 doubles, four triples, 15 home runs, and 161 total bases.

DiMaggio went on another streak of 16 consecutive games with a hit, which came to an end on August 3 when he went hitless in the first game of a doubleheader. The 16-game streak gave him hits in 72 out of 73 games. DiMaggio went on to win the American League MVP Award in 1941, despite the .406 season enjoyed by Ted Williams. ─᎗─

Did You Know?

Horace Clarke and Don Mattingly are the only Yankees to have twice spoiled no-hitters by recording the lone hits of those particular games. Clarke spoiled no-hit bids by Orioles pitcher Jim Palmer in 1967 and Tigers pitcher Joe Niekro in 1970. Mattingly broke up a perfect game bid by White Sox pitcher LaMarr Hoyt in 1984 and a no-hit bid by Milwaukee's Moose Haas in 1985.

Doubleheader Sweep Makes It Record 19 Consecutive Wins

With their 3–1 and 7–2 doubleheader sweep in Cleveland, the Yankees set a franchise record with their 19th consecutive win of the 1947 season.

In the opening game, the Yankees won their 18th game in a row as Bobo Newsom picked up career win No. 200.

The much-traveled veteran pitcher was making only his second start as a Yankee, but he went the distance.

Newsom dodged some bullets en route to the victory. In the fourth inning, the Indians had the bases loaded with one out, but Newsom struck out Joe Gordon and retired Snuffy Stirnweiss on a ground out.

George McQuinn's two-run homer in the fourth inning was the key blow.

In the second game, Vic Raschi, "the Springfield Rifle," coasted to a win on a six-hitter.

Yankees third baseman Billy Johnson drove in three runs to pace the offense.

The streak began with a win in the second game of a doubleheader at Washington on June 29. During the streak, the Yankees swept six doubleheaders.

The 19-game winning streak also tied the American League record set by the Chicago White Sox in 1906. —∞—

At a Glance

GAME 1

WP: Newsom

HR: McQuinn (9)

Key stats: Newsom wins 200th game of career; McQuinn 2-run HR

GAME 2

WP: Raschi

Key stats: Raschi 6-hitter; Johnson 3 RBIs; Yanks win 19th game in a row

Perfect Setting Leads to Perfect Game for Cone

The setting was perfect.

What were the chances that the same team would have two perfect games thrown in two years, both on Sunday afternoons, both by pitchers named David, both at the same ballpark?

The odds against that happening were enormous, considering that there had been only 15 perfect games in baseball history prior to this one.

It was Yogi Berra Day at Yankee Stadium. Berra was there for his first day back after a 14-year absence, but so was Don Larsen. The two of them formed the battery that combined on the perfect game in the 1956 World Series against

David Cone can't bear to stand as he celebrates with catcher Joe Girardi after throwing a perfect game against the Expos on July 18, 1999. It was the 16th perfect game in baseball history.

the Dodgers. Legendary Hall of Fame Broadcaster Bob Wolff, who called Larsen's gem in 1956, was watching the game from the press box.

As a tribute to Berra, Larsen threw the ceremonial first pitch to his battery-mate.

Little did the crowd of 41,930 know that in a span of just more than a year, Yankee Stadium would play host to two perfect games (see: May 17, 1998).

In a delicious twist of irony, David Cone—in front of Berra, Larsen, and millions of others watching on TV or listening on the radio—tossed the 16th perfect game in big-league history, turning the trick on the Montreal Expos in an interleague game.

Cone got Montreal's Orlando Cabrera to pop-up in foul territory, where Scott Brosius caught it for the final out to put the right-hander in the record books.

The 1994 American League Cy Young Award winner had incredible stuff that day.

"Probably as a Yankee, the best stuff I ever had," Cone said.

Cone had somewhat of an advantage, as no one in the Expos' lineup had ever faced him. With the command of a dynamite breaking pitch, not to mention a biting slider and a moving fastball, Cone kept the Montreal hitters off balance all game long.

The game was played in 98-degree heat, but Cone enjoys pitching in that climate.

"Love the hot weather," Cone said. "You can really feel the ball."

Cone struck out 10. Thirteen of the outs were either popouts or flyouts, while the Expos made only four outs on grounders. Cone threw a total of 88 pitches and didn't go to a three-ball count on any hitter.

Cone needed two defensive gems to preserve the perfecto. In the top of the first inning, the second batter of the game, Terry Jones, lined a shot toward right-center field, but Paul O'Neill made a diving catch.

The grab would take on added importance as the game wore on, but the game would have to wait as rain began to fall in the third inning. After a brief delay of 33 minutes, the game resumed and Cone

Expos	AB	R	H	RBI
W. Guerrero dh	3	0	0	0
Jones cf	2	0	0	0
Mouton cf	1	0	0	0
White lf	3	0	0	0
V. Guerrero rf	3	0	0	0
Vidro 2b	3	0	0	0
Fullmer 1b	3	0	0	0
Widger c	3	0	0	0
Andrews 3b	2	0	0	0
McGuire ph	1	0	0	0
Cabrera ss	3	0	0	0
Totals	27	0	0	0

Yankees	AB	R	H	RBI
Knoblauch 2b	2	1	1	0
Jeter ss	4	1	1	2
O'Neill rf	4	1	1	0
Williams cf	4	0	1	1
Martinez 1b	4	0	1	0
Davis dh	3	1	1	0
Ledee lf	4	1	1	2
Brosius 3b	2	1	0	0
Girardi c	3	0	1	1
Totals	30	6	8	6

MON 0 0 0 0 0 0 0 0 0 - 0 0 0
NY   0 5 0 0 0 0 0 1 X - 6 8 0

Expos	IP	H	R	ER	BB	SO
Vazquez L(2–5)	7	7	6	2	3	2
Ayala	1	1	0	0	0	0
Totals	8	8	6	2	3	2

Yankees	IP	H	R	ER	BB	SO
Cone W(10–4)	9	0	0	0	0	10

DP—Montreal 1. 2B—New York, Girardi, O'Neill. HR—New York, Ledee (3), Jeter (16). HBP—New York, Knoblauch, Brosius. LOB—Montreal 0; New York 4. Attendance—41,930.

didn't skip a beat. Cone sat down 22 straight hitters before the second defensive gem occurred. Montreal's Jose Vidro hit a ball toward the middle of the diamond that appeared to be the first base hit of the game, but second baseman Chuck Knoblauch ranged to his right, backhanded the ball, and threw a strike to Tino Martinez at first base to complete an exhilarating play.

Ironically, Knoblauch made almost the same exact play in the same exact situation (with one out in the eighth) in David Wells' perfect game the year before.

Getting the lift that he probably needed to finish the task, Cone struck out Brad Fullmer for his ninth K of the game to end the eighth inning.

Three outs to go, and the crowd was almost hoping the Yankees would go quickly in their half of the eighth inning so Cone could get back to work. It was already 5–0, but the Yankees added a run and Montreal made a pitching change. Cone would have to sit a little more before taking the mound for the ninth.

Ricky Ledee grounded out to end the eighth and it was time for the spotlight to focus strictly on the man occupying the Yankee Stadium mound.

"Going out for the ninth, I felt like my head was on fire," Cone said.

From the moment Ledee grounded out to end the eighth, the fans were on their feet.

"They wanted it more than I did," Cone said.

Chris Widger began the ninth inning with a three-pitch strikeout.

Ryan McGuire batted for Shane Andrews and there was one more "hold your breath" moment. The left-handed batter lofted a fly ball toward left field. Ledee seemed to hesitate as he ran toward the ball and it looked like he had a chance to drop it, but the left fielder recovered in time to make a two-handed grab near his belt buckle.

Cabrera would see Cone's 86th, 87th, and 88th pitches, the final one of which was popped up in foul territory on the left side. Scott Brosius settled under it, and the rest is history.

Cone dropped to his knees and grabbed his head. His catcher, Joe Girardi, was the first to reach him and embraced him in a never-ending bear hug.

As is his nature, Derek Jeter made light of the moment. Cone said while he was engulfed in the pile of players around him, Jeter told him, "Alright, it's over, get up already."

When he did get up, Chili Davis and Knoblauch hoisted him on their shoulders for a hero's ride off the field. —⁓—

Home Away from Home Leads to Win in 16th

What was unusual about this 8–7 Yankees win is that the game started at Shea Stadium and was completed at Minnesota's Metropolitan Stadium with the Bombers acting as the home team while wearing their road uniforms.

On Saturday, July 12, the Yankees and Twins played 14 innings and were tied at six before the game was suspended due to the American League curfew. No inning would begin after 1 a.m. With the Twins playing their last game in New York, the game would be resumed in Minnesota when the Yankees traveled there a week later.

On July 19, before the regularly-scheduled game, the Yankees took the field at Metropolitan Stadium in their "road grays," but as the home team that had the last at-bat.

In the top of the 16th inning, the Twins scored a run to take a 7–6 lead. Rod Carew, who was 4-for-8, singled and stole second. The future Hall of Famer scored the go-ahead run on a pinch-hit single by Tom Lundstedt, who was in the minors when the game originally began.

With two out and two on in the Yankees' half of the 16th, Graig Nettles singled off Tom Burgmeier to tie the game. Lou Piniella followed with a single to right to score Chris Chambliss with the winning run, and the Yankees had a most unusual ending to a bizarre victory.

> ## At a Glance
> **WP:** Martinez (1–0)
>
> **HR:** Coggins (1)
>
> **Key stats:** Coggins 3-for-7, 2 RBIs; Munson 3-for-5, RBI

Left-hander Tippy Martinez, who was also in the minors when the game started, picked up the win in relief by recording the final out of the 16th.

Yankees pitcher Pat Dobson was the pitcher of record when the game was suspended and he was back on the mound for the 15th inning in Minnesota. Before the game was suspended, there was a wild ninth inning. Minnesota trailed 3–2 but scored four times in the top of the ninth to grab a 6–3 lead. In the last of the ninth, Rich Coggins hit a two-run homer to make it a one-run deficit. With Rick Dempsey at second and two outs, Thurman Munson delivered an RBI single to center to tie the game at six.

The game resumed with totally different umpires than the ones who worked the game in New York. A crew that featured Russ Goetz, Merle Anthony, George Maloney, and Bill Deegan was replaced by Art Frantz, Nick Bremigan, Jim McKean, and Jerry Neudecker.

The marathon lasted 5 hours and 11 minutes in game time. —᪲—

Stottlemyre Shows Power at the Plate with Grand Slam

Mel Stottlemyre was not just a terrific Yankees pitcher, he was also a very good hitter. He showed off his offensive skills with an inside-the-park grand slam to beat the Boston Red Sox 6–3.

Stottlemyre went the distance, giving up three runs on 10 hits, but his hitting is what will be remembered from this one.

The Yankees were leading 2–1 in the fifth inning when they loaded the bases with nobody out.

Joe Pepitone began the inning with a walk. Clete Boyer bunted safely past the mound and Roger Repoz walked to set up the historic blow.

Stottlemyre took the first pitch he saw from Red Sox pitcher Bill Monbouquette (who would later pitch for the Yankees) and hit a screaming line drive toward center field.

"I guess they thought I was going to bunt to squeeze in a run," Stottlemyre said after the game. "Anyway he threw me a high fastball."

Boston left fielder Carl Yastrzemski and center fielder Jim Gosger were playing shallow, but the ball split the two and rolled to the deepest part of center field, some 460 feet away.

Pepitone, Repoz, and Boyer all scored. When Stottlemyre reached third, Yastrzemski and Gosger were just getting to the ball.

"I was surprised when [third base coach] Frank Crosetti waved me in," the 23-year-old right-hander said.

Stottlemyre raced home as the relay throw came in and skipped under the glove of Red Sox catcher Bob Tillman, giving the Yankees a 6–1 lead.

The blow was Stottlemyre's second home run of the season and the third grand slam ever hit by a

Red Sox	AB	R	H	RBI
Gosger cf	5	1	2	1
Malzone 3b	4	1	2	0
Yastrzemski lf	3	1	2	0
Mantilla 2b	4	0	1	1
Thomas 1b	4	0	0	0
Conigliaro rf	3	0	0	1
Tillman c	4	0	1	0
Petrocelli ss	4	0	1	0
Monbouquette p	2	0	0	0
Green ph	1	0	1	0
Jones ph	1	0	0	0
Totals	35	3	10	3

Yankees	AB	R	H	RBI
Richardson 2b	3	1	2	0
Kubek ss	4	1	2	2
Mantle lf	4	0	0	0
Moschitto rf	0	0	0	0
Howard c	4	0	0	0
Tresh rf,lf	4	0	0	0
Pepitone 1b	3	1	1	0
Boyer 3b	3	1	1	0
Repoz cf	2	1	0	0
Stottlemyre p	3	1	3	4
Totals	30	6	7	6

BOS	1	0	0	0	0	0	2	0	-	3	10	0
NY	0	0	0	2	4	0	0	X	-	6	7	1

Red Sox	IP	H	R	ER	BB	SO
Monbouquette L(7–11)	4	5	6	6	3	4
Earley	2	1	0	0	0	1
Duliba	2	1	0	0	0	2
Totals	8	7	6	6	3	7

Yankees	IP	H	R	ER	BB	SO
Stottlemyre W(10–5)	9	10	3	2	1	5

E—New York Richardson. DP—Boston 1; New York 1. 2B—Boston Green; New York Pepitone. HR—Boston Gosger (3); New York Kubek (3), Stottlemyre (2). SF—Boston Conigliaro. LOB—Boston 7; New York 3. Attendance: 24,594.

Yankee pitcher. Spud Chandler and Don Larsen also hit grand slam home runs while pitching for the Yankees, but those went over the fence. Stottlemyre's shot was believed to be the first inside-the-park grand slam ever hit by a pitcher.

With Stottlemyre having to run the full 360 feet around the bases, manager Johnny Keane wondered if he had enough stamina to finish the game.

In the top of the sixth, Gosger flied out to start the inning. Frank Malzone singled and Yastrzemski walked, putting runners on first and second base. Stottlemyre struck out Felix Mantilla and got Lee Thomas to fly out to end the threat.

Boston scored twice in the eighth inning to cut the margin to 6–3, but Stottlemyre got through the eighth and had a 1–2–3 ninth to wrap up a memorable day.

The pitcher who spent his entire 11-year career in pinstripes already had a reputation of being a solid hitter. The Hazleton, Missouri, native ended with 120 hits in his career, including seven home runs, 13 doubles, and six triples. In September 1964, he recorded a 5-for-5 game against the Senators at D.C. Stadium, where four years later, he would start the All-Star Game for the American League.

Stottlemyre's first full season in the big leagues was in 1965. He went on to win 164 games and throw 40 shutouts in a brilliant career. ⎯∾⎯

Yanks Make Efficient Work of Angels in Pair of Shutouts

It's rare when a team gets shut out on both ends of a doubleheader, but the Yankees did it when they swept a twin bill from the Angels 6–0 in the first game and 3–0 in the nightcap.

Fritz Peterson and Mel Stottlemyre dominated the Angels in such an efficient manner that the combined time for both games was a little more than four hours.

Peterson allowed four hits in the opener. He was backed by a pair of home runs by Bobby Murcer and solo shots from Ron Blomberg and Johnny Callison.

The left-hander did not walk a batter and allowed only one Angels hitter to advance past first base until Ken McMullen doubled in the seventh.

In the nightcap, Stottlemyre benefitted from a defense that produced four double plays.

Angels southpaw Rudy May was just as stingy, but the Yankees touched him for a run in the second on an RBI single by Gene Michael and a two-run homer in the seventh inning by catcher John Ellis.

Stottlemyre recorded his 11th straight win against the Angels and stretched his personal scoreless innings streak vs. California to 46 innings. —⁓—

At a Glance

GAME 1

WP: Peterson (9–11)

HR: Murcer 2 (12, 13), Blomberg (8), Callison (3)

Key stats: Peterson 4-hitter; Murcer 2-for-3, 3 RBIs; Munson 2-for-4

GAME 2

WP: Stottlemyre (10–11)

HR: Ellis (3)

Key stats: Stottlemyre 4-hitter; Ellis 2-for-3, 2 RBIs

Third Time's a Charm for Abbott vs. Angels

In December 1992, the Yankees traded three players to the California Angels for left-handed pitcher Jim Abbott. What made Abbott special is that he was born without a right hand yet worked his way to the major leagues to be a productive pitcher.

Abbott took the cue from a five home-run attack to go eight innings and beat his old team for the first time 12–1.

The Yankees' offense went back-to-back twice in the game, but it was the one-handed southpaw who provided the lead story.

Abbott gave up one unearned run (which scored on a double-play ball) on five hits as he beat his former teammates in his third attempt.

Abbott defied the critics who said he couldn't play defense. The 25 year old developed a method by which, after throwing the pitch, he would transfer the glove, which he balanced on his right arm, to his left hand, where he could field balls hit back to the mound.

Later that season, Abbott completed one of the most incredible feats of pitching ever seen when he tossed a no-hitter against the Cleveland Indians at Yankee Stadium (see: September 4, 1993). —⁓—

Angels	AB	R	H	RBI
Polonia lf	4	1	1	0
Curtis cf	3	0	1	0
Easley 2b	3	0	1	0
Salmon rf	3	0	0	0
Javier rf	1	0	0	0
Davis dh	4	0	1	0
R. Gonzales 3b	3	0	0	0
Snow 1b	3	0	0	0
DiSarcina ss	3	0	1	0
Correia ss	0	0	0	0
Tingley c	3	0	0	0
Totals	30	1	5	0

Yankees	AB	R	H	RBI
Boggs 3b	2	3	1	0
Meulens ph,3b	1	0	0	0
James lf	5	1	2	0
Mattingly 1b	3	2	1	3
Maas ph,1b	1	0	0	0
Tartabull dh	3	3	2	4
O'Neill rf	4	1	1	1
B. Williams cf	4	1	1	0
Stanley c	3	1	2	3
Leyritz c	0	0	0	0
Gallego ss	4	0	0	0
Kelly 2b	4	0	0	0
Totals	34	12	10	11

```
CAL  1 0 0 0 0 0 0 0 0 - 1 5 0
NY   1 0 4 0 0 3 4 0 X - 12 10 1
```

Angels	IP	H	R	ER	BB	SO
Springer L(1–5)	5.1	4	7	7	3	3
Linton	0.2	4	5	5	1	0
Patterson	2	2	0	0	0	1
Totals	8	10	12	12	4	4

Yankees	IP	H	R	ER	BB	SO
Abbott W(7–8)	8	5	1	0	1	6
Wickman	1	0	0	0	0	1
Totals	9	5	1	0	1	7

E—New York Boggs. DP—New York 2. 2B—California Disarcina; New York Boggs. HR—New York Tartabull 2 (17,18), O'Neill (13), Stanley (15), Mattingly (8). SH—California Curtis. HBP—New York Stanley. LOB—California 4; New York 3. Attendance: 25,148.

Mantle Hits for the Cycle for Only Time in His Career

A year after winning baseball's Triple Crown, Mickey Mantle added another batting achievement to his resume when he hit for the cycle for the only time in his career, leading the Yankees past the White Sox 10–6 at Yankee Stadium.

In the first inning, Mantle hit a soft fly ball to center field. Chicago center fielder Larry Doby had trouble seeing the ball, and it dropped at his feet as Mantle took second with a double.

In the third inning, Mantle laced a monstrous home run off White Sox pitcher Bob Keegan that traveled an estimated 465 feet after reaching the next-to-last row of the right-center-field bleachers.

Mantle got his single to lead off the sixth inning, and then needed only the triple to complete the rare batting feat.

With the bases loaded and no one out in the seventh, Mantle laced a shot toward the left-field corner that cleared the bases for a three-bagger to become the eighth Yankee player to hit for the cycle.

The triple turned out to be a key hit in the game as the Yankee pitchers could not keep the White Sox down. Tommy Byrne relieved starter Don Larsen, but Byrne had a terrible outing as he gave up four earned runs in 1 1/3 innings of work. —⌇—

White Sox	AB	R	H	RBI
Rivera rf	2	0	1	1
Landis ph	0	0	0	0
Northey ph	0	0	0	1
Phillips pr,rf	1	1	0	0
Fox 2b	5	0	2	1
Torgeson 1b	3	0	1	3
Minoso lf	3	0	0	0
Doby cf	4	0	0	0
Aparicio ss	5	0	1	0
Moss c	4	1	0	0
Esposito 3b	2	2	1	0
Keegan p	1	1	0	0
Dropo ph	0	0	0	0
Pierce pr	0	1	0	0
Totals	**30**	**6**	**6**	**6**

Yankees	AB	R	H	RBI
Kubek ss	5	1	4	2
McDougald 2b	4	1	1	1
Mantle cf	5	2	4	4
Simpson 1b	4	1	2	2
Berra c	4	0	0	0
Bauer rf	4	0	0	0
Howard lf	4	1	1	0
Coleman 3b	3	3	3	0
Larsen p	1	0	0	0
Byrne p	1	0	0	0
Richardson pr	0	1	0	0
Totals	**35**	**10**	**15**	**9**

CHI	0 0 0 0 2 4 0 0 0	-	6 6 2
NY	2 0 1 0 1 0 5 1 X	-	10 15 0

White Sox	IP	H	R	ER	BB	SO
Keegan	5	7	4	4	0	0
LaPalme	0.1	2	0	0	0	0
Howell	0.2	1	2	2	1	0
Harshman L(7–5)	1	2	3	3	2	1
Staley	1	3	1	1	0	0
Totals	**8**	**15**	**10**	**10**	**3**	**1**

Yankees	IP	H	R	ER	BB	SO
Larsen	4.1	2	2	2	6	3
Byrne	1.1	0	4	4	4	0
Ditmar W(7–1)	1.1	3	0	0	2	0
Grim SV(11)	2	1	0	0	1	0
Totals	**9**	**6**	**6**	**6**	**13**	**3**

E—Chicago Moss, Staley. DP—Chicago 3; New York 3. 2B—New York Mantle, Coleman. 3B—New York Howard, Mantle. HR—New York Simpson (8), Mantle (26). SH—New York Grim. LOB—Chicago 10; New York 5. SB—New York Mantle. Attendance: 42,422.

Pair of 21s Leads to Jackpot for Yankees

To say the Yankees had their "hitting shoes" on would be an understatement. The Bronx Bombers lived up to their moniker by displaying a 21-hit attack in a 21–1 rollover of the Cleveland Indians at the Stadium.

Chili Davis was the main culprit, tying a career high with five hits and driving in six runs. Jorge Posada tied a career high with four hits while driving in three and scoring three times.

The Yankees did most of their damage in the fifth and sixth innings, when they combined for 13 runs on 10 hits.

With the Yankees leading 18–0 in the top of the seventh, the crowd of 54,870 booed when Yankees left fielder Ricky Ledee "gingerly" played a single, allowing the slow-footed Jim Thome to score without a throw for the Indians' only run.

The cheers returned when the Yankees scored their 20th and 21st runs in the seventh on Ledee's two-run single.

Hideki Irabu, who would be named American League pitcher of the month twice in his career, cruised through seven innings for the win while Ed Yarnall finished it off with two scoreless innings. —⚊

Indians	AB	R	H	RBI
Lofton cf	3	0	1	0
Wilson ph,2b	2	0	0	0
Vizquel ss	4	0	2	0
R. Alomar 2b	3	0	0	0
A. Ramirez rf	1	0	0	0
M. Ramirez rf	2	0	0	0
Sexson lf	1	0	0	0
Justice dh	4	0	0	0
Thome 1b	3	1	1	0
Cruz lf,cf	4	0	3	1
Branyan 3b	4	0	1	0
Diaz c	4	0	1	0
Totals	**35**	**1**	**9**	**1**

Yankees	AB	R	H	RBI
Knoblauch 2b	4	1	1	1
Jeter ss	3	1	1	1
Sojo pr,ss	1	2	1	1
O'Neill rf	3	0	0	0
Ledee pr,rf	2	2	2	3
Williams cf	5	1	1	2
Davis dh	6	3	5	6
Martinez 1b	2	2	1	1
Manto ph,1b	3	0	1	0
Brosius 3b	5	3	2	2
Posada c	6	3	4	3
Curtis lf	4	3	2	1
Totals	**44**	**21**	**21**	**21**

CLE	0 0 0	0 0 0	1 0 0	-	1	9	1
NY	4 0 0	1 7 6	3 0 X	-	21	21	0

Indians	IP	H	R	ER	BB	SO
Langston L(1–1)	4.1	10	9	7	3	2
Assenmacher	1.1	6	7	7	3	3
Candiotti	0.2	4	5	5	3	0
Reed	1.2	1	0	0	0	2
Totals	**8**	**21**	**21**	**16***	**9**	**7**

Yankees	IP	H	R	ER	BB	SO
Irabu W(7–3)	7	7	1	1	1	7
Yarnall	2	2	0	0	1	3
Totals	**9**	**9**	**1**	**1**	**2**	**10**

E—Cleveland Branyan. DP—New York 1. 2B—Cleveland Cruz, Thome, Vizquel; New York Brosius, Curtis, Davis. HR—New York Brosius (10), Davis (14). SF—New York Knoblauch. LOB—Cleveland 9; New York 9. Attendance: 54,870.

* — Team earned runs does not equal the composite totals for all pitchers due to instances in which provisions of Section 10.18 (i) of the Scoring rules were applied. (www.retrosheet.org)

Chambliss Delivers a Rare Curtain Call after Walk-Off Home Run

Call this one a statement game.

Chris Chambliss hit a two-out, three-run, walk-off home run in the bottom of the ninth inning to lift the Yankees to a thrilling 6–5 win over the Boston Red Sox at an electric Yankee Stadium.

The remodeled icon of the Bronx had not seen an ending like this. The 49,723 on hand were so thrilled that they stayed and chanted for Chambliss to come out and take a curtain call, and the first baseman obliged.

This was reported to be the first such occurrence since Roger Maris' curtain call after his 61st home run in 1961, and began what would turn into a normal scenario in Yankee Stadium.

The Yankees were sitting pretty in the American League East (13 games ahead of second-place Cleveland entering the day), while the defending American League champion Red Sox were eight under .500 and 17 games behind.

The Yankees trailed 5–0 as they batted in the fifth inning. Thurman Munson broke the ice with a two-out RBI single to make it 5–1.

The Yankees made it a 5–2 deficit an inning later on an RBI double by Oscar Gamble and had runners at second and third base with no one out. The Red Sox went to the bullpen for right-handed reliever Tom Murphy, who struck out Willie Randolph and retired Jim Mason on an RBI ground out to make it 5–3. Murphy ended the threat when he got Mickey Rivers to ground out to first, unassisted.

Murphy held the Yankees scoreless in the seventh and eighth innings, but pinch-hitter Elrod Hendricks got the ninth-inning rally started with a single to center.

Red Sox	AB	R	H	RBI
Burleson ss	4	0	1	0
Fisk c	5	1	1	0
Lynn cf	4	0	2	1
Yastrzemski 1b	3	0	0	0
Rice lf	3	2	2	2
Miller lf	0	0	0	0
Evans rf	3	1	1	0
Darwin dh	3	0	2	2
Cooper ph,dh	1	0	0	0
Griffin 2b	4	0	0	0
Heise 3b	4	1	2	0
Totals	**34**	**5**	**11**	**5**

Yankees	AB	R	H	RBI
Rivers cf	5	2	2	0
White lf	5	0	1	0
Munson c	5	0	1	1
Chambliss 1b	5	1	1	3
C. May dh	3	1	3	0
Nettles 3b	4	1	2	1
Gamble rf	4	0	1	1
Randolph 2b	3	0	0	0
Mason ss	3	0	1	1
Hendricks ph	1	1	1	0
Totals	**38**	**6**	**13**	**6**

```
BOS  0 2 0 1 2 0 0 0 - 5 11 1
NY   0 0 0 0 1 2 0 0 3 - 6 13 1
```

Red Sox	IP	H	R	ER	BB	SO
Wise	5	9	3	3	2	1
Murphy	3.2	3	2	2	0	1
House L(1–3)	0	1	1	1	0	0
Totals	**8.2**	**13**	**6**	**6**	**2**	**2**

Yankees	IP	H	R	ER	BB	SO
Holtzman	4.1	9	5	5	1	0
Jackson	2.2	2	0	0	1	1
Tidrow W(4–1)	2	0	0	0	0	2
Totals	**9**	**11**	**5**	**5**	**2**	**3**

E—Boston Rice; New York Randolph. DP—Boston 2; New York 1. 2B—Boston Evans, Darwin; New York Gamble, Rivers. HR—Boston Rice (15); New York Chambliss (12). SH—Boston Burleson. SF—Boston Rice. LOB—Boston 6; New York 8. Attendance: 49,723.

Rivers doubled off the wall in right to put runners at second and third base with nobody out.

The Yankees nearly wasted this golden opportunity when Murphy got Roy White on a stress-free flyout to center and then retired Munson on a ground out to third without a run scoring.

At this point, Red Sox manager Don Zimmer made a controversial move when he brought in left-handed reliever Tom House to face Chambliss.

"I told him to pitch tough," Zimmer said, "not to give Chambliss anything good to hit."

Chambliss put his thinking cap on while he stood on deck and waited for House to finish his warm-ups.

"He usually throws breaking balls to me," Chambliss said.

Not this time, however, as House threw a first-pitch fastball that stayed out over the plate. Chambliss smoked it into the right-center-field bleachers for an emotional victory.

"I guess he wanted to get the fastball up and in to set me up for the curve," Chambliss said. "I was trying to hit it up the middle to tie the game. That's when I usually get a home run." —⌇—

Did You Know?

Hideki Matsui is the first player to win the World Series MVP after having a majority of his at-bats as a designated hitter. Toronto's Paul Molitor had 12 at-bats as a DH and 12 as a first baseman when he won the award in 1993.

Pitcher John Escapes Three-Error Inning to Dump Brewers

Yankees pitcher Tommy John tied a major league record with three errors in one inning, but he pitched eight innings to pick up the win in the Yankees' 16–3 rout of the Milwaukee Brewers at Yankee Stadium.

Dave Winfield was the hitting star, belting two home runs and driving in five. But John's errors stole the show. "Unfortunately, I'll be remembered more for that [the three errors] than the game I pitched," he said.

The Yankees led 4–0 when the fielding lapse occurred in the fourth. With one out, Jim Gantner walked. Jeffrey Leonard hit a dribbler to the left of [the mound. I]t was bobbled by John for the first [error. John eventually] picked up the ball, but threw [it past first] base for the second error. Gantner, [headed to th]ird, broke for home but stopped as [the throw came] in from right field. The 45-year-old [John took th]e ball off and threw it past the catcher, allowing Ga]ntner to score.

John was charged with a third error, which tied a record. J. Bentley "Cy" Seymour of the 1898 New York Giants is the only other pitcher in big-league history to commit three errors in one inning, although John's total all came during one single play.

Despite his faux pas, John had a storied major league career and is the only player to have a surgery named after him.

In 1974, John was the first to undergo a medical procedure where a ligament in the elbow is replaced by a tendon from elsewhere in the body. John returned in 1976 and went on to pitch until 1989, when he was 46 years old. —⁓—

Brewers	AB	R	H	RBI
Molitor dh	4	0	0	0
Gantner sb	3	1	1	0
Leonard lf	2	1	0	0
Adduci lf	2	0	0	0
Yount cf	4	0	1	0
Deer rf	4	1	2	0
Sveum ss	4	0	0	0
Meyer 1b	3	0	2	0
Castillo 3b	3	0	0	1
O'Brien c	3	0	0	0
Totals	32	3	6	1

Yankees	AB	R	H	RBI
Henderson lf	6	1	2	1
Mattingly 1b	5	1	1	0
Winfield rf	5	3	3	5
Washington cf	5	3	4	0
Clark dh	4	1	1	1
Slaught c	5	1	2	1
Randolph 2b	3	3	2	1
Santana ss	5	2	1	3
Velarde 3b	5	1	2	3
Totals	43	16	18	15

MIL	0	0	0	2	0	0	1	0	0	-	3 6 2
NY	4	0	0	1	2	2	3	4	X	-	16 18 3

Brewers	IP	H	R	ER	BB	SO
Bosio L(6–12)	4.1	11	7	7	1	2
Crim	1.2	2	2	2	0	0
Jones	2	5	7	3	2	0
Totals	8	18	16	12	3	2

Yankees	IP	H	R	ER	BB	SO
John W(8–3)	8	6	3	2	1	3
Guante	1	0	0	0	0	1
Totals	9	6	3	2	1	4

E—Milwaukee Sveum; New York John 3. DP—Milwaukee 1; New York 2. 2B—Milwaukee Deer; New York Randolph, Slaught, Velarde 2. HR—New York Winfield 2 (18,19), Santana. LOB—Milwaukee 3; New York 6. Attendance: 28,869.

Strawberry Comes Through with Walk-Off Two-Run Homer

A dramatic home run and a big win with a New York flavor.

Darryl Strawberry slugged a two-run walk-off homer to lift the Yankees to a 3–2 win over the Kansas City Royals at Yankee Stadium.

Kansas City's Kevin Appier held the Yankees to a run on four hits in eight innings pitched as the Royals clung to a 2–1 lead.

Jason Jacome was brought on to close it, but Strawberry took him deep for the win.

Signing Strawberry, the former Met phenom, was a risk. A suspension in 1995 for using cocaine, not to mention tax problems and numerous court appearances, made for a shaky relationship for any club.

Yankees owner George Steinbrenner was always fascinated with Strawberry and realized the potential of what he could bring to the team, which needed some more pop at the plate. So Steinbrenner signed the tall left-handed hitter, who was playing for the St. Paul Saints of the independent Northern League.

Ironically, the Yankees starter was Dwight Gooden, another former Mets phenom, and he was almost as good as Appier. Doc also went eight innings, giving up two runs on seven hits. John Wetteland pitched a scoreless ninth and got the win. ⎯⏦

Royals	AB	R	H	RBI
Offerman 1b	4	1	2	2
Goodwin cf	4	0	1	0
Lockhart 3b	4	0	0	0
Roberts 2b	4	0	1	0
Hamelin dh	4	0	1	0
Damon rf	3	0	0	0
Tucker lf	3	0	1	0
Macfarlane c	3	0	0	0
Howard ss	3	1	1	0
Totals	32	2	7	2

Yankees	AB	R	H	RBI
Boggs 3b	3	0	0	0
B. Williams cf	2	0	0	0
O'Neill rf	4	0	0	0
Martinez 1b	2	1	1	0
G. Williams pr	0	1	0	0
Strawberry dh	4	1	2	2
Sierra lf	3	0	1	0
Leyritz c	3	0	0	1
Jeter ss	3	0	1	0
Fox 2b	2	0	0	0
Aldrete ph	1	0	0	0
Howard 2b	0	0	0	0
Totals	27	3	5	3

										R	H	E
KC	0	0	2	0	0	0	0	0	0 -	2	7	0
NY	0	1	0	0	0	0	0	0	2 -	3	5	0

Royals	IP	H	R	ER	BB	SO
Appier	8	4	1	1	4	7
Jacome L(0–3)	0	1	2	2	1	0
Totals	8	5	3	3	5	7

Yankees	IP	H	R	ER	BB	SO
Gooden	8	7	2	2	0	1
Wetteland W(1–2)	1	0	0	0	0	2
Totals	9	7	2	2	0	3

DP—Kansas City 1. 2B—Kansas City Hamelin; New York Sierra. HR—Kansas City Offerman (2); New York Strawberry (3). LOB—Kansas City 3; New York 5. SB— Kansas City Goodwin; New York Strawberry. Attendance: 35,658.

Eight Homers Leaves No Doubt about Bronx Bombers Nickname

The Yankees lived up to their famous moniker of Bronx Bombers when they slammed a franchise-record eight home runs in a 16–3 rout of the Chicago White Sox at Yankee Stadium.

Hideki Matsui led the barrage with two home runs while six other players went deep.

Bobby Abreu's three-run homer and Matsui's solo shot in the first inning gave the Yankees a 4–0 lead.

The Yankees scored five times in the third inning, with Robinson Cano and Melky Cabrera going deep, while Jorge Posada added a two-run shot in the fourth inning.

Matsui hit his second home run off White Sox reliever Gavin Floyd, who also gave up long balls to Johnny Damon and Shelley Duncan to complete the power display.

"I was quite surprised," Matsui said of the eight home runs by the team. "I've never experienced something like this."

A crowd of 53,958 enjoyed the offensive show that featured 16 hits. Posada was 4-for-5 and Abreu was 3-for-4, while Matsui scored four times.

Former teammate Jose Contreras was pounded for seven runs in 2 2/3 innings pitched. Mike Mussina got the win with six solid innings. —ᵐ—

White Sox	AB	R	H	RBI
Owens cf	4	0	2	0
Fields 3b	4	0	0	0
Thome dh	4	0	1	0
Konerko 1b	3	0	2	0
Erstad 1b	1	0	1	0
Pierzynski c	3	0	0	0
Hall c	1	0	0	0
Dye rf	4	1	0	0
Podsednik lf	3	1	1	0
Uribe ss	2	1	1	3
Gonzalez ph,ss	1	0	0	0
Richar 2b	3	0	0	0
Totals	33	3	8	3

Yankees	AB	R	H	RBI
Damon dh	3	2	2	1
Jeter ss	5	1	1	0
Cairo ss	0	0	0	0
Abreu rf	4	2	3	3
Duncan rf	1	1	1	1
Rodriguez 3b	5	0	0	0
Basak 3b	0	0	0	0
Matsui lf	3	4	2	3
Posada c	5	3	4	2
Cano 2b	5	1	2	3
Phillips 1b	4	1	0	1
Cabrera cf	4	1	1	2
Totals	39	16	16	16

```
CHI   0 3 0 0 0 0 0 0 0 - 3 8 1
NY    4 0 5 2 0 3 2 0 X - 16 16 0
```

White Sox	IP	H	R	ER	BB	SO
Contreras L(5–14)	2.2	8	7	7	1	2
Haeger	1.1	2	4	2	2	0
Floyd	3	6	5	5	1	0
Logan	1	0	0	0	0	0
Totals	8	16	16	14	3	2

Yankees	IP	H	R	ER	BB	SO
Mussina W(6–7)	6	6	3	3	0	6
Farnsworth	1	0	0	0	0	1
Myers	1	1	0	0	0	1
Henn	1	1	0	0	0	0
Totals	9	8	3	3	0	8

E—Chicago Uribe. DP—New York 2. 2B—Chicago Konerko; New York Posada, Cano. HR—Chicago Uribe (10); New York Abreu (9), Matsui 2 (20,21), Cano (9), Cabrera (6), Posada (12), Damon (6), Duncan (4). SF—New York Phillips. LOB—Chicago 3; New York 4. Attendance: 53,958.

Munson's Life Cut Short in Plane Crash after Win

When Thurman Munson left the Yankees' 9–1 win at Chicago's Comiskey Park, it marked the final time that the Yankee captain ever wore a big-league uniform.

The very next day, Munson tragically perished in a plane crash.

The 1976 American League Most Valuable Player started his final game at first base. In his penultimate plate appearance, Munson walked and scored on Reggie Jackson's home run.

He struck out against the White Sox's Ken Kravec in his final at-bat in the third inning. Munson strained his right knee during the at-bat and had to leave the game. Jim Spencer replaced the captain at first base in the fourth inning.

Don Hood pitched seven scoreless innings in an emergency start. Ed Figueroa and Luis Tiant were both unavailable because of injuries.

The Yankees scored three runs in the first inning. With Munson on first base and two out, Jackson belted a two-run homer into the lower deck in left-center field at Comiskey. It proved to be the final run that Munson ever scored.

Lou Piniella followed with a solo home run for a 3–0 lead.

The Yankees broke the game open by scoring four runs in the sixth inning, keyed by a two-run single by Willie Randolph. —

Yankees	AB	R	H	RBI
Randolph 2b	4	0	1	2
Murcer cf	5	0	1	0
Munson 1b	1	1	0	0
Spencer 1b	1	1	0	0
Jackson rf	4	1	2	2
Piniella lf	5	1	3	2
Nettles 3b	3	1	1	0
White dh	5	1	1	0
Narron c	3	2	1	1
Stanley ss	4	1	2	2
Totals	35	9	12	9

White Sox	AB	R	H	RBI
Squires 1b	4	0	0	0
Bannister lf	4	0	2	0
Johnson dh	4	1	1	0
Orta 2b	3	0	0	0
Lemon cf	4	0	3	1
Washington rf	3	0	0	0
May c	3	0	0	0
Pryor ss	3	0	0	0
Bell 3b	3	0	0	0
Totals	31	1	6	1

										R	H	E
NY	3	0	0	1	0	4	1	0	0 -	9	12	0
CHI	0	0	0	0	0	0	0	0	1 -	1	6	0

Yankees	IP	H	R	ER	BB	SO
Hood W(4–0)	7	4	0	0	0	3
Kaat	2	2	1	1	1	0
Totals	9	6	1	1	1	3

White Sox	IP	H	R	ER	BB	SO
Kravec L(9–10)	5.1	7	7	7	5	3
Proly	0	2	1	1	0	0
Howard	1.2	1	1	1	2	0
Farmer	2	2	0	0	1	2
Totals	9	12	9	9	8	5

DP—New York 2; Chicago 3. 2B—New York Stanley. HR—New York Jackson (9), Piniella (10), Narron (2). HBP—Chicago May, Washington. LOB—New York 7; Chicago 6. Attendance: 21,109.

Collins Does It All with Pair of Homers

A one-man gang named Joe Collins led the Yankees to a 2–1, 10-inning victory over the Cleveland Indians at Yankee Stadium.

Collins hit a one-out walk-off home run in the bottom of the 10th inning to make a winner of Tommy Byrne, who pitched all 10 innings.

The Yankees first baseman, who spent his entire 10-year career in pinstripes, homered in the first inning to tie the game at one. Cleveland had taken a 1–0 lead in the top of the inning on a Bobby Avila sacrifice fly, but that was all they would get against the lefty Byrne.

Early Wynn matched Byrne zero for zero until the 10th. Jerry Coleman, who started at second base because Gil McDougald was hit by a line drive in batting practice, flied out to start the 10th.

Collins, who had good swings against Wynn all game long, ended the game with a shot into the lower right-field stands.

The Indians had a golden opportunity to break the deadlock in the seventh inning when they loaded the bases with one out, but Wynn, known as a good hitter, ended the threat by bouncing into a double play. —⁓—

Indians	AB	R	H	RBI
Smith rf	4	1	2	0
Avila 2b	2	0	0	1
Wertz 1b	4	0	0	0
Fain 1b	0	0	0	0
Rosen 3b	3	0	0	0
Doby cf	4	0	1	0
Evers lf	4	0	0	0
Strickland ss	4	0	1	0
Hegan c	3	0	3	0
Wynn p	3	0	0	0
Totals	31	1	7	1

Yankees	AB	R	H	RBI
J. Coleman 2b	5	0	0	0
Collins 1b	4	2	3	2
Mantle cf	4	0	1	0
Berra c	4	0	2	0
Noren lf	4	0	0	0
Bauer rf	4	0	2	0
Byrne p	4	0	1	0
Carey 3b	4	0	0	0
Hunter ss	4	0	0	0
Totals	37	2	9	2

CLE	1	0	0	0	0	0	0	0	0	-	1	7	0
NY	1	0	0	0	0	0	0	0	1	-	2	9	0

Indians	IP	H	R	ER	BB	SO
Wynn L(13–6)	9.1	9	2	2	1	5

Yankees	IP	H	R	ER	BB	SO
Byrne W(10–2)	10	7	1	1	4	5

DP—New York 2. 2B—Cleveland Smith; New York Bauer 2, Mantle. 3B—Cleveland Smith. HR—New York Collins 2 (8,9). SH—Cleveland Wynn, Avila 2. SF—Cleveland Avila. LOB—Cleveland 8; New York 8. Attendance: 43,124.

Rodriguez Becomes the Youngest to 500 HRs

Royals	AB	R	H	RBI
DeJesus cf	4	2	2	3
German ph,lf	1	0	0	0
Grudzielanek 2b	4	1	1	0
Smith 2b	1	0	0	0
Teahen rf	4	2	3	1
Butler dh	4	1	2	1
Gload 1b	4	0	3	3
Gordon 3b	5	0	0	0
Pena ss	5	0	0	0
Gathright lf,cf	3	2	2	0
LaRue c	4	0	0	0
Totals	39	8	13	8

Yankees	AB	R	H	RBI
Damon dh	6	0	0	0
Jeter ss	5	2	3	0
Cairo ss	1	0	0	0
Abreu rf	5	4	3	2
Rodriguez 3b	4	3	3	3
Duncan 1b	1	0	0	0
Matsui lf	4	2	3	2
Posada c	3	2	0	0
Molina c	0	0	0	0
Cano 2b	5	2	4	3
Betemit 1b	4	1	3	3
Phillips 1b,3b	1	0	1	1
Cabrera cf	5	0	1	2
Totals	44	16	21	16

KC	0 0 2	0 4 0	1 0 1	-	8	13	0
NY	4 0 1	1 1 4	5 0 X	-	16	21	1

Royals	IP	H	R	ER	BB	SO
Davies	3	6	5	5	3	2
Bale L(0–1)	1.2	5	2	2	0	1
Peralta	1	2	3	3	1	0
Riske	0.1	2	1	1	0	1
Greinke	0	4	5	5	1	0
Gobble	1	2	0	0	0	1
Soria	1	0	0	0	0	0
Totals	8	21	16	16	5	5

Yankees	IP	H	R	ER	BB	SO
Hughes	4.2	7	6	6	2	5
Myers W(3–0)	0.1	1	0	0	0	1
Bruney	1	0	0	0	0	3
Farnsworth	1	1	1	1	0	1
Vizcaino	1	1	0	0	0	3
Villone	1	3	1	1	0	0
Totals	9	13	8	8	3	13

E—New York Rodriguez. DP—Kansas City 1; New York 1. 2B—Kansas City Gathright, Butler; New York Matsui, Cano, Cabrera, Jeter, Phillips. 3B—New York Cano. HR—Kansas City DeJesus (6); New York Rodriguez (36), Abreu (11). SF—Kansas City Gload. LOB—Kansas City 8; New York 9. SB—Kansas City Teahen; New York Rodriguez. Attendance: 54,056.

It took 11 days and a 3-for-29 slump before Alex Rodriguez stepped into the record books.

Rodriguez blasted a three-run homer in the bottom of the first inning to become the 22nd player and the youngest in major league history to reach 500 home runs as the Yankees pounded the Kansas City Royals 16–8.

The historic blow came off Royals right-hander Kyle Davies.

With runners at first and second base and one out, Rodriguez hit the first pitch from Davies just inside the left-field foul pole to reach the coveted milestone.

Rodriguez, who won his third American League Most Valuable Player award that season, stood at home plate for a moment before throwing his hands in the air as the ball landed in the stands for his first homer since July 25. He exchanged high-fives with teammates, who gathered in front of the Yankees' dugout, while the fans gave him a standing ovation.

"That felt really good off my bat today," Rodriguez said in an interview with the YES Network. "I didn't know if it would stay fair or foul. I was so relieved it stayed fair. I acted like a goofball running around the bases but I guess you only do 500 once."

At age 32 plus eight days, A-Rod surpassed Hall of Fame first baseman Jimmie Foxx as the youngest to reach the 500 home-run mark, and he became the third player to reach the coveted milestone as a Yankee.

When asked about how many homers he thought he'd end his career with, Rodriguez said, "When I was 24, I never thought about 500, and I'm not going to think about what my destination is."

"His prime years are ahead of him, basically,"

Yankees manager Joe Torre said. "This is a stop off for him. It's not a destination."

Rodriguez was pleased to have achieved the milestone in front of the home crowd at Yankee Stadium.

"The energy of the fans just put it in perspective a little bit," Rodriguez said. "It seemed like they cared more about it than I did. For me, I wanted to do it at home. I knew it would come at some point this year, but with two days remaining before we go on the road, I wanted to make sure we did it at home."

A-Rod admitted that, after hitting his last home run on July 25, he was trying to hit No. 500 but kept coming up empty.

"I've conceded the fact that you can't will yourself to hit a home run. I tried hard for about five days," Rodriguez said.

Finally, the moment had arrived.

When the ball was hit, Torre told Don Zimmer in the Yankees' dugout, "That's it," but A-Rod was not so sure.

"I hadn't hit one in so long, I didn't know if it was going to be foul or fair," Rodriguez said. "I definitely thought, because I've been hooking the ball a little bit, where that ball started. Last week, that ball probably would have hooked foul about 20 feet." —∾—

Ruffing's Complete Game Gets Boost from Homer

It took a mere one hour and 37 minutes for the Yankees to defeat the Cleveland Indians 6–1 at Yankee Stadium.

Red Ruffing was the star of this rapidly moving contest.

Not only did the Yankees right-hander pitch a complete game, but he homered and was actually given an intentional walk.

In the fifth inning, Ruffing homered off Indians pitcher Harry Eisenstat for a 1–0 lead.

Charles Herbert "Red" Ruffing was one of the best hitting pitchers of all time. During a 22-year major league career, Ruffing had a lifetime batting average of .269. The Hall of Famer had 98 doubles, 13 triples, 36 home runs, and 273 RBIs.

> ## At a Glance
>
> **WP:** Ruffing (15–4)
>
> **HR:** DiMaggio (12), Ruffing (1)
>
> **Key stats:** Ruffing complete game, HR

The Indians tied the game in the sixth inning. Yankees catcher Bill Dickey dropped a throw from George Selkirk that allowed Bruce Campbell to score the tying run.

The Yankees scored five times in the seventh inning to put this one away.

With one out, Babe Dahlgren doubled. Ruffing, who had a homer and a single in the game already, was intentionally walked, and the strategy almost worked when Frank Crosetti forced Ruffing at second for the second out.

The victory was Ruffing's 169th as a Yankee, and he passed Bob Shawkey to become the winningest Yankees pitcher in history. He would run his total to 231, and remains, more than 70 years later, the winningest right-hander in franchise history. Only southpaw Whitey Ford, with 236, has surpassed his Yankee total. Ford passed Ruffing in 1965. —〰—

P Red Ruffing

Charles "Red" Ruffing played 15 seasons in pinstripes and was the team's winningest pitcher, with 231 wins, until Whitey Ford surpassed him in 1965.

Ruffing won 20 or more games four years in a row from 1936–1939 and appeared in seven World Series, where he posted a 7–2 record with a 2.63 ERA.

In 1932, Ruffing became the first pitcher to throw a complete game 1–0 shutout and hit a home run when he beat the Washington Senators in 10 innings.

Ruffing was an accomplished hitter who smacked 36 career home runs and had a .269 lifetime average.

The 6-foot-1 right-hander was elected to the Baseball Hall of Fame in 1967.

'That Was for You, Thurman'

In what went down as one of the most emotional wins in their history, the Yankees rallied to beat the Baltimore Orioles 5–4 on the day they buried Thurman Munson.

Four days earlier, Munson was killed when his private twin-engine jet crashed short of the runway at Akron-Canton airport in Ohio.

Bobby Murcer, who with Lou Piniella eulogized the fallen Yankee captain, drove in all five runs, including the game-winning two-run single in the bottom of the ninth inning.

On the flight back following the funeral, manager Billy Martin told Murcer to go home and skip the game. He knew he was emotionally drained.

"I kinda feel like I need to play tonight," he told his manager.

So Martin put him in the lineup.

It was a surreal day for the entire Yankees organization.

Most of the team and the executives flew to Canton at about 8 a.m. on Monday. Murcer and Piniella, along with their wives, flew on Sunday night to be with Munson's widow, Diana, and the family.

About 500 people attended the funeral service at the Canton Civic Center, while hundreds more lined up outside along the five-mile route to the Sunset Hills Cemetery where Munson was buried.

Immediately after the funeral, the Yankees flew back to New York to play a game that most really did not want to play.

Sleep was at a premium for most of the Yankees so they tried to rest up at the stadium. Luis Tiant slept on the floor of the darkened trainer's room. Willie Randolph slept on a table, a towel draped over his face. Piniella slept on another table.

Yankees owner George Steinbrenner walked

Orioles	AB	R	H	RBI
Bumbry cf	4	0	1	0
Garcia ss	4	1	0	0
Belanger ss	0	0	0	0
Singleton rf	4	1	1	2
Murray 1b	4	0	2	0
DeCinces 3b	4	0	0	0
May dh	4	2	2	1
Ayala lf	3	0	2	0
Lowenstein pr-lf	0	0	0	0
Dauer 2b	2	0	0	1
Skaggs c	3	0	1	0
Totals	32	4	9	4

Yankees	AB	R	H	RBI
Randolph 2b	4	2	2	0
Murcer lf	5	1	2	5
Chambliss 1b	4	0	1	0
Jackson rf	2	0	0	0
Nettles 3b	3	0	1	0
Spencer dh	3	0	0	0
Piniella ph-dh	1	0	0	0
Brown cf	3	0	1	0
Randle ph-cf	1	0	0	0
Gulden c	3	0	1	0
White ph	1	0	0	0
Narron c	0	0	0	0
Dent ss	2	2	0	0
Totals	32	5	8	5

BAL	0	1	0	0	1	2	0	0	0	- 4	9	2
NY	0	0	0	0	0	0	3	0	2	- 5	8	0

Orioles	IP	H	R	ER	BB	SO
D. Martinez	6.2	7	3	3	4	5
T. Martinez L(6–2)	1.1	1	2	1	1	2
Totals	8	8	5	4	5	7

Yankees	IP	H	R	ER	BB	SO
Guidry W(10–7)	9	9	4	4	0	9

E—Baltimore 2. DP—New York. 2B—Baltimore, May, Ayala; New York, Brown, Randolph. HR—Baltimore, May (16), Singleton (28); New York, Murcer (1). SH—New York, Randolph. SF—Baltimore, Dauer. LOB—Baltimore 2; New York 9. SB—New York, Randolph. Attendance—36,314.

into the clubhouse about 90 minutes before the game to try to pick up his emotionally drained team. After a brief stop in the trainer's room, the owner admitted, "It's been a long day."

Murcer firmly believed that Thurman would've wanted the team to play.

"If he was sitting here and I said I couldn't play, he'd say, 'You're crazy,'" Murcer said. "I just know that's what he would've wanted me to do."

The Yankees began the game a little sluggish as they got behind Dennis Martinez and the Orioles 4–0.

Lee May and Ken Singleton home runs off Ron Guidry provided Baltimore with the lead, but the Yankees began their comeback in the seventh inning.

Bucky Dent drew a two-out walk, and Randolph followed with a double, putting runners on second and third.

Murcer lined Martinez's fastball into the right-field stands for a three-run homer, his first since he rejoined the club on June 26, and suddenly it was 4–3.

Murcer said, "It's the first two-out base hit I've had with men in scoring position in I don't know how long."

It was Murcer's first Yankee home run since September 22, 1974, and his first at Yankee Stadium since September 28, 1973.

Orioles closer Tippy Martinez replaced Dennis Martinez in the seventh and held the lead until the ninth inning.

> **C Thurman Munson**
>
> The second Captain in the history of the New York Yankees was Thurman Munson.
>
> In 1970, Munson batted .302 with six home runs and 53 runs batted in and was named the American League Rookie of the Year.
>
> Munson was one of the best clutch hitters who ever donned the pinstripes. In 1976, he was named the American League's Most Valuable Player.
>
> In the 1976 World Series loss to Cincinnati, Munson was nearly unstoppable as he batted an incredible .529 with nine hits in 17 at-bats. The 5-foot-11 backstop was a lifetime .373 hitter in World Series play.
>
> Munson died in a plane crash on August 2nd, 1979.

In the ninth, something told Martin to let Murcer hit against the tough lefthander Tippy Martinez, a former Yankee. Tippy Martinez was emotionally drained as well; he had loved Thurman. In fact, after going ahead 0–2 on two breaking pitches to Murcer, Martinez had a flashback to a time when Munson had walked to the mound and told him to give Ron LeFlore a fastball.

Four days after Yankees captain Thurman Munson was killed in an airplane crash, the team carried on with a victory over the Baltimore Orioles. Yankees third baseman Graig Nettles bows his head in memory of his fallen teammate.

"Give him a chance to keep his [30-game] hit streak going," Munson said.

At once, Tippy Martinez decided he owed Murcer a straight pitch. Not a batting practice pitch, not a meatball, but a major league fastball on the outside corner of the plate.

"I had to get it over and he had to hit it," Tippy said. "But I wanted to give him at least one pitch he could handle."

Murcer swung and lined the game-winning walk-off hit down the left-field line, and the Yankees came from behind to win 5–4 as bedlam erupted in the stands and on the field. Martinez, walking to the Orioles' dugout, glanced at the heavens and said to himself, "That was for you, Thurman."

Somehow, someway, Murcer found the energy to leap into the air after he reached first base.

"Everybody was so tired," the Yankees icon said after the game. "I think we were playing on the spirit of Thurman. I think that's what carried us through the game. I know it did me."

When the game was over, Murcer and Piniella exchanged a hug in the dugout.

It may have been the only victory in Yankees history in which all the fans left with tears in their eyes. —⁓—

A-Rod's Blast in 15th Inning Another One for the History Books

Alex Rodriguez hit a two-run walk-off home run in the bottom of the 15th inning to give the Yankees a 2–0 victory over the Red Sox in another epic battle between the rivals at Yankee Stadium.

"That's the longest game that I've ever been involved in," Rodriguez said after the five-hour, 33-minute marathon was over.

This game started out as pitchers' duel between Boston's Josh Beckett and the Yankees' A. J. Burnett.

Both were dealing. Beckett threw seven scoreless frames while Burnett was just a little better with 7 2/3 innings of shutout ball.

The Yankees right-hander allowed a bloop hit to Boston's Jacoby Ellsbury in the first inning, but no hits thereafter. Burnett walked six and was lifted in the eighth inning to a standing ovation from the sellout crowd of 48,262.

"It was the loudest thing I ever heard," Burnett said. "It gave me goose bumps."

Yankees manager Joe Girardi was just as appreciative as the fans.

"It's important, because it's like a playoff game," Girardi said. "There's going to be games like that down the stretch here that we're playing. They're going to be tight ballgames and A. J. came up huge for us. To match zeroes with their guy, it's incredible. Both of those guys pitched great."

Both teams had chances in the extra innings but both bullpens were up to the task.

With two on and two out in the ninth inning, Red Sox pitcher Daniel Bard struck out Jorge Posada.

Red Sox	AB	R	H	RBI
Ellsbury cf	5	0	2	0
Pedroia 2b	4	0	0	0
Martinez 1b	6	0	0	0
Youkilis 3b	4	0	1	0
Ortiz dh	6	0	1	0
Drew rf	5	0	0	0
Varitek c	6	0	0	0
Reddick lf	6	0	0	0
Green ss	1	0	0	0
Kotchman ph	1	0	0	0
Woodward ss	2	0	0	0
Totals	46	0	4	0

Yankees	AB	R	H	RBI
Jeter ss	7	1	1	0
Damon lf	7	0	0	0
Teixeira 1b	6	0	0	0
Rodriguez 3b	7	1	2	2
Matsui dh	5	0	2	0
Posada c	5	0	2	0
Pena pr	0	0	0	0
Molina c	0	0	0	0
Cano 2b	6	0	2	0
Swisher rf	2	0	0	0
Hairston rf	0	0	0	0
Hinske ph,rf	1	0	0	0
Cabrera cf	5	0	0	0
Totals	51	2	9	2

```
BOS 000000000000000 - 0 4 0
NY  000000000000002 - 2 9 1
```

Red Sox	IP	H	R	ER	BB	SO
Beckett	7	4	0	0	2	7
Okajima	1.1	0	0	0	0	1
Bard	0.2	1	0	0	1	2
Ramirez	0.2	0	0	0	1	0
Papelbon	1.1	0	0	0	0	2
Delcarmen	1	0	0	0	2	0
Saito	1	0	0	0	1	0
Tazawa L(0–1)	1.2	4	2	2	0	2
Totals	14.2	9	2	2	7	14

Yankees	IP	H	R	ER	BB	SO
Burnett	7.2	1	0	0	6	6
Hughes	0.1	0	0	0	0	0
Rivera	1	1	0	0	0	2
Aceves	3	1	0	0	1	0
Bruney	2	1	0	0	1	2
Coke W(3–3)	1	0	0	0	0	1
Totals	15	4	0	0	8	14

E—New York, Posada. DP—Boston 2; New York 2. 2B—New York, Cano. HR—New York, Rodriguez (20). LOB—Boston 10; New York 12. SB—Boston, Ellsbury 2; New York, Rodriguez. Attendance—48,262.

The Red Sox had two on and two out in the top of the 10th, but Alfredo Aceves got Dustin Pedroia to fly out to left.

Derek Jeter got the winning rally started in the 15th against Boston's Junichi Tazawa with a single. After Johnny Damon failed on a sacrifice bunt attempt, Mark Teixeira struck out, leaving it up to Rodriguez.

The count was 2–1 when Tazawa hung a curveball, and A-Rod was all over it as he drove it over the left-field wall to end a stimulating regular season game.

"I was thinking little, maybe right-center and get the ball in the gap and probably win the game," A-Rod said afterward.

"I figured the game was never going to end," Jeter said.

Phil Coke got the win in relief, but it was the entire Yankees bullpen, which consisted of Phil Hughes, Mariano Rivera, Alfredo Aceves, and Brian Bruney, that was stellar in keeping the game scoreless.

"I don't know the last time I was this proud of our team," Bruney said. "It was definitely one of most exciting games I've been a part of. I could always use an outing like that. I think when you play the Red Sox it's a different level. I think everybody in park knew it would come down to one swing. Alex came through for us."

"It was a big game at the beginning, and it just kept getting bigger and bigger," Rodriguez said. "You don't want to play 15 innings and use up great pitching performances from both sides. We knew the game was very important, and it was good that we won."

According to the Elias Sports Bureau, Rodriguez's dramatic blast was the fifth game-ending home run in a scoreless game in the 15th inning or later.

It was also the 13th time in the history of their storied rivalry that the Yankees and Red Sox played 15 or more innings. The longest game between the two foes came back on August 29, 1967, when they played 20 innings in the second game of a doubleheader at Yankee Stadium. The Yankees beat Boston 4–3 in that game on Horace Clarke's walk-off RBI single.

In August 1978, the Red Sox beat the Yankees 7–5 in 17 innings in a game that had to be completed the day after it originally started because of an American League curfew. ⎯⁓⎯

Williams and Justice Need Just Two Swings to Shock Oakland

During the 1920s, the Yankees lineup was nicknamed "Murderers' Row" because it featured talented hitters such as Babe Ruth and Lou Gehrig. Those players never saw an ending like this one.

In the blink of an eye—or in baseball terms, two pitches—the Yankees stunned the Oakland A's with a 4–3 walk-off victory at Yankee Stadium.

Bernie Williams and David Justice hit back-to-back home runs in the bottom of the ninth inning on just two pitches from losing pitcher Jason Isringhausen to make a winner of Mariano Rivera.

The Yankees trailed 3–2 when Williams took the first pitch of the inning and drove it over the right-field wall for the tying blow.

Before Williams could finish receiving his accolades in the Yankee dugout, Justice ended the game with a bomb that landed in the center-field bleachers.

"That might've been the hardest he's hit a ball since he got here," manager Joe Torre said.

The Yankees acquired Justice from the Cleveland Indians in exchange for outfielder Ricky Ledee and pitchers Jake Westbrook and Zach Day in June of 2000.

"I've seen back-to-back home runs," Jeter said, "but not two pitches, bottom of the ninth, game over."

The A's took a 3–1 lead in the fifth inning off Yankees starter Roger Clemens on back-to-back home runs from Eric Chavez and Ramon Hernandez. Chavez's two-run shot turned into an inside-the-park home run when his drive bounced off the top of the center-field wall and eluded Williams.

Athletics	AB	R	H	RBI
Long cf	4	0	0	0
Velarde 2b	5	0	0	0
Jason Giambi 1b	3	0	1	0
Grieve lf	3	0	1	0
Christenson pr,lf	0	0	0	0
Stairs dh	3	0	0	0
Piatt ph,dh	2	0	0	0
Tejada ss	3	0	1	0
Jeremy Giambi rf	3	1	0	0
Chavez 3b	4	1	2	2
Hernandez c	4	1	2	1
Totals	34	3	7	3

Yankees	AB	R	H	RBI
Jeter ss	4	0	1	0
Posada c	4	0	0	0
O'Neill rf	3	1	0	0
Williams cf	4	1	1	1
Justice lf	4	1	2	2
Hill dh	3	0	1	0
Polonia pr,dh	0	0	0	0
Martinez 1b	2	0	0	0
Brosius 3b	2	1	0	0
Sojo 2b	2	0	1	0
Canseco ph	1	0	0	0
Vizcaino 2b	0	0	0	0
Totals	29	4	6	3

											R	H	E
OAK	0	0	0	3	0	0	0	0	-	3	7	1
NY	0	0	1	0	0	0	1	0	2	-	4	6	0

Athletics	IP	H	R	ER	BB	SO
Zito	6.1	3	2	1	2	4
Mecir	1.2	1	0	0	1	1
Isringhausen L(5–4)	0	2	2	2	0	0
Totals	8	6	4	3	3	5

Yankees	IP	H	R	ER	BB	SO
Clemens	7	5	3	3	4	4
Stanton	1	1	0	0	1	2
Rivera W(6–3)	1	1	0	0	2	1
Totals	9	7	3	3	7	7

E—Oakland Jason Giambi. DP—Oakland 2. 2B—Oakland Tejada; New York Hill. HR—Oakland Chavez (16), Hernandez (13); New York Williams (25), Justice (30). LOB—Oakland 11; New York 4. Attendance: 36,357.

The Yankees hadn't done much with A's left-hander Barry Zito until the seventh inning when Justice singled home their first run, and then they loaded the bases with one out. Former Yankee Jim Mecir relieved Zito and promptly struck out Scott Brosius for the second out.

In a moment of drama that only baseball can provide, Jose Canseco, in his first appearance since he was claimed on waivers from Tampa Bay, was sent up to pinch-hit against his former mates, but he flied to right on a 2–1 pitch to end the threat.

"The adrenaline was definitely pumping," the former American League Most Valuable Player said. "I told myself to drive the ball straight-away. It [Mecir's pitch] got on me pretty good."

There was some controversy over the acquisition of Canseco. The Yankees had already picked up Glenallen Hill as an extra right-handed bat. Torre said he was "surprised" by the waiver acquisition of Canseco but Yankees owner George Steinbrenner told the press that he "supported the decision of general manager Brian Cashman 100 percent."

Canseco was impressed with his new teammates, even though the Yankees told him he was claimed to block a rival from acquiring his services.

"Isringhausen came in throwing 95 miles an hour, all of a sudden, one pitch—out. Next pitch—out," Canseco said. "It was like, it's over, that quick. It was a pretty awesome ending." —∞—

Victory Keeps Yankees Inching Closer to Top of American League East

It had been nearly eight years since the Bombers last won the American League pennant, but a crowd of 45,145, the largest of the season to that point, saw a nail-biter as the Yankees nipped the American League East–leading Detroit Tigers 1–0.

The win moved the Yankees to within two games of first place, the closest the club had been to the top this late in the season since 1964.

Yankee right-hander Steve Kline dueled Detroit's Joe Coleman as both pitchers lived up to the match-up. Kline tossed eight scoreless innings and lowered his league-leading ERA to 1.69, while Coleman gave up a run on five hits in seven innings of work.

The Yankees scored the lone run of the game in the fourth inning. Bobby Murcer led off with a double, and with two outs, Johnny Callison brought him home with an infield single for an RBI.

In the top of the eighth inning, Detroit had a chance to score when the Tigers had two on and two out and a full count on Tigers third baseman and future Yankee Aurelio Rodriguez. With the runners on the move, Rodriguez slapped a grounder to Gene Michael, who flipped the ball to second baseman Horace Clarke with the hope of ending the inning. John Knox, however, beat the throw at second. Alertly, Clarke fired to Ron Blomberg at first base, and they got Rodriguez by a step.

Clarke said, "When the ball was hit, I was going over to second, not even expecting the ball to be thrown in my direction, but when he did throw it, I just reacted as quickly as possible."

Sparky Lyle pitched the ninth and walked a tightrope.

Tigers	AB	R	H	RBI
McAuliffe 2b	4	0	0	0
Rodriguez 3b	4	0	0	0
G. Brown lf	4	0	1	0
Taylor pr	0	0	0	0
Cash 1b	3	0	1	0
Sims c	2	0	0	0
Freehan ph	1	0	1	0
Northrup cf	4	0	0	0
Horton rf	3	0	0	0
Brinkman ss	3	0	1	0
I. Brown ph	1	0	0	0
Coleman p	2	0	0	0
Haller ph	1	0	0	0
Totals	32	0	5	0

Yankees	AB	R	H	RBI
Clarke 2b	3	0	0	0
Munson c	4	0	0	0
Murcer cf	3	1	2	0
White lf	4	0	0	0
Blomberg 1b	3	0	0	0
Callison rf	3	0	2	1
Swoboda rf	0	0	0	0
Sanchez 3b	3	0	1	0
Michael ss	3	0	0	0
Kline p	3	0	0	0
Totals	29	1	5	1

DET 0 0 0 0 0 0 0 0 0 - 0 5 0
NY 0 0 0 1 0 0 0 0 X - 1 5 1

Tigers	IP	H	R	ER	BB	SO
Coleman L(12–11)	7	5	1	1	1	6
Scherman	1	0	0	0	1	0
Totals	8	5	1	1	2	6

Yankees	IP	H	R	ER	BB	SO
Kline W(13–4)	8	3	0	0	0	3
Lyle SV(26)	1	2	0	0	1	2
Totals	9	5	0	0	1	5

E—New York Sanchez. DP—New York 1. 2B—Detroit G. Brown; New York Murcer 2. HBP—Detroit Sims. LOB—Detroit 8; New York 6. SB—New York Clarke. Attendance: 40,145.

Gates Brown led off the inning with a double and was replaced by pinch-runner Tony Taylor. Lyle struck out Norm Cash without the runner advancing, but pinch-hitter Bill Freehan hit an infield single to put runners on first and second with one out.

Jim Northrup grounded out as the runners moved up. Willie Horton was walked intentionally, loading the bases. Detroit and future Yankees manager Billy Martin sent up Ike Brown to bat for light-hitting shortstop and future Yankee Ed Brinkman.

Brown took ball one, and then Lyle fired a strike.

The Yankees closer got a swing and a miss for strike two and then finished off Brown as the pinch-hitter swung through a patented Lyle slider to end the game as the crowd let out a thunderous roar.

The renewed excitement about the Yankees brought out a large walk-up crowd to the stadium ticket booths. According to some reports, fans bought tickets as late as the seventh inning to watch the game live.

Traffic was so congested around the area of Yankee Stadium that many fans, stuck in cars that were not moving, got out of their cars on the Major Deegan Expressway and walked the rest of the way to the ballpark. —∞—

Torrez Brilliant in Two-Hitter against Former Team

On April 27, the Yankees acquired right-handed pitcher Mike Torrez from the Oakland A's in exchange for three players, including pitcher Dock Ellis, who was a key component of the team that won the American League pennant in 1976.

Torrez pitched his best game as a Yankee when he two-hit his former team in a 3–0 victory at Yankee Stadium.

The 30 year old from Topeka, Kansas, faced only 29 batters and did not allow a hit until Manny Sanguillen broke up the no-hit bid with a two-out single in the fifth inning.

The Yankees scored two in the first inning and one in the fourth thanks to three errors from A's second baseman Marty Perez, who was one of the three players sent to Oakland to acquire Torrez.

It was a hot night in the Bronx, but Torrez was up to the task.

"I felt sort of lazy out in the bullpen warming up," the 6-foot-5 hurler said. "I knew when the game started I would have to kick myself a little bit. It was a hot, humid day."

Oakland pinch-hitter Tim Hosley recorded the only other hit when he singled with one out in the ninth inning.

Athletics	AB	R	H	RBI
Scott 3b	3	0	0	0
Perez 2b	4	0	0	0
Tyrone rf	3	0	0	0
Page lf	3	0	0	0
Tabb 1b	3	0	0	0
Sanguillen c	3	0	1	0
Mallory dh	3	0	0	0
Murray cf	2	0	0	0
Crawford ph	1	0	0	0
Picciolo ss	2	0	0	0
Hosley ph	1	0	0	0
Alexander pr	0	0	0	0
Totals	28	0	2	0

Yankees	AB	R	H	RBI
Randolph 2b	3	1	0	1
Nettles 3b	3	0	1	0
Stanley 3b	1	0	0	0
Munson c	4	0	0	0
Jackson rf	4	1	1	1
Piniella lf	3	0	1	0
Chambliss 1b	3	1	2	1
White dh	3	0	2	0
Blair cf	3	0	0	0
Dent ss	3	0	0	0
Totals	30	3	7	3

```
OAK  0 0 0 0 0 0 0 0 0 - 0 2 4
NY   2 0 0 1 0 0 0 0 X - 3 7 0
```

Athletics	IP	H	R	ER	BB	SO
Torrealba L(3–4)	8	7	3	0	1	2

Yankees	IP	H	R	ER	BB	SO
Torrez W(12–10)	9	2	0	0	0	4

E—Oakland Perez 3, Sanguillen. DP—Oakland 1; New York 1. 2B—New York Chambliss, White. SF—New York Randolph. HBP—Oakland Scott. LOB—Oakland 2; New York 5. SB—New York Randolph, Jackson. Attendance: 16,804.

Stottlemyre's Debut Includes Patented Blast from Mantle

This game may have provided the stimulus for the Yankees to begin their push for the American League pennant.

Mel Stottlemyre went the distance in his major league debut and Mickey Mantle hit one of his patented mammoth home runs as the Yankees walloped the Chicago White Sox 7–3 at Yankee Stadium.

The 22-year-old right-hander was knocking 'em dead with the Yankees' AAA farm team at Richmond of the International League, posting a 13–3 record with a 1.42 ERA.

Going into the game, the Yankees trailed the first-place Baltimore Orioles by 3½ games and were dragging through the dog days of August.

Stottlemyre allowed three runs, two earned, on seven hits with one walk and one strikeout and was the beneficiary of some Yankee power.

The Yankees hit four home runs in the game, two by Mantle. But the first one was noteworthy. It came in the fourth inning off White Sox right-hander Ray Herbert. Mantle, the switch-hitting future Hall of Famer, connected on a 3–1 pitch for a long drive that carried over the head of Chicago center fielder Gene Stephens and landed approximately 15 rows into the center-field bleachers. The four-bagger was estimated to have traveled approximately 502 feet.

Mantle's second homer was hit right-handed off White Sox lefty Frank Baumann, a shot that went into the right-field grandstand.

Roger Maris and Clete Boyer added long balls for the Yankees, who were buoyed by the debut of the young pitcher.

Stottlemyre already showed in the minors that he could hit, and he didn't skip a beat when he

White Sox	AB	R	H	RBI
Hershberger rf	4	1	0	0
Buford 2b	4	0	0	0
Robinson lf	4	0	1	0
Ward 3b	4	2	2	0
Skowron 1b	4	0	1	1
Stephens cf	4	0	0	0
Hansen ss	4	0	1	1
Martin c	4	0	1	0
Herbert p	2	0	0	0
Peters ph	1	0	0	0
Weis ph	1	0	1	0
Totals	36	3	7	2

Yankees	AB	R	H	RBI
Kubek ss	4	0	0	0
Richardson 2b	4	1	3	0
Maris rf	4	1	1	2
Mantle cf	4	3	3	2
Lopez lf	0	0	0	0
Tresh lf,cf	4	1	2	0
Pepitone 1b	4	0	1	0
Blanchard c	3	0	0	1
Boyer 3b	4	1	1	1
Stottlemyre p	3	0	1	0
Totals	34	7	12	6

											R	H	E
CHI	0	0	1	1	0	0	0	1	0	-	3	7	1
NY	0	0	1	1	0	3	0	2	X	-	7	12	2

White Sox	IP	H	R	ER	BB	SO
Herbert L(5–4)	5	6	3	3	0	0
Mossi	0.1	3	2	1	0	0
Fisher	0.2	0	0	0	0	2
Baumann	2	3	2	2	0	0
Totals	8	12	7	6	0	2

Yankees	IP	H	R	ER	BB	SO
Stottlemyre W(1–0)	9	7	3	2	1	1

E—Chicago Buford; New York Kubek, Pepitone. DP—Chicago 2. 2B—Chicago Ward; New York Richardson, Tresh. 3B—Chicago Ward. HR—New York Boyer (8), Mantle 2 (24,25), Maris (18). SF—New York Blanchard. LOB—Chicago 7; New York 4. SB—Chicago Hershberger. Attendance: 16,945.

singled in his first major league at-bat. Stottlemyre, the 1964 *Sporting News* Minor League Player of the Year, threw 116 pitches in his initial big-league appearance. He got 19 outs on grounders, but said his curveball was not especially sharp.

Stottlemyre made 11 more starts and helped lead the Yankees to the pennant with a 9–3 record and an outstanding 2.06 ERA.

Stottlemyre won Game 2 of the World Series vs. the St. Louis Cardinals, but he came up short on two days' rest in Game 7 against Hall of Famer Bob Gibson. He never saw another postseason game for the rest of his career.

Stottlemyre pitched his entire 11-year career with the Yankees. He won 20 games three times, 40 by shutout, and lost 20 in 1966 despite posting a 3.80 ERA. The right-hander provided one of the few beacons of light during a down period of Yankees history, when he won 164 games.

In 1974, Stottlemyre endured a rotator cuff problem with his right shoulder, and it eventually ended his playing career. Stottlemyre went on to be a successful pitching coach, first with the New York Mets, where he won a World Series title in 1986, and then back with the Yankees, where he garnered four more rings. ⟶

Did You Know?

The original Yankee Stadium hosted four All-Star Games, including the 2008 game that lasted a record-tying 15 innings and set a record for the longest game by time (4 hours, 50 minutes). The National and American Leagues split the four Stadium games.

Ruffing Uses His Arm, Bat to Stop Senators in 10 Innings

Red Ruffing was literally a one-man gang as he beat the Senators with his arm and bat in a 10-inning 1–0 win at Washington's Griffith Stadium.

The future Hall of Famer hit a solo home run with two out in the top of the 10th inning off Senators losing pitcher Alphonse Thomas for the only run of the contest.

Ruffing was brilliant as he struck out 12 and allowed only three hits in going the distance for one of his 45 career shutouts.

The game had an interesting side note because it was the first meeting

The Yankees pitching staff posed before a game on May 17, 1932. (Left) Johnny Allen, George Pipgras, Red Ruffing, and Lefty Gomez proved to be a formidable foursome. On August 13, Ruffing put on quite a show against Washington. He pitched a three-hitter with 12 strikeouts in 10 innings. His solo homer with two out in the top of the 10th inning proved to be the difference.

At a Glance

WP: Ruffing (14–5)

HR: Ruffing (2)

Key stats: Ruffing shutout in 10 IP, 12 Ks, 2 BBs; Ruffing HR

between the teams since an ugly incident back in July, when Yankees catcher Bill Dickey broke the jaw of Senators outfielder Carl Reynolds.

Dickey received a 30-day suspension and a $1,000 fine for his aggression. Reynolds entered the game as a pinch-hitter in the bottom of the 10th inning and received a tremendous ovation. Dickey was booed vociferously by the reported crowd of approximately 10,000 fans each time he came to the plate.

Reynolds nearly put the Senators in position to tie the game when he lined a shot to right-center field. Yankees center fielder Earle Combs made a leaping grab to rob Reynolds of what would have been at least a triple and maybe an inside-the-park home run to help preserve the win, as Ruffing fanned David Harris for his 12th strikeout to end the game.

Washington had a chance to end the game in the ninth inning. Sam Rice led off with a single to center. After Buddy Myer fouled out, Heinie Manush drove a ball to the scoreboard in right field, where Babe Ruth hauled it in for the second out. Joe Cronin singled to send Rice to third base, but Ruffing fanned Senators first baseman Joe Kuhel for his 10th strikeout to end the threat.

The 32-year-old Washington pitcher allowed seven hits, three to Ruffing and two to third baseman Joe Sewell, as he became the first pitcher to shut out the Yankees for nine innings that season.

Tommy Thomas faced a Yankees batting order that featured Ruth, Lou Gehrig,

C Bill Dickey

Bill Dickey was a great catcher who was noted for his ability to handle pitchers and his throwing arm, but he was a gifted offensive player as well.

In 1936, the Hall of Famer recorded the highest single season batting average for a backstop when he hit .362. (Dodgers catcher Mike Piazza tied that mark in 1997)

Dickey's competitiveness was never more evident than in 1932 when he broke the jaw of Carl Reynolds with one punch after the man collided with him at the plate. Dickey was suspended for 30 days and received a $1000 fine as a result of the incident.

Tony Lazzeri, and Dickey as the Nos. 3–6 hitters, but he held that imposing quartet to a combined 1-for-16 in the game.

The incident between Dickey and Reynolds occurred in the first game of a holiday doubleheader in Washington. In the bottom of the seventh inning, Reynolds was trying to score the tying run when he collided with Dickey at home plate.

The Yankees catcher had been involved in a similar play in Boston the day before the twin bill, so his reaction was to retaliate against Reynolds with a hard right to the jaw.

Reynolds did not go down, but he suffered a double fracture of his jaw as other players and the umpires got between the two combatants.

Both players were tossed and Dickey did not play in the second game. —⚊—

Did You Know?

Six Yankees have homered in their first World Series at-bats. Chick Fewster was the first in 1921. Other players who accomplished the feat included: George Selkirk in 1936; Elston Howard in 1955; Roger Maris in 1960; Jim Mason in 1976; and Bob Watson in 1981.

Branca Gets Lone Victory with Yankees after Giving Up 'Shot'

Everyone remembers Ralph Branca as the man who gave up the "Shot Heard 'Round the World," but the former Dodgers pitcher tossed six scoreless innings to pick up his first and only win for the Yankees in a 3–1 victory over the Boston Red Sox at Yankee Stadium.

The Mount Vernon, New York, native was pitching for his Yankees career. After being released by the Detroit Tigers in early July, the Yankees signed him as a free agent.

In his first outing, he pitched one scoreless inning. His second outing was less than stellar, as he walked six batters in four innings of work against the Baltimore Orioles, so this start against Boston was probably his last chance.

Branca got through the first inning unscathed. In the second inning, Yogi Berra made a terrific play on a foul pop that was near the visiting dugout on the third-base side. Berra caught the ball and tumbled into the Red Sox dugout but held on.

The Yankees scored twice in the fifth inning on an unearned run and an RBI single by Phil Rizzuto.

After Branca set the Red Sox down in order in the top of the sixth inning, Yankees manager Casey Stengel pinch-hit for his pitcher with one out and the bases loaded. The move paid off in a run as Bill Skowron made it 3–0 thanks to an RBI infield single.

Johnny Sain tossed the final three innings to save the win for Branca. —⁓—

Red Sox	AB	R	H	RBI
Piersall rf	5	0	1	0
Williams lf	2	0	0	0
Goodman 2b	4	0	1	0
Agganis 1b	4	0	1	0
Hatton 3b	4	0	0	0
Olson cf	3	0	0	0
Owen c	4	0	1	0
Consolo ss	4	1	1	0
Kemmerer p	2	0	0	0
Maxwell ph	1	0	1	1
White ph	1	0	0	0
Totals	34	1	6	1

Yankees	AB	R	H	RBI
Rizzuto ss	4	0	2	1
Collins 1b	4	0	1	0
Mantle cf	3	0	0	0
Berra c	4	0	1	0
Noren lf	4	1	1	0
Slaughter rf	3	0	0	0
Bauer rf	0	0	0	0
Carey 3b	2	1	1	0
Coleman 2b	3	0	0	0
Branca p	2	1	1	0
Skowron ph	1	0	1	1
Totals	30	3	8	2

BOS 0 0 0 0 0 0 1 0 0 - 1 6 1
NY 0 0 0 0 2 1 0 0 X - 3 8 1

Red Sox	IP	H	R	ER	BB	SO
Kemmerer L(1–3)	4.1	6	2	1	1	0
Parnell	1.2	2	1	1	3	0
Kinder	2	0	0	0	0	2
Totals	8	8	3	2	4	2

Yankees	IP	H	R	ER	BB	SO
Branca W(4–3)	6	4	0	0	3	5
Sain SV(24)	3	2	1	1	1	1
Totals	9	6	1	1	4	6

E—Boston Olson; New York Rizzuto. DP—Boston. 2B—Boston Consolo, Maxwell. SH—New York Slaughter. LOB—Boston 10; New York 8. SB—New York Carey 2, Noren. Attendance: 45,150.

Munson's Walk-Off Homer Ends It in 13th

Thurman Munson hit a two-out, two-run, walk-off home run in the bottom of the 13th inning to give the Yankees a thrilling 9–8 win over the Chicago White Sox at Shea Stadium.

Chicago's Dick Allen hit a towering home run to dead center field off Yankees closer Sparky Lyle for an 8–7 lead in the top of the inning.

White Sox pitcher Terry Forster entered the game in the eighth inning and was on the long end as he sat down the first two Yankees in the bottom of the 13th.

Bobby Murcer kept the game alive with a single to right. Munson worked the count full against Forster. With Murcer on the move, Munson took the full-count pitch and drove it over the left-field wall for an exciting come-from-behind win.

At a Glance

WP: Lyle (7–3)

HR: Munson (11)

Key stats: Lyle 3 1/3 IP in relief, 1 H; Munson 2-for-3, 2 RBIs; Dempsey 3-for-5, 2 RBIs; Murcer 3-for-7, RBI

The dramatic blow capped off quite a slugfest at Shea.

The teams combined for 17 runs and 33 hits. White Sox second baseman Jorge Orta led the way with five hits, including two home runs, while Murcer and starting catcher Rick Dempsey had three hits apiece for New York.

The Yankees had chances to end the game when they had a runner in scoring position in the ninth, 11th, and 12th innings, but could not cash in.

In the bottom of the 12th, Mel Stottlemyre, for the second time in his career, pinch ran for Bill Sudakis. It was a significant move because it marked the final appearance for the proud pitcher in a Yankees and major league uniform.

Stottlemyre pitched the final game of his career in relief on August 4. His shoulder problems had gotten so bad that the Yankees released him at the end of spring training in 1975. —⧥—

Nettles' Ninth-Inning Blast Lifts Yankees Past Rangers

Graig Nettles led off the ninth inning with a solo home run to lift the Yankees to a 2–1 win over the Texas Rangers at Yankee Stadium.

The Bombers held a precarious 1–0 lead thanks to Doyle Alexander, but the enigmatic right-hander walked Toby Harrah on a 3–2 pitch to start the ninth inning.

To the surprise of many, manager Billy Martin decided to stick with his pitcher after the base on balls.

The first pitch in the ninth inning was all Graig Nettles needed to see from Texas Rangers pitcher Tommy Boggs. Nettles took the first pitch deep for the game-winning solo home run on August 17, 1976. Nettles was known as a rangy third baseman who could also hit for power.

Rangers	AB	R	H	RBI
Clines lf	4	0	1	0
Harrah ss	3	1	0	0
Hargrove 1b	3	0	2	0
Burroughs rf	4	0	0	1
Moates pr,rf	0	0	0	0
Lahoud dh	4	0	0	0
Howell 3b	4	0	1	0
Randle 2b	4	0	0	0
Beniquez cf	3	0	1	0
Sundberg c	3	0	0	0
Totals	**32**	**1**	**5**	**1**

Yankees	AB	R	H	RBI
Rivers cf	4	0	0	0
White lf	4	0	0	0
Munson c	4	0	0	0
Chambliss 1b	4	0	2	0
C. May dh	2	0	0	0
Nettles 3b	4	1	1	1
Gamble rf	3	1	2	1
Randolph 2b	3	0	1	0
Stanley ss	3	0	1	0
Totals	**31**	**2**	**7**	**2**

TEX 0 0 0 0 0 0 0 0 1 - 1 5 0
NY 0 0 0 0 1 0 0 0 1 - 2 7 0

Rangers	IP	H	R	ER	BB	SO
Boggs L(0–3)	8	7	2	2	2	1

Yankees	IP	H	R	ER	BB	SO
Alexander W(8–8)	9	5	1	1	2	2

HR—New York Gamble (12), Nettles (19). LOB—Texas 6; New York 7. Attendance: 20,959.

"It depends on the hitters coming up," Martin said after the game. "You try to match up the pitcher with the hitters. He had pitched good enough to show me that they weren't hitting him well."

Mike Hargrove singled, putting runners at first and third with no one out. The Rangers tied the game on a force play at second base, with Harrah scoring from third on the play. From there, Alexander managed to keep the game tied.

Tommy Boggs, the Rangers' 20-year-old pitcher, was equal to the task of matching Alexander as he limited the Yankees to one run on six hits through eight innings.

Nettles jumped all over Boggs' first pitch and drove it to deep right field.

"When I hit it, I thought for sure it was gone," Nettles said, "but then I remembered the ball wasn't carrying too well in batting practice."

The ball carried right into the stands for a dramatic finish. —⁓—

Witt's Two-Hit Shutout Gives Yankees a Cushion

Mike Witt, who pitched a perfect game on the final day of the 1984 season, was a little less than perfect as he threw a complete game two-hit shutout in beating the Seattle Mariners 6–0 at Yankee Stadium.

The Yankees acquired Witt in a trade with the California Angels that had sent Dave Winfield to the West Coast back in May 1990.

Witt had been struggling with elbow problems but he got off to a good start against Seattle by setting the side down in order in the first inning.

"I had strike one on most everybody and went from there," Witt said.

Despite giving up a hit in the second inning, the right-hander faced the minimum 18 batters through six innings.

Jesse Barfield and Kevin Maas home runs powered the offense, but it was Witt's turn to shine.

The shutout was in jeopardy in the ninth inning as Seattle loaded the bases with one out, but Witt was up to the challenge as he retired Jeffrey Leonard on a fly to right and then got former Yankee Scott Bradley on a force out at second base to end the game. —⁓—

Mariners	AB	R	H	RBI
Reynolds 2b	3	0	0	0
Schaefer pr	0	0	0	0
Briley rf	3	0	0	0
Griffey Jr. cf	3	0	0	0
Davis 1b	3	0	2	0
Leonard lf	4	0	0	0
Bradley dh	4	0	0	0
E. Martinez 3b	2	0	0	0
Valle c	3	0	0	0
Vizquel ss	3	0	0	0
Totals	28	0	2	0

Yankees	AB	R	H	RBI
Kelly cf	5	0	1	0
Sax 2b	3	2	1	0
Azocar lf	3	1	1	0
Hall dh	3	1	1	0
Balboni ph,dh	0	0	0	0
Maas 1b	3	1	1	3
Nokes c	4	0	2	1
Barfield rf	2	1	1	2
Leyritz 3b	4	0	0	0
Espinoza ss	4	0	1	0
Totals	31	6	9	6

```
SEA  0 0 0 0 0 0 0 0 0 - 0 2 0
NY   0 0 1 3 0 1 1 0 X - 6 9 0
```

Mariners	IP	H	R	ER	BB	SO
Holman L(11–9)	5.2	7	5	5	1	4
Harris	1	1	1	1	1	1
Lovelace	0.1	0	0	0	3	1
Knackert	0.2	0	0	0	0	1
Schooler	0.1	1	0	0	0	0
Totals	8	9	6	6	5	7

Yankees	IP	H	R	ER	BB	SO
Witt W(2–5)	9	2	0	0	4	4

DP—Seattle 1; New York 1. HR—New York Barfield (17), Maas (14). SF—New York Barfield. HBP—Seattle Reynolds. LOB—Seattle 6; New York 7. Attendance: 30,532.

Mantle, Howard Chalk Up 15 RBIs, Set Career Marks

Mickey Mantle and Elston Howard combined for 15 RBIs as the Yankees plastered the Athletics at Kansas City's Municipal Stadium 21–7. Both had career highs in RBIs.

Mantle hit a grand slam and drove in seven, while Howard had four hits, including a pair of three-run homers, to go along with his eight RBIs.

Howard's first home run came in the top of the first inning off Kansas City's losing pitcher, Dan Pfister. It gave the Yankees a 4–0 lead.

The Yankees blew the game open in the fourth inning with five more runs, including Mantle's slam. The bases-clearing blow came off A's reliever Jerry Walker, who gave up nine runs in three innings of work. Mantle showed off his all-around game in the third inning when he singled and promptly stole second and third base.

The Athletics made their contribution to the slugfest with four home runs off Yankees winning pitcher Ralph Terry, who went on to win the 1962 World Series MVP Award. In the bottom of the seventh, the first three batters homered off the right-hander. Gino Cimoli, Wayne Causey, and Bill Bryan went deep in succession to tie an American League record. —⁓—

Yankees	AB	R	H	RBI
Tresh lf	5	3	3	2
Richardson 2b	5	1	1	0
Linz 2b	1	0	0	0
Maris rf	2	4	2	0
Blanchard rf	1	0	0	0
Mantle cf	4	3	3	7
Reed cf	2	1	1	0
Howard c	6	4	4	8
Kubek ss	6	1	2	0
Skowron 1b	6	2	2	4
Boyer 3b	6	1	2	0
Terry p	2	1	0	0
Totals	46	21	20	21

Athletics	AB	R	H	RBI
Tartabull cf	5	0	0	0
Charles 3b	4	0	0	0
Lumpe 2b	4	1	2	0
Siebern 1b	4	2	2	2
Jimenez lf	4	1	1	1
Cimoli rf	4	1	3	1
Causey ss	3	1	2	2
Bryan c	4	1	1	1
Johnson ph	1	0	0	0
Walker p	1	0	0	0
Williams p	1	0	0	0
Alusik 1b	1	0	0	0
Totals	36	7	11	7

NY	4	0	1	5	0	4	0	4	3	-	21	20	1
KC	0	1	0	0	0	2	3	1	0	-	7	11	0

Yankees	IP	H	R	ER	BB	SO
Terry W(18–10)	9	11	7	6	0	2

Athletics	IP	H	R	ER	BB	SO
Pfister L(3–10)	3	4	5	5	2	1
Walker	3	7	9	9	3	1
Williams	2	6	4	4	0	0
Archer	1	3	3	3	0	0
Totals	9	20	21	21	5	2

E—New York Mantle. DP—New York 1. 2B—New York Boyer, Mantle, Maris, Kubek. 3B—New York Richardson, Howard; Kansas City Cimoli, Siebern. HR—New York Howard 2 (13,14), Mantle (24), Skowron (19); Kansas City Siebern (17), Cimoli (8), Causey (4), Bryan (1). SH—New York Terry. SF—Kansas City Causey. HBP—New York Terry. LOB—New York 5; Kansas City 3. SB—New York Mantle 2, Boyer. Attendance: 29,274.

Griffey's Lone Hit Is the Only One That Matters

Ken Griffey was 2-for-22 in his career vs. Geoff Zahn when he came to bat with the game on the line.

The Yankees trailed 1–0 in the bottom of the ninth inning and had the tying and winning runs at second and third with two out.

Griffey, who had been held hitless in four previous at-bats, lashed Zahn's 0–1 pitch into right field for a two-run walk-off single that gave the Yankees a thrilling 2–1 win over the California Angels at Yankee Stadium.

"He had me off balance all day," Griffey said. "After 0-for-4, I was hoping that I was going to do something."

The winning hit capped off a tremendous pitching duel between Zahn and Yankees starter Dave Righetti.

The two matched zeros for eight innings, and then the Angels broke through for a run in the top of the ninth. Righetti allowed a leadoff triple to the Angels' Daryl Sconiers. In his previous outing, Righetti had lost 1–0, so manager Billy Martin went to his fire-balling closer, Goose Gossage.

"I've given up two runs in my last 17 innings so I can't say I'm really frustrated," Righetti said.

With the infield in, Gossage struck out Rod Carew, but Doug DeCinces chopped a single to left to give the Angels the lead.

Zahn walked Roy Smalley to start the ninth inning, but he got a force at second base before retiring rookie Don Mattingly, who was pinch-hitting, on a fly to right.

Willie Randolph bounced to second base for what appeared to be the final out, but Angels second baseman Bobby Grich had the ball go off his ankle for a two-base error.

"No way that should be an error," Grich complained after the game. "I thought it was going to take about a three-foot hop, but it turned out to be a

Angels	AB	R	H	RBI
Downing lf	3	0	0	0
Sconiers 1b	4	1	1	0
Beniquez rf	2	0	0	0
Carew ph	1	0	0	0
Valentine rf	0	0	0	0
DeCinces dh	3	0	1	1
Lynn cf	4	0	0	0
Grich 2b	4	0	0	0
Ron Jackson 3b	3	0	1	0
Lubratich ss	3	0	1	0
Boone c	2	0	0	0
Totals	29	1	4	1

Yankees	AB	R	H	RBI
Randolph 2b	4	1	2	0
Griffey 1b	5	0	1	2
Winfield lf	3	0	0	0
Baylor dh	4	0	0	0
Wynegar c	3	0	0	0
Kemp rf	4	0	1	0
Smalley ss	3	0	0	0
Milbourne pr	0	0	0	0
Campaneris 3b	4	1	1	0
Moreno cf	2	0	1	0
Mattingly ph	1	0	0	0
Totals	33	2	6	2

											R	H	E
CAL	0	0	0	0	0	0	0	0	1	-	1	4	3
NY	0	0	0	0	0	0	0	0	2	-	2	6	1

Angels	IP	H	R	ER	BB	SO
Zahn L(8–9)	8.2	6	2	0	4	1

Yankees	IP	H	R	ER	BB	SO
Righetti	8	3	1	1	4	5
Gossage W(11–4)	1	1	0	0	0	1
Totals	9	4	1	1	4	6

E—California Grich, Ron Jackson, Zahn; New York Randolph. DP—New York 1. 2B—California Lubratich. 3B—California Sconiers. SH—New York Moreno. LOB—California 5; New York 10. Attendance: 50,896.

four-inch hop. There was nothing I could do with that ball."

Gossage got the win in relief. Zahn pitched 8 2/3 innings but did not give up an earned run thanks to the Grich miscue.

Righetti faced the minimum 15 batters through the first five innings before giving up his first hit, a single to Ron Jackson to start the sixth inning. He was trouble-free until the ninth.

The Yankees had a chance to score against Zahn in the first inning, but Butch Wynegar flied out to left field to leave two runners stranded.

Griffey played 4½ seasons in New York before he was traded to the Atlanta Braves in June 1986 for Claudell Washington and Paul Zuvella.

Zahn pitched better than his 11–11 career record vs. the Yankees would indicate. In 27 career appearances, Zahn tossed 12 complete games and posted a 3.16 ERA against the Bombers. —ᴡ—

P Goose Gossage

Rich Gossage was the most overpowering right-handed closer in Yankees history.

An intimidating force on the mound, "Goose" saved 151 games in a Yankees uniform.

Gossage's greatest moment came in the 1978 one-game playoff for the AL East, when he closed the game by retiring future Hall of Famer Carl Yastrzemski on a foul pop with the tying and winning runs on base.

Gossage was an eight-time All-Star as a reliever.

In 1980, Gossage finished third in the voting for the American League's MVP and Cy Young Awards.

Gossage was elected to the Hall of Fame in 2008.

Remember Me? I'm Simpson, the Grand Slam Guy

Journeyman outfielder Harry Simpson burned his old team with a grand slam to lead the Yankees past the Athletics at Kansas City's Municipal Stadium, 11–4.

Simpson, who was acquired in a trade for former Yankee second baseman Billy Martin to add some punch to the lineup, had struggled since joining the team, but he broke out against his old teammates in a big way.

The A's took a 2–0 lead in the bottom of the first inning against Yankees starter Don Larsen, but the Yankees rallied for six runs in the third inning.

The Yankees tied the game at two on a bases-loaded single by Hank Bauer. After a walk to Mickey Mantle, Yogi Berra grounded into a forceout at home, then Simpson picked up his teammate with the slam off A's pitcher Wally Burnette.

Larsen couldn't stand the prosperity of a 6–2 lead. He was rocked for a two-run homer by Kansas City's Joe DeMaestri and did not get out of the fifth inning.

Art Ditmar ended the fifth by leaving a man on base. Johnny Kucks gave the Yankees four scoreless innings to pick up the win. ―⁓―

Yankees	AB	R	H	RBI
Bauer rf	6	1	1	2
Collins 1b	5	0	1	0
Mantle cf	4	2	1	0
Berra c	5	3	2	2
Simpson lf	4	2	3	4
McDougald 2b	4	0	1	0
Kubek ss	5	2	2	2
Lumpe 3b	4	1	3	1
Larsen p	1	0	0	0
Totals	**38**	**11**	**14**	**11**

Athletics	AB	R	H	RBI
Power 1b	4	1	1	0
Hunter 2b	4	1	2	0
Zernial lf	4	0	0	0
Cerv rf	2	0	0	0
Martin 3b	4	0	1	2
Held cf	4	0	0	0
Thompson c	2	1	0	0
DeMaestri ss	3	1	1	2
Burnette p	1	0	0	0
Skizas ph	1	0	0	0
Martyn ph	1	0	0	0
Totals	**30**	**4**	**5**	**4**

NY	0 0 6 0 0 0 2 0 3	-	11	14	1
KC	2 0 0 0 2 0 0 0 0	-	4	5	0

Yankees	IP	H	R	ER	BB	SO
Larsen	4.2	5	4	4	2	5
Ditmar	0.1	0	0	0	0	0
Kucks W(8–8)	4	0	0	0	1	1
Totals	**9**	**5**	**4**	**4**	**3**	**6**

Athletics	IP	H	R	ER	BB	SO
Burnette L(6–9)	2.1	3	5	5	2	0
McDermott	0.1	2	1	1	0	0
Portocarrero	2.1	2	0	0	0	3
Hill	2	2	2	2	2	0
Morgan	2	5	3	3	1	0
Totals	**9**	**14**	**11**	**11**	**5**	**3**

DP—New York 2. 2B—New York Lumpe. 3B—New York McDougald. HR—New York Simpson (10), Berra (19); Kansas City DeMaestri (5). SH—New York Kucks 2, McDougald. LOB—New York 8; Kansas City 2. Attendance: 19,202.

Girardi's Career-Best 7 RBIs Paces Assault at the Plate

Tino Martinez, Scott Brosius, and Joe Girardi each had four hits to pace a 23-hit attack in the Yankees' 21–3 demolition of the Rangers at The Ballpark in Arlington.

The trio combined for 17 RBIs, with Girardi netting a career-high seven.

The Yankees began the barrage by putting up a six spot against Rangers starter and loser John Burkett in the first inning, with Martinez, Brosius, and Girardi each driving in two runs.

The Bombers scored five times in the sixth inning to take a 14–2 lead and added five more in the seventh, keyed by a bases-clearing triple by Girardi, to go up by 17.

Said manager Joe Torre of the offensive output, "It's not like you're trying to rub it in, but you just can't go up to the plate and stand there."

Andy Pettitte took full advantage of the support to go eight innings for the win. The Yankees southpaw gave up three runs on 10 hits.

Coming into the game, Pettitte, who lives in Texas, had never beaten the Rangers at Arlington, going 0–3 with a 16.05 ERA in those games.

"It only took 21 runs and five years for me to get a win here," a jovial Pettitte kidded after the game. ⎯⎯

Yankees	AB	R	H	RBI
Knoblauch 2b	5	1	0	0
Jeter ss	5	0	1	0
Sojo pr,ss	1	2	1	0
O'Neill rf	5	1	3	0
Spencer pr,rf	1	1	0	0
Williams cf	5	3	2	1
Curtis ph,cf	1	0	0	0
Martinez 1b	6	3	4	4
Leyritz dh	4	3	2	1
Ledee lf	5	3	2	2
Brosius 3b	6	4	4	6
Girardi c	6	0	4	7
Totals	50	21	23	21

Rangers	AB	R	H	RBI
McLemore 2b,lf	5	0	0	0
Rodriguez c	3	0	1	0
Zaun c	1	0	0	0
Greer lf	3	0	1	0
Shave 3b	1	1	1	0
Gonzalez dh	4	1	2	0
Palmeiro 1b	4	1	2	3
Zeile 3b	3	0	1	0
Alicea 2b	0	0	0	0
Kelly rf	4	0	1	0
Clayton ss	4	0	1	0
Goodwin cf	3	0	0	0
Totals	35	3	10	3

```
NY   6 0 2 0 1 5 5 2 0 - 21 23 0
TEX  0 2 0 0 0 0 0 1 0 -  3 10 0
```

Yankees	IP	H	R	ER	BB	SO
Pettitte W(11–9)	8	10	3	3	2	2
Grimsley	1	0	0	0	0	1
Totals	9	10	3	3	2	3

Rangers	IP	H	R	ER	BB	SO
Burkett L(4–7)	2.2	8	8	8	2	4
Kolb	2.1	3	1	1	1	1
Venafro	1	5	5	5	0	0
Patterson	1	5	5	5	1	1
Munoz	1	2	2	2	1	0
Crabtree	1	0	0	0	0	0
Totals	9	23	21	21	5	6

DP—New York 2. 2B—New York Girardi 2, Leyritz, Brosius, Jeter, Williams, Sojo; Texas Zeile, Shave. 3B—New York Girardi. HR—New York Brosius (14), Martinez (19); Texas Palmeiro (38). LOB—New York 7; Texas 7. SB—New York Ledee. Attendance: 38,024.

Five-Run Rally in the 9th Capped by Henderson's Single

The Yankees scored an improbable victory as they rallied for five runs in the ninth inning to score a 7–6 walk-off win over the Oakland Athletics at Yankee Stadium.

The Yankees trailed 6–2 entering the ninth inning against premier closer Dennis Eckersley, but Claudell Washington and Don Mattingly both singled and then scored when Ken Phelps blasted a three-run homer to make it a one-run game.

Phelps said, "I wanted to make sure I stayed out of the double play. I wanted to hit the ball hard somewhere, score the run and hopefully keep things going."

Dave Winfield singled to extend the rally, so A's manager Tony LaRussa replaced his closer with left-hander Greg Cadaret to pitch to the left-handed hitting Mike Pagliarulo.

"I'm shell shocked," Eckersley said after the game. "It was quick, bam, bam. They just hit the heck out of the ball."

Eckersley entered the game with 35 saves in 40 opportunities and had allowed only 12 earned runs in just over 56 innings pitched, so the meltdown was surprising, to say the least.

"Maybe I should have taken time to pause," said the closer who would eventually attain Hall of Fame status. "Maybe I threw too many strikes. All I know is I got my butt kicked."

The managerial wheels were turning as Yankee skipper Lou Piniella was in a quandry.

"The decision was to bunt with Pagliarulo or send [Gary] Ward up to pinch hit," Piniella said. After Pagliarulo got behind 0–2, Piniella sent Ward up to pinch-hit.

Athletics	AB	R	H	RBI
Phillips lf,3b	4	1	1	0
Henderson cf	3	2	1	0
Canseco rf	5	2	2	2
McGwire 1b	3	0	0	0
Steinbach c	5	0	2	3
Baylor dh	1	0	0	0
Parker dh,ph	2	0	0	0
Hubbard 2b	4	1	2	0
Gallego 3b	1	0	1	0
Polonia ph,lf	3	0	1	0
Weiss ss	4	0	2	1
Totals	35	6	12	6

Yankees	AB	R	H	RBI
Henderson lf	6	1	2	1
Washington cf	5	1	2	1
Mattingly 1b	4	1	1	0
Phelps dh	4	1	3	3
Winfield rf	5	2	3	0
Pagliarulo 3b	4	0	2	0
Ward ph	1	0	1	0
Slaught c	3	0	0	1
Velarde 2b	2	0	0	0
Clark ph	1	0	0	0
Aguayo 2b	2	1	2	0
Santana ss	5	0	1	0
Totals	42	7	17	6

OAK	2	1	0	0	1	0	0	0	2	-	6	12 2
NY	0	0	1	0	0	0	0	1	5	-	7	17 0

Athletics	IP	H	R	ER	BB	SO
Stewart	6.2	6	1	1	3	6
Honeycutt	0.1	0	0	0	0	1
Eckersley	1	7	5	5	0	1
Cadaret	0	1	0	0	0	0
Nelson L(7–5)	0.2	3	1	1	0	0
Totals	8.2	17	7	7	3	8

Yankees	IP	H	R	ER	BB	SO
Candelaria	1.1	6	3	3	2	0
Nielsen	7.1	6	3	3	3	0
Guante W(5–6)	0.1	0	0	0	0	0
Totals	9	12	6	6	5	0

E—Oakland Phillips, Steinbach. DP—Oakland 1; New York 3. 2B—Oakland Canseco, Steinbach; New York Pagliarulo, Washington. HR—Oakland Canseco (33); New York Phelps (20). SH—Oakland Phillips. SF—New York Slaught. LOB—Oakland 8; New York 13. SB—New York Henderson. Attendance: 34,520.

"With two strikes, that's one shot, not three," Ward said. "I told myself anything looks close, I got to swing. I was shaking. I didn't even think I'd be able to control the bat because I was shaking so much."

Ward took a pitch for ball one, then fouled off the next two against Cadaret. On the fourth pitch, Ward stroked the ball to right-center field for a single that sent Winfield scampering to third.

Gene Nelson, who began his career with the Yankees, replaced Cadaret and induced Don Slaught to ground into a double play. Winfield scored the tying run, but the rally was not done yet.

Luis Aguayo and Rafael Santana ripped two-out singles and Rickey Henderson ended the game with an RBI infield single off the glove of A's third baseman Tony Phillips.

"This was a good come-from-behind win," Piniella said.

The Yankees got behind when the A's took advantage of an ineffective John Candelaria to take a 3–0 lead.

Oakland took a 6–2 lead in the ninth inning on a solo home run by Jose Canseco before the Yankees staged their remarkable rally. —⌇—

ıst 25, 1950

ıs 10, Browns 0

Ford Begins His Rookie Campaign by Turning Heads

Edward Charles "Whitey" Ford was less than two months into his big-league career, and he was already giving indications that he was going to be special.

Ford tossed a complete game four-hit shutout as the Yankees walloped the Browns in St. Louis, 10–0.

Since his call-up on July 1, the Yankee southpaw had worked 35 1/3 innings and had given up only two runs (one earned).

Whitey Ford, getting warmed up at spring training in St. Petersburg, Florida, didn't take long to show he had Hall of Fame stuff. On August 25, 1950, the rookie tossed a four-hit shutout of the St. Louis Browns. In his first 35 1/3 innings pitched, he allowed two runs (one earned).

199

Ford was cruising when he ran into a bit of a problem in the fifth inning.

Ken Wood led off with a single. After Les Moss struck out, Owen Friend singled, sending Wood to third base. At this point, Ford bore down to strike out Billy DeMars and Ned Garver to stymie the threat.

Hank Bauer tied a career high with five hits, while Yogi Berra had three hits and a home run to key a 16-hit attack.

The Yankees put a three-spot on the board in the first inning to give "the Chairman of the Board" all the support he would need.

Phil Rizzuto singled and eventually scored on an unusual play. There were runners at first and third base when Joe DiMaggio lined a ball to shortstop. Tom Upton fielded it and then tried to double up the runner at first, who dove back in and was safe. Rizzuto took advantage of the throw to scoot home and score the first run.

Berra then homered deep into the right-center-field bleachers for a 3–0 lead.

Ford walked two and struck out seven to raise his record to 5–0. —⟨w⟩—

P Whitey Ford

Edward Charles "Whitey" Ford spent his entire 18-year career with the Yankees and became the winningest pitcher in franchise history as he compiled 236 victories.

Ford grew up in Queens and was signed as an amateur free agent in 1947. The crafty left-hander began his big-league career in 1950, when he won his first nine decisions and was named the American League's Rookie of the Year.

Ford was given the moniker "Chairman of the Board" for his composure and command in pressure situations.

The Yankees southpaw won the 1961 Cy Young Award and the World Series MVP in the same year.

Ford broke Babe Ruth's World Series record of 29 2/3 consecutive scoreless innings by reaching 33 2/3 (the record was broken by Mariano Rivera in 2000).

Ford was elected to the Hall of Fame in 1974.

Tartabull's Grand Slam Holds Up in the End

Danny Tartabull provided all the offense the Yankees would need as they topped the Milwaukee Brewers 4–3 at Yankee Stadium.

Tartabull hit a grand slam off Milwaukee starter and loser Bruce Ruffin in the third inning, and three Yankee pitchers made that stand up.

Starter Scott Kamieniecki went seven innings, giving up two unearned runs, to qualify for the win. Rich Monteleone gave up a run in one inning of work while closer Steve Farr pitched a scoreless ninth for the save.

Ruffin walked two batters on nine pitches to set up the third-inning rally.

Tartabull worked the count to 2–2 against the Milwaukee southpaw and then jumped on a fastball and put it into the left-field seats for the big blow.

The Brewers scored two unearned runs in the fourth inning and could have had more, but Greg Vaughn was thrown out at the plate on the front end of a double-steal attempt to end the inning. ~~~

Brewers	AB	R	H	RBI
Listach ss	4	1	1	0
Hamilton cf	4	0	1	0
Molitor 1b	4	1	2	1
Stubbs 1b	4	1	1	0
Bichette rf	4	0	1	0
Vaughn lf	2	0	1	0
Seitzer 3b	3	0	0	0
Nilsson ph	1	0	0	0
Surhoff c	4	0	0	0
Fletcher 2b	2	0	0	0
Totals	32	3	7	1

Yankees	AB	R	H	RBI
B. Williams cf	4	1	1	0
Velarde 3b	3	1	0	0
Mattingly 1b	0	0	0	0
Hall rf	3	1	1	0
Tartabull dh	2	1	1	4
R. Kelly lf	3	0	1	0
Stanley c	4	0	1	0
Hayes 1b,3b	2	0	1	0
Stankiewicz ss	3	0	0	0
P. Kelly 2b	2	0	1	0
Totals	26	4	7	4

```
MIL  0 0 0 2 0 0 0 1 0 - 3 7 0
NY   0 0 4 0 0 0 0 0 X - 4 7 1
```

Brewers	IP	H	R	ER	BB	SO
Ruffin L(1–6)	3	5	4	4	3	2
Bones	3	1	0	0	2	0
Austin	2	1	0	0	2	1
Totals	8	7	4	4	7	3

Yankees	IP	H	R	ER	BB	SO
Kamieniecki W(4–10)	7	4	2	0	3	1
Monteleone	1	3	1	1	0	0
Farr SV(21)	1	0	0	0	0	0
Totals	9	7	3	1	3	1

E—New York Velarde. DP—Milwaukee 2. 2B—Milwaukee Bichette. HR—New York Tartabull (18). LOB—Milwaukee 5; New York 5. SB—Milwaukee Stubbs; New York P. Kelly. Attendance: 17,864.

Pearson Throws First Yankee Stadium No-No

A slim right-handed pitcher named Monte Pearson made history as he threw the first no-hitter in the history of Yankee Stadium in a 13–0 blanking of the Cleveland Indians, the team that dealt him to New York in December 1935.

Pearson, six days shy of his 30th birthday, faced 29 batters, two over the minimum because of a pair of walks. Otherwise, he made it look easy against the Indians' lineup.

The Yankees took a 7–0 lead as Pearson sat down the first nine Indians in order. In the fourth inning, he walked Indians shortstop Lyn Lary and Bruce Campbell to start the inning.

After Jeff Heath fanned for the first out of the inning, Pearson got future Hall of Famer Earl Averill on an infield roller and then ended the inning by striking out Hal Trosky. Pearson retired the next 12 hitters and went to the ninth inning with the no-hitter intact.

At a Glance
WP: Pearson
HR: Gordon 2 (18, 19), Henrich 2 (15, 16)
Key stats: Pearson throws first no-hitter at Yankee Stadium; Gordon 2 HR, 6 RBIs; Henrich 2 HR, 4 RBIs

The Yankees built Pearson a very nice cushion thanks to a pair of two-home run games by Tommy Henrich (4 RBIs) and Joe Gordon (6 RBIs).

Joe DiMaggio batted cleanup and went 1-for-5 with two runs scored, while Lou Gehrig was 2-for-4 with three runs scored while batting fifth.

Cleveland manager Ossie Vitt was desperate to fight off the ignominy of being no-hit, so he sent up a pair of pinch-hitters to start the ninth inning. Alas, Julius Solters struck out, and Frankie Pytlak grounded out.

While those who were at Yankee Stadium had to be feeling an incredible sense of excitement over the prospect of witnessing history, DiMaggio calmly called for time and ran toward the dugout to get a pair of sunglasses. The Yankee Clipper was the only one on the field who was basking in the late afternoon sun that emerged, so he wanted to be sure in case the ball was hit to him.

The final out did come in the outfield but it wasn't to center. Campbell was the final batter and he hit a low liner toward left field, where George Selkirk broke in and secured the ball for the final out.

The fans were going crazy and some ran on the field to hinder Pearson and the Yankees from getting into their clubhouse.

After posting a 63–27 career mark as a Yankee, Pearson was traded to the Cincinnati Reds following the 1940 season. —⚒—

Murcer Hits for the Cycle in Comeback Victory over Texas

Johnny Callison's walk-off RBI single in the bottom of the 11th inning gave the Yankees a come-from-behind 7–6 win over the Texas Rangers, but it was Bobby Murcer who was the star at Yankee Stadium.

Murcer became the ninth Yankee player to hit for the cycle when he homered in the bottom of the ninth to tie the game at six and send it into extra innings.

The Rangers took a 6–2 lead against Yankees starter Steve Kline, who came into the game sporting a 1.61 ERA but simply did not have it in this one. The right-hander was touched up for six runs (five earned) on 13 hits in seven innings pitched.

The Yankees scored three runs in the seventh inning to cut the deficit to 6–5, in part thanks to run-scoring singles from Horace Clarke and Thurman Munson.

The Yankees had a chance to tie the game in the eighth inning, but Munson grounded out to short, leaving the tying run on third base.

After striking out in his first at-bat, Murcer tripled with one out in the fourth inning and scored on an RBI single by Roy White.

The Yankees center fielder doubled in the fifth inning and singled in the seventh, leaving him a home run shy of putting his name in the record books.

With Murcer scheduled to lead off the ninth inning, Texas went with left-hander Steve Lawson to try and close it out.

Lefties or righties, it didn't matter for Murcer, who had his previous three hits off left-handers Mike Paul and Paul Lindblad.

Rangers	AB	R	H	RBI
Maddox cf	5	2	1	0
Mason ss	5	0	3	2
Biittner lf,1b	5	1	2	1
Billings c	5	0	1	0
Jones 3b	5	1	1	0
Howard 1b	4	0	1	0
Lovitto lf	1	0	0	0
Ford rf	5	1	3	3
Harris 2b	5	0	0	0
Paul p	3	1	2	0
Ragland 3b	1	0	0	0
Totals	44	6	14	6

Yankees	AB	R	H	RBI
Clarke 2b	5	1	1	1
Munson c	5	1	1	1
Murcer cf	5	2	4	1
White lf	5	1	2	1
Alou 1b	3	0	0	0
Blomberg ph,1b	2	1	0	0
Sanchez 3b	3	0	1	0
Allen ph,3b	2	0	0	1
Swoboda rf	3	0	2	1
Callison ph,rf	3	0	1	1
Michael ss	5	0	2	0
Kline p	1	0	0	0
Lanier ph	1	1	1	0
Klimkowski p	1	0	0	0
Ellis ph	0	0	0	0
Stottlemyre pr	0	0	0	0
Totals	44	7	15	7

TEX 0 0 1 0 0 3 2 0 0 0 0 - 6 14 2
NY 0 0 0 2 0 0 3 0 1 0 1 - 7 15 2

Rangers	IP	H	R	ER	BB	SO
Paul	6	9	3	3	1	4
Lindblad	0	3	2	2	0	0
Cox	2	1	0	0	1	1
Lawson	1.1	1	1	1	2	1
Pina L(2–6)	0.2	1	1	1	3	0
Totals	10	15	7	7	7	6

Yankees	IP	H	R	ER	BB	SO
Kline	7	13	6	5	0	3
Klimkowski	3	1	0	0	1	1
Lyle W(8–3)	1	0	0	0	0	2
Totals	11	14	6	5	1	6

E—Texas Biittner, Billings; New York Allen, Michael. DP—New York 3. 2B—Texas Paul; New York Murcer, Swoboda, Lanier, Clarke. 3B—New York Murcer. HR—Texas Ford (11); New York Murcer (23). SH—New York Kline. LOB—Texas 6; New York 15. SB—New York Michael. Attendance: 15,987.

A crowd of 15,987 went nuts when Murcer drove a 2–2 pitch from Lawson into the right-field seats for his 23rd home run of the season to tie the game.

Lawson was in the game because of an unusual maneuver made by Rangers manager Ted Williams in the top of the ninth inning.

The Splendid Splinter allowed his pitcher Casey Cox to bat, and after he walked, Williams pinch ran for Cox. That meant he had to insert another pitcher in the last of the ninth.

Following Murcer's homer, the Yankees put the potential winning run on thanks to an error by Texas first baseman Larry Biittner, but Lawson worked out of it to send the game to extra innings.

The Yankees had a chance in the 10th inning, when they put two runners on with one out, but Rangers reliever Horacio Pina came in and shut the door on the potential winning rally.

In the 11th, Pina walked Ron Blomberg to start the inning. Bernie Allen then walked to put runners on first and second base, and Callison followed with his walk-off hit. —∿—

Did You Know?

The Yankees have finished in first place a total of 46 times, the most in professional team sports history. The Montreal Canadiens of the National Hockey League are second in that category with 32 first-place finishes.

Peckinpaugh's Four Hits Power Yanks Past Senators

Roger Peckinpaugh tied a career high with four hits to power the Yankees to a 10–3 win over the Senators at Washington's Griffith Stadium.

Peck's game keyed a 14-hit attack for the Bombers, who knocked out Senators starter Eric Erickson before he could record an out.

Errors by future Hall of Fame outfielder Sam Rice and third baseman Howie Shanks did not help Erickson's cause as he gave up five runs, but only one was earned against the Swedish-born hurler.

Babe Ruth hit behind Peckinpaugh in the third slot and was 1-for-2 with two runs scored, but the Bambino left the game in the fifth inning after he twisted his ankle running to first base.

Bob Meusel, Aaron Ward, and Elmer Miller had two hits apiece, with Meusel and Ward adding three RBIs.

Right-hander Carl Mays went the distance, giving up three runs on eight hits for his 21st win.

Peckinpaugh managed the Yankees for 20 games at age 23 in the 1914 season, making him the youngest manager in baseball history. He was also captain of the team from 1914 to 1921. —⁓—

Yankees	AB	R	H	RBI
Miller cf	5	2	2	0
Peckinpaugh ss	4	3	4	1
Ruth lf	2	2	1	1
Fewster rf	1	0	0	0
Meusel rf,lf	5	1	2	3
Pipp 1b	5	1	1	0
Ward 2b	4	0	2	3
McNally 3b	5	0	1	1
Hofmann c	4	1	0	0
Mays p	3	0	1	0
Totals	**38**	**10**	**14**	**9**

Senators	AB	R	H	RBI
Bush ss	5	2	1	0
Milan rf,cf	5	1	2	1
Judge 1b	3	0	2	1
Rice cf,rf	5	0	1	0
B. Miller lf	4	0	0	1
Harris 2b	4	0	1	0
Shanks 3b	2	0	1	0
Gharrity c	4	0	0	0
Acosta p	1	0	0	0
Brower ph	1	0	0	0
Courtney p	1	0	0	0
Smith ph	1	0	0	0
Totals	**36**	**3**	**8**	**3**

```
NY   5 2 0 2 1 0 0 0 0 - 10 14 3
WAS  2 0 0 0 0 0 0 0 1 -  3  8 2
```

Yankees	IP	H	R	ER	BB	SO
Mays W(21–9)	9	8	3	2	3	2

Senators	IP	H	R	ER	BB	SO
Erickson L(7–8)	0	4	5	1	1	0
Acosta	4	8	4	4	0	2
Courtney	5	2	1	1	2	1
Totals	**9**	**14**	**10**	**6**	**3**	**3**

E—New York Peckinpaugh, Pipp, Ward; Washington Rice, Shanks. DP—New York 1; Washington 3. 2B—New York Ruth, Meusel, Pipp; Washington Milan, Judge. SH—New York Ruth; Washington Judge. HBP—New York Hofmann. LOB—New York 7; Washington 10. Attendance: NA.

O'Neill Joins Elite Group of Yankees with 3 Homers in One Game

Paul O'Neill became the 14th player in franchise history to hit three home runs in one game as the Yankees outlasted the California Angels 11–6 at Yankee Stadium.

"It's a great thing, something I've never done before," O'Neill said, "even hitting in my backyard during home run derby."

O'Neill's first home run came in the top of the first inning off Angels left-hander Brian Anderson to give the Yankees a 3–0 lead. The blow also snapped a 0-for-16 skid for the emotional outfielder.

Going into the game, O'Neill was 5-for-10 vs. Anderson with two home runs, so it was no surprise when the Yankees right fielder went deep for a second time against the southpaw in the second. A second three-run homer gave the Yankees a commanding 7–0 lead.

Paulie completed his trifecta when he homered off Mike Harkey on a 3–2 pitch to lead off the fifth inning. Three home runs in his first three at-bats, and the 25,633 fans in attendance wanted more.

When O'Neill came to bat in the sixth inning, he had a chance to match what Lou Gehrig accomplished 63 years earlier (see: June 3, 1932).

Facing lefty Bob Patterson, O'Neill singled to drive in his eighth run of the game.

At a Glance

WP: Hitchcock (7–9)

HR: O'Neill 3 (17, 18, 19), Stanley (17)

Key stat: O'Neill 4-for-5, 8 RBIs, 4 runs

In the eighth inning, he struck out against Angels pitcher Troy Percival, but he got one more raucous ovation from the appreciative Yankee fans. —∾—

Skowron's Game-Winning Single Sends 'Em Home Happy

A crowd of 65,566 packed Yankee Stadium to see Moose Skowron's RBI single score Elston Howard from third base with the winning run in an exciting 1–0 win over the Detroit Tigers.

It was a battle of southpaws as Detroit's Don Mossi hooked up with Whitey Ford in a matchup that lived up to the hype, at least for a little while.

Ford, who had allowed no runs on four hits, had to leave the game in the fifth inning after suffering a strained hip muscle. He was replaced by Bud Daley.

Mossi was holding down the powerful Yankees lineup that included Roger Maris and Mickey Mantle. The Tigers left-hander struck out both in succession in the first inning and held the pair to a combined 0-for-8 on the day.

Daley ran into some trouble in the eighth inning, but was helped by his defense. With one out and Bill Bruton on first, Al Kaline lined a ball to left field. Bruton took third base and Kaline tried to stretch the hit into a double, but left fielder Yogi Berra threw him out to kill the rally.

With two out and none on in the ninth inning, Howard singled and took third when Berra followed with a single. Skowron stepped to the plate and hit a bouncer toward third base that got past Steve Boros (a future major league manager) to end a thrilling game. —~—

Tigers	AB	R	H	RBI
Wood 2b	4	0	0	0
Bruton cf	3	0	1	0
Kaline rf	4	0	3	0
Colavito lf	2	0	0	0
Cash 1b	3	0	1	0
Boros 3b	4	0	0	0
Fernandez ss	4	0	0	0
Roarke c	4	0	2	0
Mossi p	3	0	0	0
Totals	31	0	7	0

Yankees	AB	R	H	RBI
Richardson 2b	4	0	1	0
Kubek ss	4	0	1	0
Maris rf	4	0	0	0
Mantle cf	4	0	0	0
Howard c	4	1	2	0
Berra lf	4	0	2	0
Skowron 1b	4	0	1	1
Boyer 3b	2	0	1	0
Ford p	1	0	0	0
Daley p	1	0	0	0
Lopez ph	1	0	0	0
Totals	33	1	8	1

DET	0 0 0 0 0 0 0 0 0 -	0	7	0
NY	0 0 0 0 0 0 0 0 1 -	1	8	0

Tigers	IP	H	R	ER	BB	SO
Mossi L(14–4)	8.2	8	1	1	1	7

Yankees	IP	H	R	ER	BB	SO
Ford	4.2	4	0	0	1	2
Daley	3.1	3	0	0	3	2
Arroyo W(12–3)	1	0	0	0	0	1
Totals	9	7	0	0	4	5

DP—Detroit 1. 2B—New York Boyer. 3B—Detroit Kaline. LOB—Detroit 8; New York 7. Attendance: 65,566.

Mussina Near Perfect in Shutout Victory

It was as close to perfection as you could get without being perfect.

Mike Mussina came within one strike of becoming the fourth pitcher in Yankees history to toss a perfect game when he shut out the Boston Red Sox at Fenway Park 1–0.

Mussina set down the first 26 Red Sox hitters before pinch hitter Carl Everett blooped a single into short left field to break up the bid.

"I'm going to think about it," Mussina admitted, "until I retire."

The no-hitter and the game were on the line in this one as the Yankees held a slim 1–0 lead.

The irony of this game was that the Red Sox pitcher was David Cone, who had tossed a perfect game two years earlier while wearing the pinstripes.

The Yankees got the only run of the game in the top of the ninth inning.

With runners on first and third base and one out, Enrique Wilson's double scored pinch-runner Clay Bellinger, so it was left up to Mussina to try for the glory, not to mention a big win at Fenway Park.

> ## At a Glance
> **WP:** Mussina (14–11)
>
> **Key stats:** Mussina 1-hitter, 13 Ks, 0 BB; Wilson 1-for-1, RBI; Martinez 2-for-3

Troy O'Leary led off the ninth inning as a pinch hitter and grounded out. Mussina struck out Lou Merloni for his 13th strikeout of the game and was one out away.

The Yankees right-hander got ahead of Everett 1–2, but the left-handed batter got enough of Mussina's next pitch to spoil the run at the history books.

There was still the matter of winning the game, and Mussina put that to rest by retiring Trot Nixon on a groundout to second base. —∞—

Lyle Gives Way to Gossage, and the Goose Saves the Day

This game signified the passing of the torch as the Yankees held off the Seattle Mariners 4–3 at Yankee Stadium.

The Yankees had a 4–0 lead but the Mariners scored twice in the eighth inning to cut the lead to 4–2.

Sparky Lyle came into to try and save it, but the 1977 Cy Young Award winner gave up a run on a Bill Stein double. Seattle had the tying run at third base and the go-ahead run at second with nobody out.

On September 3, 1978, Goose Gossage replaced Sparky Lyle in relief, and a Hall of Fame career as a closer was born. After the Mariners had cut the Yankees' lead to 4–2 in the ninth inning against Lyle, Gossage entered and struck out the only three batters he faced.

At this point, Yankees manager Bob Lemon went to Goose Gossage, who had been signed for moments like this.

Lyle had been the Yankees' star closer ever since he joined the team for the 1972 season, but he was 34 years old. The team felt it needed a younger arm to close the games, and the hard-throwing Gossage was available.

Seattle's Tom Paciorek was the first batter Gossage faced, and he went down swinging.

Bob Robertson was sent up to hit to pinch-hit. Robertson once hit three home runs in a 1971 National League Championship Series game, so Seattle manager Darrell Johnson was hoping that his slugger off the bench could get his bat on one.

Gossage was firing as he sat down Robertson on three pitches.

Now there were two outs, and Seattle's hopes rested with Julio Cruz. The Mariners' second baseman was difficult to strike out, but Gossage got Cruz with a blazing fastball to preserve the win for the Yankees and Jim Beattie, who tossed eight strong innings. —⁓—

Mariners	AB	R	H	RBI
Cruz 2b	5	1	1	0
Reynolds ss	4	0	0	0
Ruppert Jones cf	2	0	2	2
Roberts rf	4	0	0	0
Bochte dh	4	0	1	0
Hale pr,dh	0	1	0	0
Meyer 1b	4	0	1	0
Stein 3b	4	0	1	1
Paciorek lf	4	0	1	0
Plummer c	2	0	0	0
Milbourne ph	1	1	1	0
Pasley c	0	0	0	0
Robertson ph	1	0	0	0
Totals	35	3	8	3

Yankees	AB	R	H	RBI
Rivers cf	5	1	2	0
Randolph 2b	3	1	1	0
Munson c	4	0	0	0
Jackson rf	4	0	2	0
Thomasson pr,rf	0	0	0	0
Piniella lf	3	2	0	0
Chambliss 1b	4	0	1	3
Nettles 3b	4	0	2	0
Johnson dh	4	0	2	1
Dent ss	4	0	2	0
Totals	35	4	12	4

											R	H	E
SEA	0	0	0	0	0	0	2	1	-		3	8	1
NY	3	0	1	0	0	0	0	X	-		4	12	0

Mariners	IP	H	R	ER	BB	SO
Honeycutt L(5–8)	8	12	4	4	2	3

Yankees	IP	H	R	ER	BB	SO
Beattie W(3–7)	8	5	2	2	2	5
Lyle	0	3	1	1	0	0
Gossage SV(21)	1	0	0	0	0	3
Totals	9	8	3	3	2	8

E—Seattle Reynolds. DP—Seattle 1. 2B—Seattle Ruppert Jones, Stein. 3B—Seattle Ruppert Jones; New York Piniella. LOB—Seattle 7; New York 9. SB—Seattle Ruppert Jones; New York Rivers. Attendance: 22,386.

Abbott Tosses Eighth No-Hitter in Yankees Franchise History

Yankees left-hander Jim Abbott tossed the eighth no-hitter in franchise history as the Bombers blanked the Cleveland Indians 4–0 at Yankee Stadium.

What makes this particular no-hitter even more remarkable is that Abbott was born without a right hand.

The courageous southpaw was a star pitcher at the University of Michigan and was a member of the 1988 U.S. Olympic gold medal–winning team.

"So many things have been nice in my career, and this is certainly at the top of them," Abbott said.

The game didn't start out like it was going to be a gem. Abbott walked Indians leadoff hitter Kenny Lofton on five pitches. The lefty fell behind in the count to the next hitter, Felix Fermin, but induced a double-play grounder, which seemed to relax the 25 year old.

The Yankees scored three runs in the third inning and added their fourth run on a solo home run by Randy Velarde in the fifth.

The closest that the Indians came to a hit was in the seventh inning. Albert Belle hit a hot smash toward the hole between third base and shortstop. Wade Boggs dove to his left, stabbed the grounder and threw to Don Mattingly at first base for the out.

Abbott admitted he was starting to feel fatigued.

"I was feeling a little tired in the seventh inning," he said, "but in the eighth and ninth, with the crowd, I didn't feel it at all."

An announced crowd of 27,225 was standing for every pitch of the final two innings.

In the eighth inning, Abbott struck out Manny Ramirez and got Candy Maldonado on a ground out to Velarde at shortstop. With two outs, he walked Jim Thome, but he ended the inning by getting

Indians	AB	R	H	RBI
Lofton cf	3	0	0	0
Fermin ss	4	0	0	0
Baerga 2b	4	0	0	0
Belle lf	3	0	0	0
Milligan 1b	1	0	0	0
Ramirez dh	3	0	0	0
Maldonado rf	3	0	0	0
Thome 3b	2	0	0	0
Ortiz c	1	0	0	0
Alomar ph,c	1	0	0	0
Totals	**25**	**0**	**0**	**0**

Yankees	AB	R	H	RBI
Boggs 3b	4	1	1	0
James lf	4	1	2	1
G. Williams lf	0	0	0	0
Mattingly 1b	3	0	1	0
Tartabull dh	4	0	1	0
O'Neill rf	4	0	0	0
B. Williams cf	3	0	1	0
Nokes c	4	0	1	0
Gallego 2b	3	1	0	0
Velarde ss	3	1	1	1
Totals	**32**	**4**	**8**	**2**

CLE	0 0 0	0 0 0	0 0 0	- 0 0 2						
NY	0 0 3	0 1 0	0 0 X	- 4 8 0						

Indians	IP	H	R	ER	BB	SO
Milacki L(0–1)	5.1	6	4	2	3	2
Wertz	2.2	2	0	0	0	2
Totals	**8**	**8**	**4**	**2**	**3**	**4**

Yankees	IP	H	R	ER	BB	SO
Abbott W(10–11)	9	0	0	0	5	3

E—Cleveland Lofton, Thome. DP—New York 2. 2B—New York James. HR—New York Velarde (6). LOB—Cleveland 3; New York 7. SB—New York B. Williams. Attendance: 27,125.

Sandy Alomar Jr. on a ground out to third. The Yankees came to bat in the bottom of the eighth inning and it seemed like the crowd was rooting for a 1–2–3 inning because they wanted to see Abbott to take his shot at history.

In the ninth, the crowd went ballistic when Lofton attempted a bunt to break up the no-hitter. It's considered taboo in baseball to try to spoil a no-hitter with a bunt late in the game, especially when it's a four-run deficit, so Lofton became an instant bad guy.

The crowd roared when Lofton bounced out to second base for the first out of the inning.

Center fielder Bernie Williams chased down Fermin's fly ball to the warning track in center for the second out.

It was Abbott vs. Carlos Baerga as the final act of this stirring drama. In the ninth inning, Baerga, a switch-hitter, decided to bat left-handed. Doing so gave him a better look at Abbott's slider, which was terrific all game long.

"You never want to get no-hit," Baerga said. "That was really on my mind in my last at-bat."

Baerga grounded to shortstop, where Velarde threw to Mattingly to complete the gem. Abbott put his arms up and looked for his catcher, Matt Nokes, who ran out to hug his pitcher.

In a rare display to the fans, Abbott insisted that Nokes share the bow with him as the fans roared their approval and the two players acknowledged the appreciation together. —⁓—

Two Homers in Inning Put A-Rod in the Books

Alex Rodriguez hit two home runs in one inning to power the Yankees to a 10–2 win over the Seattle Mariners at Yankee Stadium.

Rodriguez became the fourth Yankee to accomplish the feat and the first since Cliff Johnson turned the trick (see: June 30, 1977).

Seattle held a 2–1 lead heading to the home half of the seventh inning, but the Yankees exploded for eight runs, with three of those coming off the bat of Rodriguez.

A-Rod led off the inning with a solo home run on a 3–2 pitch from Mariners left-hander Jarrod Washburn. He added a two-run blast later in the inning off Brendan Morrow.

Derek Jeter was on base for Rodriguez's second home run of the inning.

"I can't relate to it. It's unbelievable," Jeter said. "I haven't seen anything like it in all my years playing. It's not that easy."

After A-Rod's first home run, Jorge Posada drew a bases-loaded walk to give the Yankees a 3–2 lead. Jeter's two-run double blew the game open, and then Rodriguez did his thing.

Joba Chamberlain was the beneficiary of the offensive outburst as he got his first major league win, but he had to admire what his teammate did.

"The man's incredible," Chamberlain said. "He's one of the best in the game, and he still works every day to become better. That's a tribute to him and his workout. He understands that it takes hard work. You can't get at the top and stay there. You have to work even harder." —∞—

At a Glance

WP: Chamberlain (1–0)

HR: Molina (1), Rodriguez 2 (47, 48)

Key stats: Rodriguez 2-for-3, 3 RBIs; Molina 2-for-2, RBI; Jeter 2 RBIs

---

It's Fun in Minnesota as Maris Hits Key Double to Win Game

Roger Maris drove in the game-winning run with an RBI double in the top of the 11th inning to give the Yankees a 5–4 win over the Twins at Minnesota's Metropolitan Stadium.

The Yankees took a 4–0 lead thanks to home runs by Tony Kubek, leading off the game, and Maris, who hit a two-run shot in the fifth inning. Jim Bouton was cruising to a win until the eighth inning, when he ran into trouble.

With two outs, the Twins' Bob Allison hit a pinch-hit two-run homer. Rich Rollins' single chased Bouton, who was replaced by Pete Mikkelsen. The Yankees right-hander gave up a double to Zoilo Versalles and was relieved by left-hander Steve Hamilton.

Tony Oliva couldn't touch Hamilton's first two offerings, but he managed to muscle a ball past Kubek at shortstop for the game-tying hit.

In the 11th inning, Kubek was at second base with two outs when Maris lined a double off the Twins' Al Worthington to give the Yankees the lead.

A rare throwing error by third baseman Clete Boyer allowed Minnesota's Harmon Killebrew to reach first base to start the 11th inning, but the Yankees got a break when Don Mincher lined into a double play.

> ## At a Glance
>
> **WP:** Reniff (5–3)
>
> **S:** Ford (1)
>
> **HR:** Kubek (8), Maris (21)
>
> **Key stats:** Kubek 3-for-6, RBI; Maris 4-for-5, 3 RBIs

With two outs, Jimmie Hall singled and Ron Henry walked.

Whitey Ford relieved Bill Stafford and got the Twins' Jerry Kindall to bounce into a force out at third base to end the game and get a rare save. —⁓—

It's Yogi Time! Berra Blasts Pair of Three-Run Homers

Yogi Berra hit a pair of three-run homers and drove in six runs to power the Yankees to a 13–0 thrashing of the Kansas City Athletics at Yankee Stadium.

Bob Turley held up the pitching end with a five-hitter. The Yankees right-hander walked three and struck out seven.

Berra's first three-run blast off A's pitcher Art Ceccarelli keyed a six-run rally in the third inning as the Yankees took a 6–0 lead.

The Yankees began the inning with a single by Billy Martin and a walk to Phil Rizzuto. After Martin was forced out at third base, Rizzuto tried to steal third, but Kansas City third baseman and future Yankee Hector Lopez let the throw get by him for an error, and the Scooter scored the first run.

Gil McDougald drove in the second run with a single before Berra homered. Elston Howard's RBI single produced the sixth run.

In the eighth inning, it was Yogi's three-run homer off Cloyd Boyer (Clete and Ken's brother) that was the key blow of a second six-run rally that capped off the scoring. —⁓—

Athletics	AB	R	H	RBI
Power 1b	3	0	0	0
Littrell 1b	1	0	1	0
Simpson cf	3	0	0	0
Stewart lf	1	0	0	0
Slaughter rf	3	0	0	0
Valo lf,cf	3	0	1	0
Lopez 3b	3	0	1	0
Finigan 2b	4	0	0	0
Schypinski ss	3	0	0	0
Billy Shantz c	3	0	1	0
Ceccarelli p	1	0	1	0
Harrington p	1	0	0	0
Renna ph	1	0	0	0
Totals	30	0	5	0

Yankees	AB	R	H	RBI
Bauer rf	3	2	0	0
McDougald 3b	5	2	2	1
Berra c	4	2	2	6
Mantle cf	4	1	1	0
Skowron 1b	4	0	0	0
Collins 1b	1	0	0	0
Howard lf	3	0	1	1
Noren lf	0	1	0	0
Martin 2b	4	0	1	0
Rizzuto ss	2	3	1	0
J. Coleman ss	0	0	0	0
Turley p	3	2	1	2
Totals	33	13	9	10

```
KC   0 0 0 0 0 0 0 0 0 - 0 5 4
NY   0 0 6 1 0 0 0 6 X - 13 9 0
```

Athletics	IP	H	R	ER	BB	SO
Ceccarelli L(4–7)	3	5	6	4	2	1
Herbert	0.1	1	1	1	3	0
Harrington	3.2	0	0	0	1	0
Cloyd Boyer	1	3	6	2	1	0
Totals	8	9	13	7	7	1

Yankees	IP	H	R	ER	BB	SO
Turley W(15–13)	9	5	0	0	3	7

E—Kansas City Lopez 2, Finigan, Schypinski. DP—Kansas City 2; New York 2. 2B—New York Mantle, Rizzuto. HR—New York Berra 2 (24,25). SH—New York Turley. LOB—Kansas City 6; New York 4. SB—New York Mantle. Attendance: 8,425.

A Special Night as Jeter Ties Gehrig for Most Yankees Hits

It was Jorge Posada's pinch-hit three-run home run that beat Tampa Bay 4–2, but it was Derek Jeter's night at Yankee Stadium.

Jeter tied Lou Gehrig for the most hits in Yankees franchise history when he singled down the right-field line in the bottom of the seventh inning.

It was a typical Jeter hit that tied the record, a smash to right that eluded the dive of Rays first baseman Chris Richard.

A crowd of 45,848 fans roared as Jeter took off his helmet not only to acknowledge the cheers, but also his family and friends who were in the third deck of the new Yankee Stadium.

"You look at all the great players that have played in this organization throughout the years," Jeter said. "To say that you have more hits than them or at least tied for the most hits in the history of the organization is definitely hard to believe. It means a lot."

Jeter came into the game riding a 0-for-12 streak, but he put that to rest with a nifty bunt single to lead off the first inning.

"I saw he [Rays third baseman Evan Longoria] was playing back," the captain said.

The 2000 World Series MVP grounded out in his next at-bat, but in the fifth inning, he hit a loud double to the deepest part of center field, which left him one hit shy of tying the Iron Horse.

> ## At a Glance
>
> **WP:** Albaladejo (5–1)
>
> **S:** Coke (2)
>
> **HR:** Posada (21)
>
> **Key stats:** Posada 3-run HR; Jeter 3-for-4

In the meantime, Tampa starting pitcher Jeff Niemann was throwing a great game. The young right-hander gave up one run on eight hits in seven innings with eight strikeouts. He will, however, go in the books as the pitcher who gave up the hit that tied a Yankee icon.

Niemann was gracious about it afterward.

"It was just a fastball, I wasn't trying to pitch around him or anything like that," Niemann said. "I went right at him with my best stuff. And if he did it, he did it, and he did. It's what he's been doing his whole career, so I can't feel bad about that at all."

Following Jeter's record-tying hit, there was the simple matter of winning the game. The Yankees trailed 2–0 entering the eighth inning, but scored a run on Richard's throwing error before Posada took Rays' reliever Grant Balfour deep for a three-run homer and the lead.

Here was Jeter tying a coveted mark in Yankee history, while his best friend on the team, Posada, the captain's teammate in the organization since 1992, got the big hit to secure a win.

Jeter's moment was an emotional one for Posada as well.

"When he came off the field after the third out, after he did it, I went out there, and he was still emotional about it," Posada said. "So that tells you [the moment] was still with him." —⁕—

On September 11, 2009, Derek Jeter surpassed Lou Gehrig as the Yankees' all-time hit leader, further solidifying his place as the greatest shortstop in franchise history.

Jeter was penciled in as the Yankees starting shortstop for the 1996 season, and he responded with a .314 batting average, while taking home the American League's Rookie of the Year Award.

The sixth overall selection of the 1992 draft has authored some memorable moments in Yankee history.

In Game 3 of the 2001 American League Divisional Series, Jeter made a play that many consider to be one of the best of all time, considering how it occurred and when.

The Yankees trailed the Oakland A's two games to none in the best-of-five and had a slim 1–0 lead.

With a runner on first, Oakland's Terrence Long lined a double into the right-field corner.

Yankee right fielder Shane Spencer threw the ball toward home, but it was wide of the cutoff man. Somehow, Jeter was there to intercept the throw and use a backhanded flip toward home to nail the runner at the plate.

The Yankees went on to win the game and the playoff series as Jeter's play took on monumental status.

Massacre Complete: Yankees Outscore Sox 42–9 in Series

In the finale of a four-game set at Fenway Park, a 7–4 score was the closest the Red Sox came to getting a win against the Yankees in the series, a four-game sweep that came to be known as the Boston Massacre.

The Bronx Bombers, who were once 14½ games behind, came to Fenway Park and swept their long-time rivals by an accumulated run total of 42–9.

Reggie Jackson's RBI single with two outs in the first inning gave the Yankees a 1–0 lead. Later in the inning, Graig Nettles made it 3–0 with a two-run single.

The Yankees were up 6–0 when the Red Sox finally started to make it a game by scoring two runs in the fourth inning against starter and winning pitcher Ed Figueroa. Figgy tossed six innings, giving up three runs on three hits.

Goose Gossage pitched the final three innings and gave up one unearned run in a precursor to the one-game playoff that was to be played less than a month later. —⁓—

Yankees	AB	R	H	RBI
Rivers cf	4	1	0	0
Blair cf	1	0	0	0
Randolph 2b	4	2	2	0
Munson c	5	0	3	0
Jackson dh	5	1	2	2
Piniella rf	2	2	2	2
Chambliss 1b	4	0	0	0
Nettles 3b	4	0	3	2
White lf	4	0	3	0
Dent ss	5	1	3	1
Totals	38	7	18	7

Red Sox	AB	R	H	RBI
Burleson ss	3	0	0	0
Lynn cf	3	2	1	1
Rice dh	4	0	0	0
Yastrzemski lf	3	1	0	0
Fisk c	4	0	1	1
Hancock rf	3	0	0	1
Scott 1b	2	1	0	0
Hobson 3b	4	0	2	0
Remy 2b	2	0	0	0
Brohamer ph,2b	2	0	1	0
Totals	30	4	5	3

```
NY   3 2 0 1 0 0 1 0 0 - 7 18 1
BOS  0 0 0 2 0 1 1 0 0 - 4  5 1
```

Yankees	IP	H	R	ER	BB	SO
Figueroa W(16–9)	6	3	3	3	3	3
Gossage SV(23)	3	2	1	0	2	2
Totals	9	5	4	3	5	5

Red Sox	IP	H	R	ER	BB	SO
Sprowl L(0–2)	0.2	1	3	3	4	0
Stanley	3	10	3	3	0	1
Hassler	2.2	4	1	1	2	2
Drago	0.1	1	0	0	0	0
Lee	2.1	2	0	0	2	0
Totals	9	18	7	7	8	3

E—New York Chambliss; Boston Fisk. DP—New York 1; Boston 3. 2B—Boston Hobson, Fisk, Brohamer. HR—Boston Lynn (21). SF—New York Piniella; Boston Hancock. LOB—New York 13; Boston 5. SB—New York Rivers, Dent. Attendance: 32,786.

The Rains Come, and the Yanks Get a Quick Win in Chicago

The Yankees beat the White Sox 4–3 in a rain-shortened six-inning game at Comiskey Park.

The Yankees put three runs on the board in the top of the first inning. Bobby Richardson, who had three hits, singled to center. After Tony Kubek struck out, Roger Maris walked, but Mickey Mantle struck out as well.

Elston Howard tripled in two runs and scored on Moose Skowron's single.

Yankees pitcher Ralph Terry kept the White Sox off the board until the third inning. A two-out error by Kubek kept the inning alive and allowed Roy Sievers to cash in the chance with a two-run single.

Howard came through again in the fifth inning with what proved to be the deciding run when he singled in Maris.

The White Sox narrowed the gap on a solo home run by future Hall of Famer Luis Aparicio in the fifth inning.

At a Glance

WP: Terry (14–2)

Key stats: Terry complete-game in 5 2/3 IP, 7 H, 1 ER; Howard 2-for-3, 3 RBIs; Richardson 3-for-4

In the bottom of the sixth, the White Sox nearly tied it. Al Smith led off with a double and was sacrificed to third base by future Hall of Famer Nellie Fox. With one out and the infield in, Terry got Jim Landis to ground out to Clete Boyer at third base for the second out.

At this point, the game was stopped, and the Yankees got the win. —⁓—

Bouton's 20th Win Gives Yankees AL Pennant

Jim Bouton tossed a six-hit shutout and the Yankees clinched the 1963 American League pennant with a 2–0 win over the Twins at Minnesota's Metropolitan Stadium.

Yankees third baseman Clete Boyer recorded the final out when he fell into his team's dugout after catching a pop foul off the bat of future Yankee Bernie Allen.

Fourth-inning home runs by Joe Pepitone and John Blanchard provided enough offense for Bouton, who won his 20th game of the 1963 campaign.

In the eighth inning, the Twins threatened to curtail the celebration.

Allen walked and pinch-hitter Tony Oliva singled. After Rich Rollins sacrificed the runners to second and third base, Bouton got Vic Power to foul out to first. Jimmie Hall walked to load the bases for Harmon Killebrew.

Bouton fell behind in the count 3–1, but he got Killebrew to hit a hard grounder to Tony Kubek at short. Kubek flipped to Bobby Richardson for the force at second to kill the rally.

The Yankees played without Mickey Mantle and Roger Maris, both of whom were nursing injuries. Phil Linz played center field while Blanchard was in right.

Camilo Pascual gave up only two runs on four hits in eight innings pitched, but he was the tough-luck loser. —m—

Yankees	AB	R	H	RBI
Kubek ss	4	0	1	0
Richardson 2b	4	0	0	0
Lopez lf	3	0	0	0
Pepitone 1b	3	1	1	1
Howard c	4	0	0	0
Blanchard rf	3	1	2	1
Reed rf	1	0	0	0
Linz cf	3	0	0	0
Tresh cf	0	0	0	0
Boyer 3b	3	0	0	0
Bouton p	3	0	0	0
Totals	31	2	4	2

Twins	AB	R	H	RBI
Rollins 3b	3	0	1	0
Power 1b	4	0	0	0
Hall cf	3	0	0	0
Killebrew lf	4	0	1	0
Allison rf	3	0	0	0
Battey c	4	0	2	0
Versalles ss	4	0	1	0
Allen 2b	3	0	0	0
Pascual p	2	0	0	0
Oliva ph	1	0	1	0
Totals	31	0	6	0

											R	H	E
NY	0	0	0	2	0	0	0	0	0	-	2	4	0
MIN	0	0	0	0	0	0	0	0	0	-	0	6	1

Yankees	IP	H	R	ER	BB	SO
Bouton W(20–6)	9	6	0	0	3	11

Twins	IP	H	R	ER	BB	SO
Pascual L(18–9)	8	4	2	2	2	8
Dailey	1	0	0	0	0	2
Totals	9	4	2	2	2	10

E—Minnesota Rollins. DP—New York 1; Minnesota 1. HR—New York Pepitone (25), Blanchard (16). SH—Minnesota Rollins. HBP—New York Linz. LOB—New York 5; Minnesota 8. Attendance: 32,445.

Crouching Jackson, Bye-Bye Baseball

Reggie Jackson clubbed a two-run walk-off home run in the bottom of the ninth inning to lift the Yankees to a thrilling 2–0 win over the Boston Red Sox at Yankee Stadium.

Thurman Munson led off the ninth with a single to center off losing pitcher Reggie Cleveland.

Jackson squared to bunt on the first pitch from Cleveland but took ball one. On the second pitch, Jackson swung and missed. The left-handed slugger eventually worked the count to 3–2 and then nailed a fastball that was low and away and drove it into the right-center-field bleachers for the game-winner.

"It should have been ball four," Cleveland said. "Low and outside, where I wanted it to be, looking for a ground ball."

"I crouch at the plate," Jackson said, "so to me it was the perfect pitch."

Yankees owner George Steinbrenner had a prophetic meeting with Jackson the night before the game.

"I met George Steinbrenner in P. J. Clarke's and he told me I'd win the next game with a home run," the right fielder said.

The game featured numerous defensive plays on both sides that kept the game scoreless.

Yankees starter Ed Figueroa matched Cleveland as he took advantage of the glove work displayed throughout the game.

In the fourth inning, the Red Sox had a runner on first base with no one out when Yankees center fielder Mickey Rivers ran down a long drive by Boston's Carlton Fisk near the 430-foot sign in left-center field. George Scott lined a ball to right field, but Jackson made a nice play near the wall.

Not to be outdone, Willie Randolph ran down a pop fly into short right field to end the inning.

Boston had the bases loaded with no one out in the fifth inning, but Figueroa got Fred Lynn to

Red Sox	AB	R	H	RBI
Burleson ss	3	0	2	0
Carbo rf	2	0	0	0
Lynn cf	4	0	0	0
Yastrzemski lf	4	0	0	0
Rice dh	4	0	2	0
Fisk c	4	0	0	0
Scott 1b	3	0	1	0
Hobson 3b	4	0	0	0
Doyle 2b	4	0	2	0
Totals	32	0	7	0

Yankees	AB	R	H	RBI
Rivers cf	3	0	0	0
White lf	3	0	0	0
Munson c	4	1	1	0
Jackson rf	4	1	2	2
Chambliss 1b	3	0	0	0
Nettles 3b	3	0	1	0
Piniella dh	3	0	0	0
Randolph 2b	3	0	0	0
Dent ss	3	0	2	0
Totals	29	2	6	2

BOS	0	0	0	0	0	0	0	0	0	-	0	7	0
NY	0	0	0	0	0	0	0	2	-	2	6	0

Red Sox	IP	H	R	ER	BB	SO
Cleveland L(9–8)	8	6	2	2	1	3

Yankees	IP	H	R	ER	BB	SO
Figueroa W(15–9)	9	7	0	0	3	2

DP—Boston 1; New York 1. 3B—Boston Rice. HR—New York Jackson (26). SH—Boston Burleson. HBP—New York Rivers. LOB—Boston 9; New York 5. SB—Boston Rice. Attendance: 54,365.

DH Reggie Jackson

Reggie Jackson earned the nickname, "Mr. October" for his World Series accomplishments over a 21-year major league career.

Jackson hit 563 career home runs, but his World Series numbers were off the charts.

In 27 World Series games, Jackson batted .357 with 10 home runs and 24 RBIs.

In the 1977 World Series, Jackson hit four consecutive home runs, including three in a historic sixth game, to lead the Yankees to their first World Championship in 15 years.

"Mr. October" played on five World Series winners (3 with Oakland, 2 with the Yankees) and was named the 1973 American League MVP Award winner.

Jackson was elected to the Baseball Hall of Fame in 1993.

bounce into a 1–2–3 double play and Carl Yastrzemski to bounce back to the mound to end the threat.

In the Yankees' half of the eighth inning, Randolph was robbed of a hit on a diving play by Boston third baseman Butch Hobson.

Jackson signed a three-year, $5 million dollar contract to play for the Yankees and do things like hit game-winning home runs, so it was very satisfying for the slugger to come through.

"I'm not Joe DiMaggio, I'm not Mickey Mantle, I'm not Lou Gehrig," he said. "I never will be. The thing that stands out in my mind is that I went for the most money and I got the money and landed here in New York. So I have to perform and I'm glad the people got something back." —⚊—

Guidry Two-Hits Red Sox for Second Time in a Week

It was like the "Boston Massacre, Part II."

Ron Guidry tossed a masterful two-hit shutout as the Yankees blanked the Boston Red Sox 4–0 at Yankee Stadium.

Gator was making his second start in six days against Boston, and the result was exactly the same, a two-hit shutout.

The Yankees scored all of their runs in the fourth inning as Chris Chambliss and Graig Nettles keyed the rally with home runs.

Guidry walked three and struck out five and had two men on base in one inning when the Red Sox tried to come from behind in the seventh.

With one out, Carlton Fisk walked and Fred Lynn singled to right, putting runners at first and second base.

The Yankees left-hander, who went on to win the 1978 American League Cy Young Award, struck out Butch Hobson and got Bob Bailey on a fly out to center field to squash the threat. —∼—

Red Sox	AB	R	H	RBI
Burleson ss	3	0	1	0
Remy 2b	4	0	0	0
Rice lf	4	0	0	0
Yastrzemski 1b	4	0	0	0
Fisk c	3	0	0	0
Lynn cf	2	0	1	0
Hobson 3b	3	0	0	0
Bailey dh	3	0	0	0
Evans rf	3	0	0	0
Totals	29	0	2	0

Yankees	AB	R	H	RBI
Rivers cf	4	1	1	0
Blair cf	0	0	0	0
Randolph 2b	3	0	1	0
Piniella lf	3	0	0	0
Jackson rf	3	1	0	0
Chambliss 1b	4	1	1	2
Nettles 3b	4	1	1	1
White dh	3	0	2	0
Dent ss	4	0	1	0
Heath c	3	0	0	0
Totals	31	4	7	3

```
BOS  0 0 0 0 0 0 0 0 0 - 0 2 2
NY   0 0 0 4 0 0 0 0 X - 4 7 1
```

Red Sox	IP	H	R	ER	BB	SO
Tiant L(10–8)	3.2	5	4	4	2	1
Hassler	4.1	2	0	0	2	3
Totals	8	7	4	4	4	4

Yankees	IP	H	R	ER	BB	SO
Guidry W(22–2)	9	2	0	0	3	5

E—Boston Yastrzemski 2; New York Heath. DP—Boston 1. 2B—Boston Burleson; New York Dent, White. HR—New York Chambliss (11), Nettles (26). LOB—Boston 5; New York 7. SB—New York Randolph. Attendance: 54,901.

Shawkey's Gem Marred When Witt Is Injured by Thrown Bottle

Yankees right-hander Bob Shawkey gave up one run on seven hits in a complete game 2–1 victory over the St. Louis Browns that was marred by an ugly incident in the bottom of the ninth inning at Sportsman's Park.

Browns third baseman Eddie Foster led off the ninth with a fly to right-center that was hauled in by Yankees right fielder Bob Meusel.

While converging with Meusel, Yankees center fielder Whitey Witt was hit in the face with a bottle that was thrown from the right-field bleachers. Witt dropped to the ground while players and umpires rushed to his side.

Mounted police galloped onto the field as the crowd threatened to spill out of the stands. Order was restored, and the 5-foot-7 Witt was carried off the field, unconscious, on the shoulders of his 5-foot-11 teammate, catcher Freddy Hofmann.

Reportedly, the blow suffered by Witt was so severe that the bottom of the bottle was knocked out by the impact. Witt was examined in the dressing room and was diagnosed with a painful cut.

The Orange, Massachusetts, native went on to play four years in pinstripes. He was the first batter for the Yankees in the first game ever played at Yankee Stadium.

One of the seven Browns hits came off the bat of future Hall of Famer and St. Louis first baseman George Sisler, who extended his hitting streak to 40 games. —⁓—

Yankees	AB	R	H	RBI
Witt cf	4	0	1	0
Smith rf	0	0	0	0
Dugan 3b	4	1	1	0
Ruth lf	4	0	1	0
Pipp 1b	2	0	1	1
Schang c	4	0	0	0
Meusel rf,cf	3	1	3	0
Ward 2b	3	0	0	0
Scott ss	4	0	2	1
Shawkey p	4	0	0	0
Totals	**32**	**2**	**9**	**2**

Browns	AB	R	H	RBI
Tobin rf	4	0	1	0
Foster 3b	4	0	1	1
Sisler 1b	4	0	1	0
Williams lf	4	0	1	0
Jacobson cf	3	0	1	0
McManus 2b	3	0	0	0
Severeid c	3	0	1	0
Gerber ss	2	1	1	0
Shocker p	3	0	0	0
Totals	**30**	**1**	**7**	**1**

NY	0	1	1	0	0	0	0	0	0	-	2	9	0
STL	0	0	0	0	0	1	0	0	0	-	1	7	1

Yankees	IP	H	R	ER	BB	SO
Shawkey W(19–10)	9	7	1	1	0	5

Browns	IP	H	R	ER	BB	SO
Shocker L(24–16)	9	9	2	2	2	6

E—St. Louis Jacobson. DP—New York 2; St. Louis 1. 2B—New York Meusel; St. Louis Sisler, Jacobson. SH—New York Pipp, Ward; St. Louis Gerber. LOB—New York 7; St. Louis 0. Attendance: 30,000.

Scooter's Squeeze Bunt a Success as DiMaggio Scores Game-Winner

Phil Rizzuto executed a perfect squeeze bunt to score Joe DiMaggio from third base with the winning run in the bottom of the ninth inning as the Yankees outlasted the Cleveland Indians 2–1 at Yankee Stadium.

Bob Lemon was the tough-luck loser. Lemon threw an 0–1 pitch at Rizzuto's head, but Scooter, who was one of the best bunters of all time, somehow got his bat on the ball and put it in play.

Lemon could only corral the ball as DiMaggio scored the winning run.

When Rizzuto passed away in August of 2007, the *New York Times* referred to this game in his obituary:

"Rizzuto was at bat [he was right-handed] against Bob Lemon of the Cleveland Indians. It was the bottom of the ninth inning, in the middle of a pennant chase. The score was tied at 1. DiMaggio was on third base. Rizzuto took Lemon's first pitch, a called strike, and argued the call with the umpire. That gave him time to grab his bat from both ends, the sign to DiMaggio that a squeeze play was on for the next pitch. But DiMaggio broke early, surprising Rizzuto. Lemon, seeing what was happening, threw high, to avoid a bunt, aiming behind Rizzuto. But with Joltin' Joe bearing down on him, Rizzuto got his bat up in time to lay down a bunt."

"If I didn't bunt, the pitch would've hit me right in the head," Rizzuto said. "I bunted it with both feet off the ground, but I got it off toward first base."

DiMaggio scored the winning run. Yankees manager Casey Stengel called it "the

---

SS Phil Rizzuto

Phil Rizzuto was one of the most popular Yankees of all time, on and off the field.

During his 13-year career, Rizzuto won seven World Series championships. "The Scooter" was named the American League's Most Valuable Player in 1950 after finishing second in the 1949 voting to Ted Williams.

Williams once said of the Scooter, "Rizzuto was the main difference between the Yankees and Red Sox. If we had Rizzuto in Boston, we would have won all those pennants [during that era] instead of the Yankees."

The Hall of Famer was a slick-fielding shortstop who overcame a lack of height to become one of the best to play the position in pinstripes.

After his playing career, Rizzuto became a broadcaster and was adored by Yankees fans for more than 40 years.

greatest play I ever saw." (Rizzuto would in fact become one of the first players in the major leagues to voluntarily wear a batting helmet).

As the winning run scored, Lemon angrily threw both the ball and his pitching glove into the stands.

The game was a terrific pitchers' duel between Lemon and Eddie Lopat, who was the winner and picked up his 20th victory of the 1951 season.

At a Glance

WP: Lopat (20–8)

Key stats: Rizzuto 3 hits, 2 RBIs, including game-winning squeeze bunt that scored DiMaggio in bottom of the 9th

Rizzuto drove in both runs for the Yankees. In the fifth inning, Rizzuto brought home Bobby Brown with an RBI single, one of three hits in the game.

Bobby Avila's RBI single in the sixth inning tied the game at one until the ninth.

DiMaggio beat out an infield hit to lead off the inning and took third base on a single by Gene Woodling.

The Indians loaded the bases with an intentional walk to Brown, but Rizzuto made them pay with his brilliant maneuver. —⁓—

Phil Rizzuto, named AL MVP in 1950, had plenty to be happy about while sitting on the lap of Yankees manager Casey Stengel. Rizzuto had just signed a new contract. "The Scooter" came through with an MVP-type play on September 17, 1951, when his squeeze bunt made the difference in a 2–1 win over Cleveland.

New Life Granted Thanks to Fan, and Mattingly Makes Red Sox Pay

Don Mattingly's walk-off two-run single gave the Yankees a 4–3 victory over the Boston Red Sox after an overzealous fan ran onto the field and nullified what would have been the final Yankees out at Yankee Stadium.

The Yankees trailed Boston 3–1 with two out and no one on when Mike Gallego was hit by a pitch by Red Sox reliever Greg Harris to bring the tying run to the plate.

Mike Stanley hit a fly ball to left that appeared to be the final out, but after Red Sox left fielder Mike Greenwell caught the ball, third base umpire Tim Welke ruled that time was called because a fan ran on the field before the 0–1 pitch was thrown.

"It's too bad a situation like that has to happen," Welke said. "I can't wait to see what a guy will do. I called timeout way before the pitch. I'd do the same thing again. I'd have to."

Stanley took advantage of his good fortune by hitting a single to left to put runners at first and second base.

Wade Boggs hit a slow roller toward short right field that eluded the dive of Red Sox second baseman Scott Fletcher to score Gallego and cut the lead to 3–2.

Harris walked Dion James on a close 3–2 pitch to load the bases for Mattingly.

The Yankees first baseman smacked a 1–1 pitch from Harris between first and second base to score two runs and cap a most improbable victory. —⁓—

Red Sox	AB	R	H	RBI
Fletcher 2b	5	1	2	0
Greenwell lf	5	0	1	0
Naehring 3b	3	1	2	0
Cooper ph,3b	0	0	0	0
Vaughn 1b	3	1	2	2
Deer dh	5	0	1	0
Quintana rf	3	0	0	1
Riles ph	1	0	0	0
Lyons cf	0	0	0	0
Valentin ss	4	0	0	0
Zupcic cf,rf	4	0	1	0
Pena c	4	0	2	0
Totals	37	3	11	3

Yankees	AB	R	H	RBI
Boggs 3b	3	0	1	1
Stankiewicz pr	0	1	0	0
Mattingly 1b	4	0	0	0
Tartabull dh	5	0	1	2
O'Neill rf	4	0	2	0
Nokes c	4	1	1	1
B. Williams cf	4	0	1	0
Gallego 2b	4	0	1	0
Velarde ss	3	0	2	0
Stanley ph	1	0	1	0
G. Williams pr	0	1	0	0
Totals	35	4	10	4

```
BOS  2 0 1 0 0 0 0 0 0 - 3 11 0
NY   0 0 0 0 0 0 1 0 3 - 4 10 2
```

Red Sox	IP	H	R	ER	BB	SO
Minchey	6	6	1	1	1	3
Ryan	1.1	0	0	0	1	2
Fossas	0.1	0	0	0	0	0
Harris L(6–5)	1	4	3	3	1	1
Totals	8.2	10	4	4	3	6

Yankees	IP	H	R	ER	BB	SO
Key	6	9	3	3	2	10
Munoz	2	2	0	0	0	0
Assenmacher	0.1	0	0	0	1	0
Wickman W(13–4)	0.2	0	0	0	0	1
Totals	9	11	3	3	3	11

E—New York James, Velarde. DP—Boston 1; New York 1. 2B—New York Velarde 2, Tartabull. 3B—Boston Zupcic. HR—Boston Vaughn (26); New York O'Neill (19). SH—Boston Naehring, Cooper. HBP—New York Gallego. LOB—Boston 12; New York 9. Attendance: 55,672.

Gura Sees Familiar Faces in 3–0 Shutout

Left-hander Larry Gura spun a six-hit shutout to lead the Yankees to a 3–0 win over the Cleveland Indians at Shea Stadium.

Gura matched up against former Yankee Fritz Peterson, who gave up all three runs in 5 1/3 innings pitched.

The Yankees got their runs on a sacrifice fly and an RBI single by Lou Piniella and an RBI double by Chris Chambliss.

The Yankees acquired Gura from Texas in May as the player to be named later in the Duke Sims trade.

The southpaw pitched a relatively stress-free game as he faced an Indians lineup that had four ex-Yankees or players who would go on to play for the Bombers.

Cleveland's pitchers, Peterson and Fred Beene, were both former Yankees who were dealt to the Indians in the seven-player trade that brought Chambliss to New York in April 1974.

With only one walk issued by either side, the game time was an impressive one hour and 46 minutes.

In May 1976, Gura was traded to the Kansas City Royals in exchange for back-up catcher Fran Healy. —m—

Indians	AB	R	H	RBI
Duffy ss	4	0	2	0
Gamble lf	3	0	0	0
Robinson dh	4	0	0	0
Spikes rf	4	0	0	0
Ellis 1b	4	0	0	0
Hendrick cf	3	0	0	0
Torres cf	1	0	1	0
Bell 3b	4	0	2	0
Duncan c	3	0	0	0
Hermoso 2b	3	0	1	0
Totals	33	0	6	0

Yankees	AB	R	H	RBI
White dh	4	0	0	0
Maddox cf	4	2	2	0
Murcer rf	2	1	0	0
Piniella lf	2	0	1	2
Munson c	3	0	1	0
Chambliss 1b	3	0	2	1
Nettles 3b	3	0	0	0
Alomar 2b	3	0	0	0
Michael ss	3	0	1	0
Totals	27	3	7	3

											R	H	E
CLE	0	0	0	0	0	0	0	0	0	-	0	6	1
NY	0	0	2	0	1	0	0	X		-	3	7	0

Indians	IP	H	R	ER	BB	SO
Peterson L(9–13)	5.1	7	3	3	0	1
Beene	2.2	0	0	0	0	0
Totals	8	7	3	3	0	1

Yankees	IP	H	R	ER	BB	SO
Gura W(5–0)	9	6	0	0	1	1

E—Cleveland Ellis. DP—Cleveland 1. 2B—New York Munson, Maddox 2, Chambliss. SF—New York Piniella. HBP—New York Murcer. LOB—Cleveland 7; New York 2. Attendance: 21,641.

Historic Yankee Stadium Closed Out with Victory

A grand finale for a grand ol' gal.

Yankee Stadium I officially closed its doors following the Yankees' 7–3 win over the Baltimore Orioles in the final game ever played at the historic edifice.

The final out was a grounder to first base that Cody Ransom handled to become part of the answer to a trivia question. It was fitting that Mariano Rivera was on the mound to throw the final pitch.

"It was emotional, it was a great night," Rivera said. "It's something that I'll never forget. I was thankful for the opportunity to be on the mound for the last out."

There was a moving pregame ceremony in which Yankee greats from the past along with widows and children took their positions in the field for one last time.

Catcher Jose Molina joined the list of trivia answers when he hit the final home run in the history of the stadium, a two-run shot in the fourth inning that snapped a 3–3 tie. The Yankees never trailed again.

"It feels great," Molina said. "I feel happy. It's one of those things you're going to remember for the rest of your life."

Johnny Damon's three-run homer in the third inning gave the Yankees a 3–0 lead. "It's at the top," Damon said. "I know I've had some big home runs here, but being able to close out the stadium, I have no regrets whatsoever about donning the pinstripes. I'm happy I got to enjoy this day."

Mariano Rivera, collecting some dirt from the mound following the final game at the old Yankee Stadium, threw the last pitch at the iconic venue on September 21, 2008. Rivera said the ball was headed to Yankees owner George Steinbrenner.

Orioles	AB	R	H	RBI
Roberts 2b	5	1	1	1
Markakis rf	4	0	1	0
Mora 3b	4	0	1	1
Cintron 3b	0	0	0	0
Huff dh	4	0	0	0
R. Hernandez c	4	0	0	0
Jones cf	4	1	2	0
Millar 1b	3	1	1	0
Payton lf	4	0	1	1
Castro ss	2	0	0	0
Salazar ph	0	0	0	0
Fahey pr-ss	0	0	0	0
Scott ph	1	0	0	0
Totals	35	3	7	3

Yankees	AB	R	H	RBI
Damon cf-lf	4	1	1	3
Cabrera lf	0	0	0	0
Jeter ss	5	0	0	0
Abreu rf	0	0	0	0
A. Rodriguez 3b	2	0	0	0
Giambi 1b	3	0	1	1
Gardner pr-cf	0	1	0	0
Nady lf	4	0	0	0
Ransom 1b	0	0	0	0
Cano 2b	2	1	1	1
Matsui dh	3	1	1	0
I. Rodriguez ph-dh	1	0	0	0
Molina c	4	2	3	2
Totals	32	7	9	7

```
BAL  0 1 1 1 0 0 0 0 0 - 3 7 1
NY   0 0 3 2 0 0 2 0 X - 7 9 1
```

Orioles	IP	H	R	ER	BB	SO
Waters L(3–4)	5.2	6	5	5	4	2
Cormier	0.2	2	1	1	1	1
Walker	0	1	1	0	0	0
Cherry	1.2	0	0	0	0	0
Totals	8	9	7	6	5	3

Yankees	IP	H	R	ER	BB	SO
Pettitte W(14–14)	5	7	3	2	1	3
Veras	0.2	0	0	0	1	1
Coke	0.2	0	0	0	0	1
Chamberlain	1.2	0	0	0	0	1
Rivera	1	0	0	0	0	0
Totals	9	7	3	2	2	6

E—Baltimore 1; New York 1. DP—Baltimore 1. 2B—Baltimore Millar. 3B—Baltimore Jones. HR—New York Cano. SF—New York Cano. LOB—Baltimore 7; New York 7. SB—Baltimore Roberts, Jones; New York Abreu. Attendance—54,610.

Andy Pettitte, the second-winningest pitcher at the remodeled Yankee Stadium (Ron Guidry is first with 99 wins), earned his 94th win in the Bronx. The classy left-hander also recorded his 2,000th career strikeout when he fanned Ramon Hernandez leading off the second inning.

As Rivera's signature theme song, *Enter Sandman*, by the heavy metal band Metallica, played on the stadium loudspeakers, Mo made his way to the mound for the final time.

In the ninth inning, Jay Payton grounded out to shortstop for the first out. Pinch-hitter Luke Scott grounded to Robinson Cano at second base, and the crowd started anticipating the end.

At this point, Yankees manager Joe Girardi lifted shortstop Derek Jeter so that he could get his due from the crowd—a loud standing ovation.

Brian Roberts, who was the final batter in the history of the famous ballpark, hit a bouncer that stayed fair inside the first-base line. Ransom gloved it, took the putout himself, and immediately put the historic ball in Rivera's glove. The longtime closer said that he was holding it for Yankees principal owner George Steinbrenner, who watched the final game from home in Florida.

"I'm going to give it to George," Rivera said. "He deserves it. He's the one that put this team together. He deserves it and more than that."

The game officially ended at 11:41 p.m. and the crowd continued to stand and cheer. Jeter went atop the mound and took the microphone for one final tribute.

"For all of us up here, it's a huge honor to put this uniform on every day and come out here and play," he said. "And every member of this organization, past and present, has been calling this place home for 85 years. There's a lot of tradition, a lot of history, and a lot of memories. Now the great thing about memories is you're able to pass it along from generation to generation. And although things are going to change next year, we're going to move across the street, there are a few things with the

P Mariano Rivera

Mariano Rivera has been called the best closer in the history of baseball and with good reason.

"Mo" has made his legacy by mastering one pitch called "the cutter."

Rivera is a 10-time All-Star and was on the mound for the final out in four of the Yankees' recent World Series wins.

"Mo" surpassed 500 career saves during the 2009 season. He was named the 1999 World Series MVP as the Yankees swept the Atlanta Braves.

Rivera is the last big-league player to wear #42 because Major League Baseball retired the number in honor of Jackie Robinson. Since Rivera already had the number, he is allowed to wear it until his career is over.

New York Yankees that never change, it's pride, it's tradition, and most of all, we have the greatest fans in the world."

Jeter acknowledged that he had been asked to speak a few days before the finale but he didn't know what he would say.

"We're relying on you to take the memories from this stadium and add them to the new memories that come to the new Yankee Stadium, and continue to pass them on from generation to generation. On behalf of this entire organization, we want to take this moment to salute you, the greatest fans in the world."

Following Jeter's speech, the Yankee players took off their caps, waved at the crowd, and followed the captain around the field for one final lap as Frank Sinatra's *New York, New York* played in the background.

It was a memorable evening that went on for another hour as players, media, and others remained on the field to soak it all in. —

Did You Know?

Four pitchers have hit grand slams for the Yankees. Red Ruffing was the first in 1933, followed by Spud Chandler in 1940, and Don Larsen in 1956. Mel Stottlemyre was the last to do it in 1965, and that was an inside-the-park grand slam.

Berra's Debut Includes Single, Two-Run Homer

The Yankees beat the Philadelphia A's 4–3 at Yankee Stadium, but the score doesn't tell the significance of this contest.

The game marked the major league debut of future Hall of Famer and Yankee icon Yogi Berra.

Berra was 2-for-4 in his first game, including his first home run off of A's right-hander Jesse Flores, a two-run shot that gave him his first two big-league RBIs.

Yogi batted eighth and caught right-hander Spud Chandler, who earned his 19th win of the 1946 season.

Berra wasn't the only player to make his big-league debut in this game. Bobby Brown, who was the runner-up to Jackie Robinson for the 1946 International League batting championship, started at shortstop and went 1-for-2. Brown, who batted third in front of Joe DiMaggio, went on to earn a medical degree from Tulane University while he was playing ball.

Dr. Bobby Brown became the president of the American League and held that post for 10 years.

Berra went on to become one of the great American success stories of all time, a genius in his profession, owner of more than 40 championship and All-Star rings (as player, coach, and manager), quoted by presidents, a best-selling author, featured in six decades worth of television commercials, and the guiding light of a museum and learning center bearing his name.

Not bad for a man with an eighth-grade education and the only Major Leaguer to fight at Normandy on D-Day. ―⌁―

At a Glance

WP: Chandler (19–8)

Key stats: Berra 2-for-4 in first game in majors, 2-run HR, 2 RBIs; Chandler wins 19th game of season

Ruth's Doubles Help Bombers Double-Up on the Indians

Babe Ruth was 3-for-3 (all doubles) to lead the Yankees to a come-from-behind 4–2 victory over the Cleveland Indians at the Polo Grounds.

The Indians took a 2–0 lead off pitcher Waite Hoyt in the fourth inning. Larry Gardner singled and Joe Sewell drove him in with a triple that eluded Ruth in right field. The future Hall of Famer scored Cleveland's second run on a wild pitch.

A pair of doubles by Ruth and Wally Pipp produced the first run for the Yankees in the fourth inning.

Ruth hit his second double and scored in the sixth inning on Bob Meusel's single. Meusel eventually scored on an RBI single by Pipp.

The Ruth/Pipp combination clicked again in the eighth inning, when the Bambino stroked his third double and scored his third run on Pipp's sacrifice fly.

Hoyt outpitched Indians ace Stanley Coveleski, who came into the game having already won 22 games during the 1921 season.

The right-hander for the Yankees allowed two runs on six hits while walking three and striking out seven.

A reported crowd of 33,000 saw the Yankees take a one-game lead over Cleveland in the race for the 1921 American League pennant. The Yankees would prevail and capture their long-overdue first championship in their 19th season of play. —⁓—

Indians	AB	R	H	RBI
Jamieson lf	3	0	0	0
Wambsganss 2b	2	0	1	0
Wood cf	3	0	0	0
Smith rf	4	0	0	0
Gardner 3b	4	1	2	0
J. Sewell ss	4	1	2	1
Johnston 1b	4	0	0	0
O'Neill c	3	0	1	0
Coveleski p	3	0	0	0
Speaker ph	1	0	0	0
Totals	**31**	**2**	**6**	**1**

Yankees	AB	R	H	RBI
Miller cf	3	0	0	0
Peckinpaugh ss	4	0	0	0
Ruth lf	3	3	3	0
Meusel rf	3	1	1	1
Pipp 1b	3	0	2	3
Ward 2b	4	0	0	0
McNally 3b	3	0	0	0
Schang c	2	0	0	0
Hoyt p	3	0	0	0
Totals	**28**	**4**	**6**	**4**

											R	H	E
CLE	0	0	0	2	0	0	0	0	0	-	2	6	0
NY	0	0	0	1	0	2	0	1	X	-	4	6	1

Indians	IP	H	R	ER	BB	SO
Coveleski L(22–12)	8	6	4	4	3	1

Yankees	IP	H	R	ER	BB	SO
Hoyt W(18–13)	9	6	2	2	3	7

E—New York Pipp. 2B—Cleveland O'Neill; New York Ruth 3, Meusel, Pipp. 3B—Cleveland J. Sewell. SH—Cleveland Wambsganss; New York Meusel, Pipp. LOB—Cleveland 7; New York 5. SB—Cleveland Wambsganss. Attendance: 33,000.

Yankees Set Benchmark with 112 Wins in Season

The Yankees set an American League record with their 112th victory of the season after they defeated the Tampa Bay Devil Rays 6–1 at Yankee Stadium.

The 1954 Cleveland Indians were the previous record holders when they won 111 games in a 154-game season. The Yankees went on to win 114 games in 1998, but this particular win was the record-setter. (The 2001 Seattle Mariners broke the record with 116 wins.) On this day, it was hard to believe the Yankees started the season 0–3.

"It's astounding, and it's really a credit to my ballclub," manager Joe Torre said. "They've come to play every day."

Orlando "El Duque" Hernandez went five innings to pick up his 12th win of the season. "It's a great thing, a great feeling, and I have great emotions," El Duque said. "It's nice to know we all have something to do with 112 victories."

The Yankees snapped a 1–1 tie by scoring five runs in the third inning.

At a Glance

WP: Hernandez (12–4)

Key stats: Williams 2-for-2, RBI; Brosius 2 RBIs

Tampa right-hander Dave Eiland (who became the Yankees pitching coach in 2007) was touched for six runs on six hits and was knocked out in the third inning following an RBI double by Jorge Posada.

With the Yankees having already clinched the AL Eastern Division title, Torre took the opportunity to get some of the non-starters into the historic game, including Ricky Ledee, Shane Spencer, and a young third baseman named Mike Lowell.

Bernie Williams, who was in a heated battle for the American League batting championship with Boston's Mo Vaughn, went 2-for-2 to lift his average to .337. Williams went on to win the batting title with a .339 average, two points better than Vaughn's .337.

After Tampa Bay shortstop Aaron Ledesma struck out against Mariano Rivera to end the game, the scoreboard flashed the No. 112 in large numbers and the crowd of 32,447 acknowledged the feat with a loud standing ovation.

The Yankees would go on to win an amazing 125 games including the post-season, losing only 50, and cemented their candidacy in the argument of "greatest Yankees team ever." —⁓—

Bernie Williams won the 1998 American League batting crown with a .339 average. The Yankees won 114 games to stake their claim as the greatest Yankees team ever.

Munson Scampers Home for Win after Wild Pitch

Thurman Munson scored from third base on a wild pitch in the bottom of the ninth inning to give the Yankees a 2–1 win over the Cleveland Indians at Yankee Stadium.

Munson started the ninth with a single off Indians losing pitcher Jim Bibby, who uncorked a wild pitch to send the captain to second base.

Cleveland issued an intentional walk to Reggie Jackson, and Lou Piniella sacrificed the runners to second and third.

Dave Kingman, who was a late-season acquisition, was at the plate when the game ended.

With the count at 1–1, Bibby bounced a pitch past Indians catcher Fred Kendall to allow Munson to scamper home with the winning run.

Dick Tidrow made his seventh start of the season and pitched very well, giving up a run on five hits in 7 1/3 innings pitched. Sparky Lyle, who would go on to win the 1977 Cy Young Award, tossed scoreless ball for the final 1 2/3 innings and got the win.

The Yankees took a 1–0 lead in the fifth inning on an RBI single by Cliff Johnson, but Cleveland tied the game in the eighth on a pinch-hit RBI single by Ron Pruitt. —

Indians	AB	R	H	RBI
Norris rf	3	0	1	0
Pruitt ph,rf	1	0	1	1
Oliver 2b	3	0	1	0
Blanks 3b	4	0	0	0
Thornton 1b	3	0	0	0
Carty dh	4	0	0	0
Bochte lf	4	0	0	0
Manning cf	3	0	2	0
Kendall c	3	1	1	0
Griffin ss	2	0	0	0
Lowenstein ph	1	0	1	0
Duffy ss	0	0	0	0
Totals	31	1	7	1

Yankees	AB	R	H	RBI
Randolph 2b	3	0	0	0
Nettles 3b	4	0	0	0
Munson c	4	1	1	0
Jackson rf	3	0	1	0
Piniella lf	3	1	2	0
Kingman dh	3	0	1	0
Johnson 1b	3	0	2	1
Chambliss 1b	0	0	0	0
Blair cf	2	0	0	0
Rivers ph,cf	1	0	0	0
Dent ss	3	0	0	0
Totals	29	2	7	1

CLE 0 0 0 0 0 0 0 1 0 - 1 7 0
NY   0 0 0 0 1 0 0 0 1 - 2 7 2

Indians	IP	H	R	ER	BB	SO
Waits	6	6	1	1	1	3
Bibby L(12–13)	2.1	1	1	1	1	3
Totals	8.1	7	2	2	2	6

Yankees	IP	H	R	ER	BB	SO
Tidrow	7.1	5	1	1	1	4
Lyle W(13–5)	1.2	2	0	0	0	0
Totals	9	7	1	1	1	4

E—New York Munson, Tidrow. DP—Cleveland 2; New York 2. 2B—New York Kingman. SH—New York Piniella. HBP—Cleveland Oliver. LOB—Cleveland 5; New York 5. SB—Cleveland Manning. Attendance: 14,138.

Sparky Lyle, who would go on to win the 1977 American League Cy Young Award, pitched the final 1 2/3 innings to earn the victory in a 2–1 win over the Indians on September 27, 1977.

Yanks Pound Out 30 Hits

This game could've been the precursor of the 1978 Boston Massacre.

The Yankees set a franchise record with 30 hits in a 24–4 destruction of the Red Sox at Fenway Park.

Babe Ruth and catcher Wally Schang led the barrage with five hits apiece. Lou Gehrig was 4-for-7 with three doubles and four RBIs, while the winning pitcher, Sad Sam Jones, had three hits.

The Yankees sent 16 players to the plate in the sixth inning and scored 11 runs to break the game open. Ruth came to plate twice, and in his second at-bat, he clubbed his 38th home run into the center-field bleachers.

Boston's Howard Ehmke gave up 17 runs (16 earned) on 21 hits in six innings of work.

Clarence Blethen relieved Ehmke in the seventh inning and yielded seven runs (six earned) on nine hits in the final three frames.

The Yankees set an American League record with 44 total bases in this one-sided affair.

Jones went the distance, giving up four runs on 11 hits. ―᷍―

> ## At a Glance
>
> **WP:** Jones (21–8)
>
> **HR:** Ruth (38), Ward (10)
>
> **Key stats:** Jones CG; Ruth 5-for-6, 5 RBIs; Gehrig 4-for-7, 4 RBIs; Schang 5-for-6, 5 RBIs

September 28, 1930

Ruth Bats Third, Pitches Complete Game

Babe Ruth took the mound for the first time in 10 years and went the distance in the 1930 season finale to beat his old team at Fenway Park, 9–3.

Ruth, who pitched for the 1918 World Series champion Red Sox, dazzled his former club with an assortment of fastballs and off-speed pitches.

No Red Sox runner reached second base until the sixth inning. The win gave Ruth a 4–0 record as a Yankee pitcher.

Lou Gehrig made the last of his three career starts in left field and had three hits to capture the 1930 American League batting title. The Iron Horse edged Al Simmons .382 to .381. Simmons sat out the final game of the season.

Season's Sixth Slam Sets a Record for Mattingly

Don Mattingly set a major league record by hitting his sixth grand slam of the season to lead the Yankees to a 6–0 win over the Boston Red Sox at Yankee Stadium.

Mattingly's record-setting shot came in the third inning off Red Sox left-hander Bruce Hurst. It was a "no-doubter," as it landed in the upper deck in right field.

"It feels good to do this," Mattingly said, "to do something nobody has done before."

The Yankees loaded the bases in the third inning on singles by Roberto Kelly and Rickey Henderson and a walk to Willie Randolph.

The count was 1–2 when Hurst offered a changeup.

Mattingly said, "I didn't want to pull off. He got me with two changeups the first time."

Mattingly was right on this one as he lofted it high and far into the night, where it landed approximately 11 rows into the third tier of the stadium.

The 1985 American League MVP hit four of his slams against left-handers, and he did not hit his first until May 14 of the 1987 season. The six slams, compressed into one season, would be the only ones Mattingly would hit in his entire career.

Mattingly's blast gave the Yankees 10 grand slams on the season, which tied the major league record previously set by the 1938 Detroit Tigers —⁘—

Red Sox	AB	R	H	RBI
Burks cf	4	0	1	0
Barrett 2b	4	0	2	0
Horn dh	4	0	0	0
Evans 1b	4	0	0	0
Greenwell lf	3	0	0	0
Benzinger rf	3	0	0	0
Romero 3b	3	0	1	0
Reed ss	3	0	0	0
Marzano c	3	0	0	0
Totals	31	0	4	0

Yankees	AB	R	H	RBI
Henderson dh	5	1	3	0
Randolph 2b	2	1	1	1
Mattingly 1b	5	1	2	4
Winfield rf	3	1	0	0
Ward lf	4	0	3	0
Royster 3b	3	0	2	0
Meachem ss	3	0	0	1
Skinner c	4	1	1	0
Kelly cf	4	1	1	0
Totals	33	6	13	6

```
BOS   0 0 0 0 0 0 0 0 0 - 0 4 1
NY    0 0 5 0 0 0 0 1 X - 6 13 0
```

Red Sox	IP	H	R	ER	BB	SO
Hurst L(15–13)	2.1	6	5	5	3	2
Bolton	5.2	7	1	0	2	5
Totals	8	13	6	5	5	7

Yankees	IP	H	R	ER	BB	SO
Hudson W(11–6)	9	4	0	0	1	3

E—Boston Greenwell. DP—Boston 2. 2B—Boston Barrett. HR—New York Mattingly (29). SF—New York Randolph. LOB—Boston 5; New York 9. SB—New York Kelly, Henderson. Attendance: 20,204.

Ruth Breaks Own Mark, Smacks 60th Home Run

Babe Ruth hit his 60th home run to set a major league mark as the Yankees beat the Washington Senators 4–2 at Yankee Stadium.

The score was tied at two in the bottom of the eighth inning when Ruth came to bat against Washington left-hander Tom Zachary with Mark Koenig on third base.

Ruth hit a 1–1 pitch from the southpaw and drove it deep into the right-field bleachers for a two-run homer that gave the Yankees the lead. The Bambino had broken his own record of 59 home runs, which he set in 1921.

At a Glance

WP: Pennock (19–8)

HR: Ruth (60)

Key stats: Ruth 3-for-3, 2 RBIs; Pennock 3 scoreless IP in relief

OF Babe Ruth

The greatest player in baseball history is George Herman "Babe" Ruth, who made his mark with the Yankees during a 15-year career.

Ruth was the impetus for baseball's popularity, as the fans became enamored with his majestic home runs.

The Babe set the single season mark for home runs when he slammed 60 in 1927.

Ruth held the career mark with 714 until 1974, when Hall of Famer Hank Aaron surpassed it.

Ruth broke into the big leagues as a pitcher with the Boston Red Sox, but he was dealt to the Yankees in one of the most famous trades ever made.

On December 26th, 1919, Red Sox owner Harry Frazee sold Ruth to the Yankees for $125,000 in cash and three $25,000 notes payable every year at 6% interest.

The deal later prompted the moniker, "The Curse of the Bambino," as the Yankees went on to win four World Series with Babe and 26 overall before Boston won another one in 2004.

While the reported crowd of 10,000 roared, Ruth took a triumphant run around the bases. He jogged slowly and made doubly sure to touch each base. When he got to home plate, he emphatically embedded his spikes into the vaunted pentagon, at which point hats were tossed into the air.

When Ruth trotted out to right field for the top of the ninth inning, he acknowledged the crowd with a number of military salutes.

Zachary was not pleased that he became a part of history. When the ball left the park, the Washington left-hander tossed his glove to the ground, muttered to himself, and looked for support from his teammates, which he never received. ⟶

Maris Launches 61st Home Run to Break Ruth's Record

Roger Maris broke Babe Ruth's single-season record by slamming his 61st home run to account for the only run of the game in a 1–0 win over the Boston Red Sox at Yankee Stadium.

Maris' record-setting blow came in the fourth inning off Red Sox right-hander Tracy Stallard.

With the 1961 American League pennant already in hand, all that was left was to see if Maris could break the Babe's 34-year-old record.

Maris batted in the first inning and flied out to left field.

In the fourth inning, the Yankees right fielder took the first two pitches, getting ahead in the count as the crowd booed Stallard for appearing to pitch around Maris.

The historic pitch was a fastball that appeared to be waist high, and the Yankee slugger did not miss it. Maris connected for a long drive toward right field, and the crowd of 23,154 rose to its feet as they sensed that this would be the record breaker.

The ball landed approximately 10 rows back and about 10 feet to the right of the Yankees bullpen in the lower right-field stands.

A 19-year-old truck driver from Coney Island named Sal Durante caught the ball and was given a $5,000 award, a round trip to Sacramento, California, courtesy of a restaurateur, and a round trip to the 1962 World's Fair in Seattle.

Maris circled the bases like the pro he was and when he rounded third base, an overzealous fan ran on the field to congratulate him.

When Maris reached the Yankees dugout, the fans were still roaring, so his teammates urged him

Red Sox	AB	R	H	RBI
Schilling 2b	4	0	1	0
Geiger cf	4	0	0	0
Yastrzemski lf	4	0	1	0
Malzone 3b	4	0	0	0
Clinton rf	4	0	0	0
Runnels 1b	3	0	0	0
Gile 1b	0	0	0	0
Nixon c	3	0	2	0
Green ss	2	0	0	0
Stallard p	1	0	0	0
Jensen ph	1	0	0	0
Totals	30	0	4	0

Yankees	AB	R	H	RBI
Richardson 2b	4	0	0	0
Kubek ss	4	0	2	0
Maris cf	4	1	1	1
Berra lf	2	0	0	0
Lopez lf,rf	1	0	0	0
Blanchard rf,c	3	0	0	0
Howard c	2	0	0	0
Reed lf	1	0	1	0
Skowron 1b	2	0	0	0
Hale 1b	1	0	1	0
Boyer 3b	2	0	0	0
Stafford p	2	0	0	0
Tresh ph	1	0	0	0
Totals	29	1	5	1

											R	H	E
BOS	0	0	0	0	0	0	0	0	0	-	0	4	0
NY	0	0	0	1	0	0	0	0	X	-	1	5	0

Red Sox	IP	H	R	ER	BB	SO
Stallard L(2–7)	7	5	1	1	1	5
Nichols	1	0	0	0	0	0
Totals	8	5	1	1	1	5

Yankees	IP	H	R	ER	BB	SO
Stafford W(14–9)	6	3	0	0	1	7
Reniff	1	0	0	0	0	1
Arroyo SV(29)	2	1	0	0	1	1
Totals	9	4	0	0	1	9

3B—Boston Nixon. HR—New York Maris (61). SH—Boston Stallard. LOB—Boston 5; New York 5. SB—Boston Geiger. Attendance: 23,154.

to step out and take a bow (as he had done when he hit his 60th a few days earlier).

The record-setting slugger was reserved about accepting the plaudits of the crowd as he stepped out of the dugout to acknowledge the cheers.

Maris took off his cap and waved to the fans and did not return to the dugout until he took four reluctant bows.

The record was already dripping with controversy. On July 17, commissioner Ford C. Frick said that Ruth's mark would stand unless someone could surpass it within 154 games, since that was the schedule in 1927.

The move was short-sighted and took much of the drama out of the season's final week. (Maris had lost a home run in a rainout earlier in the year).

Maris hit 59 home runs in the first 154 games, but a look at the total plate appearances should demonstrate the symmetry of the two players.

Ruth had 691 total plate appearances (these include sacrifice bunts, sacrifice flies, walks, hit by pitch, and reaching base on interference or obstruction), while Maris had 698.

Maris and Mickey Mantle staged a two-man pursuit of Ruth's record, but the slugging switch-hitter had to shut it down late in the season when he came down with an infection. Mantle finished the season with 54 home runs.

Maris' season was a model of consistency as he hit 31 of his home runs on the road.

The Yankees slugger captured the RBI crown with 142 and was named the American League's Most Valuable Player for a second straight season.

Thirty years later, commissioner Fay Vincent eliminated the asterisk from the records, effectively declaring that Maris had indeed beaten Ruth's mark. Maris still held the American League record through the 2009 season. ⁓

Green Monster, Please Meet Bucky Dent

Bucky Dent's three-run home run in the top of the seventh inning turned the game around, and the Yankees went on to a 5–4 win in what is widely considered one of the greatest games ever played.

The one-game playoff was needed because a historic pennant race did not end as the teams were tied at 99–63 after 162 games.

The Red Sox had a 14½ game lead in July, but the Yankees rallied to grab the divisional lead in September. Boston, to its credit, continued to apply pressure to the Yankees as the Red Sox stayed in the race.

Bucky Dent's three-run homer in the seventh inning over the Green Monster at Fenway Park is one of the most storied blasts in Yankees history. Reggie Jackson (left) and Dent were all smiles in the locker room after the game. Jackson led off the eighth inning with a homer of his own.

The Yankees hosted Cleveland on the final Sunday, while Boston was hosting Toronto.

Yankee-killer Rick Waits went the distance in New York to beat the Yankees 9–2.

Some 300 miles north of Yankee Stadium, the final score from the Bronx went up on the Fenway Park scoreboard and the crowd of more than 29,000 roared while there was a lull in the action on the field.

Boston shut out the Blue Jays and the one-game playoff was set.

Because the Red Sox won a coin toss, the ultimate game to decide the American League East would be played at Fenway Park.

The Yankees had their ace, Ron Guidry, ready to go. Boston sent right-hander Mike Torrez to the hill because Luis Tiant had to pitch on the final day to force the playoff.

In a twist of irony, Torrez had been the winning pitcher in the clinching game of the 1977 World Series in the Yankees' win over the Dodgers. Now the veteran right-hander was trying to beat his former team in a one-game playoff to give the Red Sox the AL East title.

On a bright, sunny day in New England, the Sox drew first blood in the second inning when future Hall of Famer Carl Yastrzemski led off with a home run for a 1–0 lead.

The Yankees trailed 2–0 when Dent batted with two on and two out in the fateful seventh inning.

With the count 1–0, Dent fouled a ball off his foot and took a few moments to gather himself. Mickey Rivers, who was on deck, gave Dent his bat after the foul ball, and the Yankees shortstop used it well.

Dent drove a 1–1 pitch from Torrez high and deep toward left field. At the very least, the ball would hit off the wall and the Yankees would be on the board.

The wind was blowing out at the time and the ball carried all the way over the Green Monster for one of the most famous home runs in baseball history.

Yankees	AB	R	H	RBI
Rivers cf	2	1	1	0
Blair ph,cf	1	0	1	0
Munson c	5	0	1	1
Piniella rf	4	0	1	0
Jackson dh	4	1	1	1
Nettles 3b	4	0	0	0
Chambliss 1b	4	1	1	0
White lf	3	1	1	0
Thomasson lf	0	0	0	0
Doyle 2b	2	0	0	0
Spencer ph	1	0	0	0
Stanley 2b	1	0	0	0
Dent ss	4	1	1	3
Totals	35	5	8	5

Red Sox	AB	R	H	RBI
Burleson ss	4	1	1	0
Remy 2b	4	1	2	0
Rice rf	5	0	1	1
Yastrzemski lf	5	2	2	2
Fisk c	3	0	1	0
Lynn cf	4	0	1	1
Hobson dh	4	0	1	0
Scott 1b	4	0	2	0
Brohamer 3b	1	0	0	0
Bailey ph	1	0	0	0
Duffy 3b	0	0	0	0
Evans ph	1	0	0	0
Totals	36	4	11	4

```
NY   0 0 0 0 0 0 4 1 0 - 5 8 0
BOS  0 1 0 0 0 1 0 2 0 - 4 11 0
```

Yankees	IP	H	R	ER	BB	SO
Guidry W(25–3)	6.1	6	2	2	1	5
Gossage SV(27)	2.2	5	2	2	1	2
Totals	9	11	4	4	2	7

Red Sox	IP	H	R	ER	BB	SO
Torrez L(16–13)	6.2	5	4	4	3	4
Stanley	0.1	2	1	1	0	0
Hassler	1.2	1	0	0	0	2
Drago	0.1	0	0	0	0	0
Totals	9	8	5	5	3	6

2B—New York Rivers, Munson; Boston Scott, Burleson, Remy. HR—New York Dent (5), Jackson (27); Boston Yastrzemski (17). SH—Boston Brohamer, Remy. LOB—New York 6; Boston 9. SB—New York Rivers 2; Boston. Attendance: 32,925.

All of a sudden, the Yankees had a 3–2 lead and the Fenway crowd of 32,925 sat in stunned silence as Dent rounded the bases.

The entire Yankees team spilled out of the dugout to congratulate Dent, but there was still work to be done.

After the home run, Rivers walked, and the Red Sox brought in Bob Stanley to relieve Torrez.

Rivers stole second and scored on an RBI double to left-center field by Thurman Munson.

In the top of the eighth inning, Reggie Jackson led off with what proved to be the winning run as he hit a long home run to dead center field that landed in the bleachers for a 5–2 lead.

The Red Sox scored twice in the last of the eighth inning to cut the deficit to one and had the tying and go-ahead runs on base. Goose Gossage, who had relieved Guidry in the seventh inning, struck out George Scott to end the threat.

With one out and the Yankees leading 5–4 in the last of the ninth, Rick Burleson walked.

Jerry Remy lined a single toward right field and it appeared Yankees right-fielder Lou Piniella could not see the ball as he was immersed in the bright afternoon sun.

Piniella stuck out his glove hand and snagged the ball, which prevented Burleson from going to third base. This would be the pivotal play of the game because the next hitter was Rice, who flew out to deep right field. Burleson took third base and would have scored if he already been there with one out.

The game came down to a matchup of future Hall of Famers, Gossage vs. Yastrzemski.

Gossage got behind 1–0 and then delivered a fastball on the inside part of the plate. Yaz swung and hit a pop fly toward the third-base side in foul territory. Nettles caught it and the Yankees had one of the most thrilling and important wins in their entire history. —⁓—

World Series

1. October 18, 1977
Yankees 8, Dodgers 4

Reggie Jackson hits three home runs in a record-setting performance in Game 6 to give the Yankees their 21st world championship.

2. October 16, 1962
Yankees 1, Giants 0

Second baseman Bobby Richardson snares a vicious line drive by the Giants' Willie McCovey with the tying and winning runs on second and third to secure a Game 7 victory.

Reggie Jackson launches the last of his three consecutive homers in the clinching Game 6 of the 1977 World Series against the Los Angeles Dodgers.

3. October 9, 1958
Yankees 6, Braves 2

The Yankees avenge the previous year's loss to Milwaukee by rallying from a 3–1 Series deficit to stun the Braves by taking Game 7.

4. October 27, 1996
Yankees 3, Braves 2

Joe Girardi's Game 6 triple keys the Yankees' first World Series win in 18 years.

5. October 7, 1952
Yankees 4, Dodgers 2

Mickey Mantle's home run and a great catch by Billy Martin lead the Yankees past Brooklyn in Game 7 for their fourth straight world title.

6. October 26, 2000
Yankees 4, Mets 2

Bernie Williams catches Mike Piazza's deep fly to center to lock up Game 5 and the Yankees' third straight championship.

7. October 15, 1923
Yankees 6, Giants 4

The Yankees wrap up their first world championship by winning Game 6 at the Polo Grounds.

ACKNOWLEDGMENTS

Thanks to those who helped complete this extensive project, including the New York Yankees' public relations department, (Jason Zillo, Michael Margolis, Jason Latimer, Lauren Moran, Connie Schwab, and Kenny Leandry and the entire staff).

Thanks also to John Labombarda of the Elias Sports Bureau for his friendship and his help in making this project a reality, and the outstanding resource Baseball-Reference.com.

Howie Karpin deserves a Yankee Stadium curtain call of his own for his work on this project, and it's one he can take from his spot at the official scorer's seat in the press box one day. His wife, Kathy, and his two sons, Danny and Jake, also deserve a bow for all the time they allowed him to plunge into this project, and I'd also like to thank my wife Lourdes for the same.

REFERENCES

- RETROSHEET.ORG
- Baseball-reference.com
- Proquest-Historical NY Times, assorted publications
- MLB.com

ABOUT THE AUTHOR

Marty Appel, former New York Yankees public relations director and their Emmy Award–winning TV producer, is the author of 18 books including the *New York Times* best seller *Munson: The Life and Death of a Yankee Captain,* the Yankees classic memoir *Now Pitching for the Yankees,* and collaborations with Tom Seaver, Bowie Kuhn, Larry King, and umpire Eric Gregg. He runs Marty Appel Public Relations (www.AppelPR.com) out of New York City.